LEARNING WITH CORPORA

Guy Aston, Silvia Bernardini, Franco Bertaccini,
Ruey Brodine, Laura Gavioli, Alan Partington,
Federico Zanettin, Daniela Zorzi

Learning with corpora

edited by Guy Aston

CLUEB

© CLUEB, Bologna, Italy
© 2001 Athelstan (This edition)
This book is not for sale in Italy.

Other titles from Athelstan:
Concordances in the Classroom
Writing in an Electronic Medium
MonoConc Pro

Athelstan
2476 Bolsover, Suite 464
Houston, TX 77005
U.S.A.
Tel: 713 523 2837
Fax: 713 523 6543

info@athel.com
www.athel.com

ACKNOWLEDGEMENTS

This book has taken a long time to write and to publish, with much of the work behind it going back to the early and mid-1990s. It was born when the authors were working together in the University of Bologna's School for Interpreters and Translators in Forlì, Italy, and were meeting regularly to discuss the roles of corpora in language and translation teaching, and experimenting in our classes with Scott and Johns' extraordinary *MicroConcord* (1993), which the School was the first institution in the world to purchase. Notwithstanding the subsequent pace of software development, we believe that this book's emphasis on the use of corpora with learners, seen from both a theoretical and an applied perspective, makes what it has to say still relevant for teachers and learners. While the literature testifies to the ever-growing interest in the pedagogic use of corpora, there is still a chasm between the research laboratory and the classroom and self-access centre. It is this gap which this book aims to fill a little, providing a theoretically-motivated but practical view of what we believe is one of the most exciting resources for learner-centred language pedagogy at intermediate and advanced levels.

We would like to thank our colleagues in Forlì for their continuing support, the many interested colleagues from other institutions who have nagged us about this book's publication, and the reviewers of earlier versions who suggested various improvements. Our students have shown perhaps the greatest patience, but also in surprisingly many cases the greatest enthusiasm. Last but not least, we are grateful to the School for Interpreters and Translators in Forlì and the Department of Interpreting, Translation, Language and Culture Studies of Bologna University for their financial assistance in finally getting the book into print, and to Michael Barlow of Athelstan for agreeing to publish and distribute it on the world market.

Forlì, February 2001

CONTENTS

Preface		1
1.	Learning with corpora: an overview *Guy Aston*	7
2.	Corpora and their uses in language research *Alan Partington*	46
3.	Corpus-based description in teaching and learning *Alan Partington*	63
4.	The pedagogic use of spoken corpora: learning discourse markers in Italian *Daniela Zorzi*	85
5.	The learner as researcher: introducing corpus concordancing in the classroom *Laura Gavioli*	108
6.	Integrating corpus work into an academic reading course *Ruey Brodine*	138
7.	Swimming in words: corpora, translation, and language learning *Federico Zanettin*	177
8.	Going to the Clochemerle: exploring cultural connotations through ad hoc corpora *Franco Bertaccini and Guy Aston*	198
9.	'Spoilt for choice': a learner explores general language corpora *Silvia Bernardini*	220
References		250
Name index		267
Subject index		271

PREFACE

> Looking farther ahead, perhaps, we need in the world of *information*, classroom access to language databases, lexicographic and grammatical corpora, oriented towards learners' interlanguages and displayed in terms that learners (not only lexicographers and grammarians) can understand.
> (Leech and Candlin 1986: xvi)

Fifteen years after Leech and Candlin made this prediction, most language teachers and learners have probably heard of corpora - carefully-designed collections of written texts and/or spoken transcripts, stored on computers. Many dictionaries of English, several grammars, and a growing number of EFL courses and supplementary materials now proclaim themselves to be 'corpus-based', meaning that their contents have been partly determined by counting and examining in one or more corpora the instances of particular linguistic features. Leech and Candlin's proposal for classroom access to such tools, however, has yet to be widely realized: relatively few teachers and learners have had the opportunity to use corpora themselves. This book aims to encourage such use, presenting a variety of ways in which teachers and learners can work with different kinds of corpora in order to develop linguistic, communicative, and cultural competence, engaging and improving their interpretative and productive skills and their capacity for learning.

In one of the earliest discussions of corpora in language teaching, Kennedy (1992: 364-7) suggested there were three reasons why few attempts had been made to use corpora directly in the classroom:

- poor communication between researchers using corpora and classroom teachers, who should not just be told "that curricula, reference works or teaching materials are based on corpus analysis";
- confusion over the distinction between "what is scientifically interesting and what is pedagogically useful";
- the predominant interest in communicative language teaching in facts which are not strictly speaking linguistic, so that "teachers tended to show more interest in the learner and the learning process than in what was being learned".

As far as concerns the first of these reasons, there are now a number of accessible introductions to work in corpus linguistics which illustrate how corpora can be constructed, describe the kinds of information which can be derived from them, and outline methods for doing so (e.g. Sinclair 1991a, McEnery and Wilson 1996, Barnbrook 1996, Stubbs 1996, Kennedy 1998, Biber et al. 1998, Aston and Burnard 1998). Generally speaking, however, their aim is to promote the use of corpora by students of linguistics rather than by language teachers and learners, and there is still relatively little material that approaches corpus linguistics from the specific perspective of language pedagogy. In consequence Kennedy's second reason for the neglect of corpora in teaching, namely the need to distinguish between the "scientifically interesting" and the "pedagogically useful", is still a matter needing clarification (for recent debate, see Carter 1998, Cook 1998, Widdowson 2000, Gavioli and Aston 2001). What is clear is that we should not expect descriptive and pedagogic approaches to corpora to share the same methods and concerns, since language learners are not trained linguists, and are generally not concerned to analyze the language for its own sake, but only insofar as this helps them to use it (Aston 1995b).

This brings us to Kennedy's third point, and the need to evaluate the compatibility of corpus use in pedagogy with the predominant interests of communicative language teaching, with its emphases on 'meaning-focussed' and 'learner-centred' instruction. Predominant interests in language pedagogy can change rapidly, and since Kennedy formulated his observations, there has been a general revival of interest in 'form-focussed' instruction, emphasizing the language by which meanings are conveyed, which has complemented the dominant emphasis of the 1980s on the meanings conveyed by language. In a recent review of empirical research on form-focussed instruction, Spada notes that

> the learners who benefitted the most in these studies were those who received FFI [form-focussed instruction] which was operationalized as a combination of metalinguistic teaching and corrective feedback provided within an overall context of communicative practice.
>
> (Spada 1997: 77)

The question remains as to how the use of corpora can be successfully integrated into a programme of this kind: whether it serves only for form-focussed work (and if so how this can best be communicatively contextualized), or whether it can also constitute a basis for meaning-focussed activity; whether it is simply a teacher-controlled classroom aid, or whether it can be a motivating instrument which enables learners to take control of their own learning.

To Kennedy's three reasons for the relative neglect of corpora in language pedagogy, we should add one more, that of accessibility. Language teachers and learners have not generally had widescale access to computing resources, and publishers and researchers who have gone to the expense of compiling corpora have often been reluctant to allow others to access them freely. This situation is now however changing rapidly. Computers are now available in many language learning settings, and the growth of the Internet and the spread of text archives on CD-ROM (from newspapers and encyclopedias to research papers and literary works) means that it is feasible for teachers and learners to compile and exploit substantial collections of electronic text for themselves. A variety of software tools to analyze such 'home-made' corpora have been produced, some explicitly designed for language teaching and learning purposes (Chandler 1989, Scott and Johns 1993, Barlow 1996b, Scott 1996, Barlow 1998). At the same time, publishers and researchers have begun to allow more general access to the corpora they have compiled, developing dedicated software for this purpose, such as the SARA system for interrogating the British National Corpus (Dodd 1997).

It is thus now technically and economically feasible for many language teachers and learners to use corpora if they so desire. This change of climate makes it all the more important that the roles of corpora in language teaching and learning should be discussed and evaluated. The papers in this volume provide detailed examples of practical work using corpora, accompanied in each case by discussions of their relevance in terms of current theories of language use and of language learning. They start from two main pedagogic premises:

- learning a language is a matter both of learning *about* how the language is used, and of learning *how to* use it, thereby developing what Widdowson (1984) terms competence and capacity;
- pedagogy should aim to develop learners' learning skills, leading them to greater autonomy.

In terms of Kennedy's three points, they aim to show how:

- corpora can provide teachers and learners with information about the language and the culture which can complement and integrate that available from other sources, such as textbooks, teachers, and reference materials. This can effectively increase their competence and awareness, as well as developing their ability to evaluate information from other sources more critically;

- corpora have a wide range of potential pedagogic uses, many of them very different from those of descriptive linguistics;
- work with corpora need not simply focus on linguistic 'facts', but can be fully compatible with a focus on the learner and on the learning process, from a meaning- as well as from a form-focussed perspective.

The volume is structured so as to illustrate these arguments in a progression from theory to practice. In chapter 1, Aston provides an introductory overview to the uses of corpora in pedagogy, focussing both on the previous literature and on the contributions to this volume, for which his paper provides a general interpretative framework. He argues that corpora can help learners to discover and check descriptive 'facts' of various kinds about the language and the culture, and to consolidate their existing knowledge; to understand and produce particular texts and text-types; to develop reading and writing skills; to provide communicative practice; to increase linguistic awareness; and to develop learning autonomy. He also discusses criteria for the selection and grading of corpus-based activities. This overview is complemented by chapter 2, in which Partington provides a description of the concerns and methods of corpus linguistics - the "scientifically interesting" background of linguistic description from which pedagogic applications aiming to develop competence have developed, and the changed conception of language use which underlies them.

The remaining chapters focus on specific uses of corpora in pedagogy, in contexts which range from all-but-total teacher control to total learner independence. In chapter 3, Partington illustrates activities aimed at helping learners to discover and check 'facts' about a variety of lexical, syntactic and discursive features of written English. In chapter 4, Zorzi instead focusses on the spoken language, considering how corpus-based work can enable learners to discover for themselves how such poorly-understood features as discourse markers are used, and to develop their sensitivity to contextual constraints on their use. In chapter 5, Gavioli takes up one of the themes to emerge from Zorzi's paper, that of training learners to make discoveries in corpora, increasing their linguistic awareness and technical ability as researchers, and illustrates ways of encouraging them to make use of their findings in their own production. Chapter 6, by Brodine, focusses on a specific EAP teaching context, considering how corpora can help learners to develop their reading skills with respect to academic texts. In chapter 7, Zanettin focusses on the use of corpora as aids in translation, both as a means of understanding the source text and of formulating and evaluating hypotheses in the construction of the target text. In chapter 8, again starting from a translation context, Bertaccini and Aston show how learners can design and analyse their own corpora to resolve particular problems in reading and writing specific texts. Finally, in chapter 9, Bernardini considers the potential of corpora for autonomous learning, taking a general perspective. She illustrates how a large corpus can provide a wealth of opportunities for learning and for communicative practice, be this with respect to the workings of the language as a whole or to those of particular texts and text-types.

All these chapters are illustrated with practical examples drawn from their authors' experience with undergraduate learners of English, French, and Italian as foreign languages. Corpora are seen as resources for learning activities which can:

- improve competence, increasing learners' knowledge of the language and the culture, and their awareness of how the former is used in the latter;
- engage capacity, helping learners develop their ability to use the language as a means of communication, both in reception and in production;
- increase autonomy, providing learners with learning instruments which they can exploit independently, and developing their ability to do so.

We believe that the uses of corpora in language learning presented are both theoretically warranted and potentially practically profitable from all of these perspectives.

While it is assumed that the reader has some experience of personal computing, and is familiar with such notions as files and bytes, this book does not call for any particular technical expertise. Those readers wishing to further explore the ideas it contains for themselves will, however, require corpus-analysis software, such as *Wordsmith Tools* (Scott 1996), *MonoConc* (Barlow 1996b, 1998), or the more limited but easier-to-use (and free) *MicroConcord* (Scott and Johns 1993). They will also require quantities of machine-readable text, such as:

- personal collections of word-processed files (letters, documents, e-mail etc.), preferably in .txt (ASCII) format (most word processors allow documents to be saved in this format using the *Save As* option);
- collections of text published on diskette or CD-ROM, such as *MicroConcord Corpus A* and *B* (Murison-Bowie 1993b, 1993c), the

- various corpora contained on the *ICAME* CD-ROM (see chapter 2: note 3), or the *BNC sampler* (Burnard 1999);
- other CD-ROMs from which texts can be selected and downloaded to disk, such as those of newspapers and encyclopedias;
- texts downloaded from World Wide Web sites (again, preferably as .txt files).

Readers with Internet access are also urged to experiment with corpora available online: for instance, limited free access is available to both the 100-million word *British National Corpus* (http://info.ox.ac.uk/bnc), and a 50-million word portion of the 300-million word *Bank of English* (http://titania.cobuild.collins.co.uk). A particularly interesting recent development is web concordancing, which treats the entire world-wide web as a corpus (http://www.webcorp.org.uk).

Where computing facilities are only available to the teacher, outside the classroom, these tools can only be used to prepare printed materials for students to work with. While much can be done with such materials, a wider variety of pedagogic activities is possible if facilities are available in the classroom or the self-access centre, for teachers and learners to use as and when they see fit. Obviously, such availability will be essential if learners are to learn to exploit corpora independently, as resources making for a growing autonomy in language learning.

1 LEARNING WITH CORPORA: AN OVERVIEW

Guy Aston

1. Premise

This chapter aims to provide a critical introduction to the uses of corpora in language pedagogy, in relation to both the previous literature and the contributions to this volume. It starts by examining the influence of work in corpus linguistics, which has above all viewed corpora as resources for the description of language use, as attested in large quantities of text. In pedagogy, corpora have been seen as a means of similarly helping not only teachers, but also learners to check linguistic 'facts' of various kinds: the process of analyzing corpus data, it has been argued, may also help to consolidate existing knowledge, to extend linguistic awareness, and to refine learning skills (Johns 1991a). While valid, it will be argued that this view seems unnecessarily restricted: as well as providing a means of learning about the language (and the culture), corpora can also be seen as providing opportunities for using it communicatively, with a focus on situated textual meanings rather than just their linguistic forms. Corpora can also be used to aid the development of reading and writing skills, and the understanding and production of particular texts and types of texts. From these perspectives too, they arguably offer a means to increase learners' motivation and to render them more autonomous.

2. Corpora and linguistic description: learning about the language

The use of corpora to help describe aspects of a language goes back to well before the computer. West's *General service list of English words* (1953), which ranked the most common words in English by frequency, and was widely used to design EFL graded reading programmes, was based on a manual analysis of several million words of text. Computers have made such tasks far easier, and lexicographers and grammarians now regularly use corpora in order to establish the frequency and exemplify the use of a wide range of lexicogrammatical features, either in the language as a whole, or in particular types of speech or writing (for examples, cfr. Partington, this volume, chapter 2). Their research has shown that native-speaker intuition is an unreliable guide to actual occurrence: many uses which occur in corpus data are not recognized by traditional descriptions, and many uses enshrined in traditional descriptions do not in fact occur with any frequency. Corpus linguists have consequently proposed the application of these new descriptive insights to the design of language teaching syllabuses and materials. A glance at some of this work will allow us to clarify ways in which such findings may be relevant to language pedagogy, as well as to illustrate the aims and methods of corpus-based description.

In the pioneering Cobuild project, Sinclair used a computerized corpus some ten times the size of West's in order to establish what words and uses of those words merited inclusion in a learner dictionary of English, and to exemplify their typical usage (Cobuild 1987, Sinclair 1987a). This corpus was also used to outline a 'lexical syllabus' based on the most frequent uses of the most frequent words in the language (Sinclair and Renouf 1988, Willis and Willis 1988, Willis 1990). Similar techniques were subsequently employed to obtain information on grammatical structures for the Cobuild learner grammar (Cobuild 1990: for subsequent work in this area see Hunston and Francis 2000). Researchers have also focussed their attention on specific areas of lexicogrammar - for instance irregular verbs (Grabowski and Mindt 1995) and ways of expressing futurity (Mindt 1997) - or on specific discourse varieties, for instance academic writing (Biber, Conrad and Reppen 1994) and informal conversation (Carter and McCarthy 1995, McCarthy and Carter 1995, Carter 1998). If the most frequent features in the target variety are prioritized in language teaching syllabuses, the utility and 'surrender value' of the latter can arguably be maximized: even if the learner gives up half-way, s/he will have learned the most frequent features of the language - often ones which were ignored or delayed in traditional syllabuses.

While it is unlikely that frequency should be the sole criterion to determine the selection and grading of syllabus content, it is clearly an important one. Insofar as frequency data from corpora can indicate whether a particular feature is likely to be worth learning, this fact makes it relevant to teachers and learners as well as to syllabus and materials designers. Conversely, the inclusion or prioritization in the syllabus of infrequent features, and the exclusion or delay of frequent ones, needs to be justified by other criteria. These criteria may include range (whether the item occurs in many types of texts), availability (whether it is necessary for particular key situations), coverage (the number of different uses the item has), and learnability (whether it is regular, brief, transparent, similar to the L1, or otherwise easily acquired: Mackey 1965: 176-190), as well as prototypicality (whether the item is prototypical in a psychological sense, from which the meanings of other uses can be inferred: Widdowson 1991). Corpora can also provide useful information regarding some of these other criteria, casting light on the range, availability, and coverage of particular items (though for learnability and prototypicality we need to turn to second language acquisition research and teaching experience). In all of these respects, pedagogy clearly has to gain from the 'improved descriptions' of the language that corpora make possible - improved in the sense that they are based on systematically observing actual use rather than intuiting what uses are possible and probable (Sinclair 1991b).

As an example, let us take one of the largest published corpora, the *British National Corpus*, with its 100 million words of written and spoken English, and search for the word-forms *hand* and *foot*. We find that *hand* is much the more frequent of the two: it occurs 35,352 times in the corpus (roughly once every 2,800 words), nearly five times as often as *foot* (7,544 times, or once every 13,300 words).

Figure 1 shows a random selection of 20 occurrences of *hand*. The various instances, or *citations* from the corpus, are displayed here in a one-per-line format known as KWIC (key word in context). A KWIC concordance places the key word (*hand*) in the centre of the line, surrounded by as much of the context as will fit on that line. As only a few words of context are given, some citations may be difficult to understand; and annoyingly, the first and last words of the citation may be truncated. The virtue of KWIC format, however, is that it makes it easy to identify and compare the words which precede and follow the key word in the various citations. In this example, the citations have been sorted alphabetically according to the word immediately preceding *hand*: thus the three occurrences of *other hand* are listed together. (All the programs listed in the preface to this volume allow citations to be automatically sorted in a variety of manners.)

Most textbooks, probably in accord with most people's intuitions, consider *hand* to denote a body part, and stress its use with possessives (*my/your/her hand*). In this concordance, however, we find the body-part meaning in fewer than half the instances. More often, *hand* appears to be used metaphorically - in the contrastive connectors *on the one hand/on* the other hand, and in the phrasal verb *hand over*, for instance. And where it is used literally, this is not always with a possessive: just as often, we find the determiners *a/one/each*.

We should of course resist the temptation to draw general conclusions from such a small number of citations: corpus linguists may analyze thousands of concordance lines in trying to establish the uses of a word. Nonetheless, this tiny concordance can remind us that use with a possessive

```
1   tained from a client.  The 'invisible hand" of market forces will mean that when faced
2   er in a few hours."  Niall held out a hand to steady her as she stepped off the gangway
3   But first..."  He stood up and with a hand on the Dalmatian's collar took the bitch to
4   uch he could tell Neill - he couldn't hand over Brimmer's illegal accounts until he had
5   Roger made off with a bottle in each hand and Luke had vanished again.  ¦ Caroline led
6   when he stretched out his thick hairy hand, she was surprised at the calluses on the pa
7   hing else we've got".  He flicked his hand and I thought I saw a few spots of red appea
8   r struggle anyway, and stood with his hand supporting her head, as his warm lips presse
9   have it in hand.  It should be out of hand and all over the bloody media by now.  Is an
10  ice off his chin with the heel of one hand.  "Well, Tom..."  He took the second bite.
11  o get, at one time, Dulles on the one hand and Khrushchev on the other, to answer him w
12  he representative of God.  On the one hand, this new-born child received the homage of
13  d have been among them.  On the other hand, it was not until 1973 that good Chardonnay,
14  sacre of the Innocents.  On the other hand, it has been argued that the burning of gene
15  still quite buildable.  On the other hand, there are certainly some projects which are
16  side as you.  i.e. fig 52 is a right hand holding pattern...  The needle will come on
17  he back upwards, in his strong square hand.  Alice's hand shrank a little, but she made
18  intended trying before, one trembling hand hesitating over the latch, Isabel could only
19  e, took the package and said he would hand it over to the lady next time she visited th
20  ou saying?  Benedicite!  Lift up your hand and cross yourself!  For it is both sinful a
```

Figure 1. *hand* in the BNC (random 20 lines)

to refer to a body-part is only one use of *hand*, and perhaps not even the main one. From a pedagogic viewpoint, it is clear that a larger and more reliable analysis might help in the preparation and evaluation of syllabuses and materials. Given their respective frequencies we might decide to teach *hand* before *foot*; or we might decide to place *on the one/other hand* near the beginning of a list of senses of *hand* in a learner dictionary. A large, heterogeneous corpus like the BNC can provide credible indications of the relative frequencies of the main words and structures in British English and of their various uses. Homogeneous corpora of texts of a particular type can provide similar indications for that text-type, facilitating the design of ESP syllabuses and materials (for examples see Flowerdew 1993; Biber, Conrad and Reppen 1994: cfr. section 5 below).

We have suggested that analyses of this kind may not only be of value to researchers and materials designers. Given access to concordancing facilities and a suitable corpus, teachers and learners can similarly discover for themselves how often and how particular words are used. If (as the concordance above would suggest) the most common uses of *hand* are metaphorical ones like *on the one/other hand* and *hand over*, then the teacher might want to check that these uses are adequately covered by the textbook s/he is using. Likewise, learners can use corpora in order to find out about the language for themselves. Given the concordance in Figure 1, even learners who have never seen one before are likely to notice the frequency of *on the one/other hand*; with help and practice, they may also notice more subtle regularities - for instance that this phrase tends to occur at the beginning of sentences and to be followed by a comma. Or they may be made curious as to the differences between *a hand*, *one hand* and *his hand*, as to what the *heel* of a hand is, or as to how *hand over* is used; and with encouragement and initiative, they may go on to seek further information about such features - in a grammar, a dictionary, or in further corpus examples. In each case, their linguistic competence is likely to be increased, as they discover things about the language of which they were previously unaware or uncertain.

Obviously, teachers and learners cannot expect to match the descriptions of professional linguists, which may be based on years of training and experience, as well as on many more citations and many different corpora. The objectives of teachers and learners are however rather different, so that smaller-scale, less systematic analyses may still provide useful information. In the first place, as our concordance of *hand* suggests, some macroscopic features can be noticed without sophisticated analyses of enormous amounts of data. Second, as there is rarely only one descriptive insight to be gained from a concordance of this kind, users can

```
1   ro Energy subsidiary was able to hand over $20m to its boss, Andrew Hall.¦ On line¦¦ IB
2   BL} (...) yeah you hand your railcard over and get ^ (...) ^ (PS0BK} ^ Yeah, free rape
3   ressures have forced councils to hand over debt recovery to private agents known as she
4   eanwhile the BBC have refused to hand over film of alleged rioting at an acid house par
5   laize of breaking his promise to hand over more than £2 million in back pay.¦Obituary:
6   ver, as I didn't smoke I used to hand over my cigarette coupons, and received the equiv
7   eelings which are strong, but to hand over my Precious little one to a Young and Foreig
8   yan government might hand the two men over to the Arab League, and thus pre-empt the ap
9   ade it clear that they would not hand over Noriega. Officials admit that the administra
10  en to President Bush offering to hand over part of her late husband's fortune for distr
11  . Medical ethics. I ought not to hand over the case notes until it's authorised."¦Damn.
12  d holder who would prefer not to hand over the file is entitled to refuse unless the pa
13  al illness he had been forced to hand over the leadership of the State to the military,
14  are outdated, Westminster should hand over the powers which it does have to Brussels.¦¦
15  rléans refused Stair's demand to hand over the ships and their contents to Byng but did
16  Now I am delighted to be able to hand over the spot-light to my three management collea
17            Now, er, before I hand over to Frank (.) er, a word about the dividend
18  the Tizi n'Test road, they would hand over to Mohammed, who had meantime brought his mu
19  h of his salary he would have to hand over to the Inland Revenue heavy mob for the past
20  e.¦ They point out that when you hand over your housekeeping at the Sainsbury checkout,
```

Figure 2. *hand over* in the BNC (random 20 lines)

decide for themselves what to focus on, according to their own criteria of relevance and learnability. Third, such descriptions need not be fully accurate: since learning a language involves gradual approximation to the target system, then provided users are aware that their descriptions are partial and approximate, these may still be of value to them.

To further exemplify these points, let us consider the verb *hand over*. Figure 2 provides a randomly-selected set of occurrences from the British National Corpus, sorted alphabetically according to the words following *over*. A glance at this concordance suggests that among the things which people and institutions hand over are money, valuable property, prisoners, and potentially incriminating information. While not complete, this list captures a fair proportion of these occurrences, and the user who is able to infer such a list from the concordance will form quite a good idea of some of the ways in which the verb is used. What s/he should not do is treat this account as definitive, but rather as one which can be refined and expanded in the future. Some of its limits will be immediately apparent: it makes, for instance, no reference to the fact that many occurrences imply some kind of obligation on or reluctance of the agent; intransitive uses are not considered; nor are inflected forms of the verb.

As well as trying to generate their own descriptions from the data, teachers and learners can use corpora to exemplify and integrate the descriptions provided by other sources. The concordance of *hand over* may help to consolidate and expand the information in the following dictionary entry:

> **hand over** 1 T [...] to give someone or something to someone else to take care of or to control: *The resistance fighters agreed to hand over their hostages.* 2 I,T [...] to give power or responsibility to someone else: *The captain was unwilling to hand over the command of his ship.* | *Before handing over to Jim, I'd like to thank you all for your support.*
> (LDOCE 1995)

Compared with the dictionary's broad generalizations, the concordance reveals a wider range of lower-level patterns, casting light on more specific aspects of this verb's use. It also provides a wider range of examples, some of which may be more memorable than those in the dictionary - handing over the housekeeping at the Sainsbury checkout, for instance (line 20), or handing over part of one's salary to the Inland Revenue heavy mob (line 19).

A first way corpora can be used by teachers and learners is thus to generate and test linguistic descriptions, deriving knowledge *about* the language. Recent work in second language acquisition has challenged the extreme positions of the 1980s, when scholars as far apart as Krashen (1982) and Prabhu (1987) argued that knowledge of linguistic 'facts' was irrelevant to an ability to use the language: there is now substantial empirical evidence to suggest that provided it takes appropriate forms and is suitably contextualized, explicit knowledge can play an important role in the development of linguistic and sociolinguistic competence (R. Ellis 1994, Williams 1995; Robinson 1996; Spada 1997). Some methods by which such descriptively-focussed work can be carried out by learners are discussed in greater detail in 2.2 below, and in the papers in this volume by Partington (chapter 3), Zorzi (chapter 4) and Gavioli (chapter 5).

As well as helping them learn specific lexicogrammatical items and their uses, such descriptive work may benefit learners in more general ways. Corpus linguistics has helped develop new ways of looking at, and thinking about, language knowledge and language use, and using corpora can arguably help learners to similarly refine their own perspectives. Hymes (1972) sees communicative competence as consisting of four components, relating to linguistic grammaticality, psychological feasibility, sociological appropriacy, and attestedness. Since they document what is recurrently done in actual texts (rather than what might in theory be done in hypothetical ones), corpora above all highlight attestedness: concordances show the tendencies of particular items to recur in particular contexts. Analyzing corpus data can thus develop sensitivity to a range of contextual factors to which attestedness can be related (for a more detailed description, see Sinclair 1996b):

- *collocational* - the tendency of an item to occur in particular lexical company (Sinclair 1991a). Our concordance of *hand* (Figure 1 above) suggests some interesting possibilities here. Is *invisible* a frequent collocate of *hand*? What about *heel*? Such questions can be answered by examining a larger number of examples of *hand*, or, more economically, by searching for co-occurrences of these words or phrases in close proximity. (All the software cited in the preface to this volume allows for such searches.)
- *colligational* - the tendency of an item to occur in particular grammatical company (Mitchell 1958), or in particular structural positions in texts (Hoey 1997, 2000). Does *hand over* regularly occur in modal or semi-modal environments? Is *on the one/other hand* typically sentence-initial?
- *semantic* - the tendency of an item to occur together with items from a particular semantic field, as where *hand over* appears with

valuables.
- *pragmatic* - the tendency of an item to occur in contexts which have a particular function, for instance that of a positive or negative evaluation by the speaker/writer (Louw 1993, 1997; cfr. Partington, this volume, chapter 3: 4). A question which might be posed about *on the one/other hand* is whether there a tendency for one of the two forms to introduce an alternative which is less favourably, and the other to introduce one which is more favourably evaluated by the speaker or writer.
- *generic* - the tendency of an item to occur in a particular type of text. Is *on the one hand* particularly common in academic discourse? Does it turn out to be rare in informal conversation?

The fact that an item tends to occur in certain types of context may have little to do with traditional grammatical or sociolinguistic rules. For instance, it is difficult to imagine a general rule which would explain why *problem* should occur after *main* much more often than after *principal* - yet the relative frequencies of these collocations in the BNC are 20:1. It is not that we cannot speak of a *principal problem*, but that in practice, *main* is far more frequently attested. *Main* and *problem* appear to be conventionally associated, perhaps being stored, interpreted and retrieved as a single unit - as, in a sense, a single lexeme - following what Sinclair (1991a: 110ff) has called the "idiom principle". Similarly, it is difficult to imagine a sociolinguistic rule which would account for the rarity of *on the other hand* in informal conversation: nonetheless the BNC shows that it is strongly associated with formal writing.

There is a growing literature in applied linguistics which emphasizes the importance of such contextual patterns in language use and language learning (e.g. Fillmore 1979; Pawley and Syder 1983; Peters 1983; Nattinger and De Carrico 1992; Wray 2000). Insofar as different words appear to have distinctive collocational, colligational, semantic, pragmatic, and generic associations, it has been argued that every word may have its own grammar in these respects, a grammar which can only be acquired through experience of its typical contextual patternings (Sinclair 1991a; Clear 2000; cfr. Partington, this volume, chapter 2: 4.2). Such patternings may be first learnt as idiomatic chunks, and subsequently analyzed into their components (Bolinger 1976; Peters 1983); or, where their single components have first been acquired, they may be subsequently synthesized into single units (Schank 1982; N. Ellis 1996). Hoey (2000) similarly argues that more general grammatical rules are acquired through the analysis of recurrent collocational and colligational patterns.

Concordancing corpora can help teachers and learners to identify recurrent patternings of these kinds. By so doing they may not only acquire the patterns, but also become aware of the extent to which these and other schemata - and not just single words and morphemes - constitute the building blocks of language use. They may also develop their ability to analyze and synthesize them, restructuring their previous knowledge in the process (Widdowson 1984; Aston 1995b; Aston 1997a; Skehan 1998). Learners who have come to associate *a hand*, *one hand*, and *his/her hand* with distinct typical contexts arguably have a competence which is richer, more articulated, and more readily available for use than learners who have only a generic 'dictionary' knowledge of the word *hand*; and learners who are aware that such patterns are worth noticing, and are able to identify them, are in a position to extend and deepen their competence in these respects. They are also likely to develop, through practice, their capacity to do so. In this sense the process of describing may be as useful for the acquisition of competence as the actual descriptions obtained.

2.1 Objects of description

For the reasons just outlined, corpora can be useful tools of linguistic description for learners and teachers, as well as for syllabus and materials designers. To draw on corpora effectively, however, it is necessary to identify features which lend themselves to productive analysis, and employ appropriate procedures for carrying these analyses out. This section lists some of the many features which have been suggested in the literature, and Partington (this volume, chapter 3) provides practical examples illustrating some of the different types of contextual patternings which can be evidenced. Procedures of analysis are discussed in 2.2 below.

Let us begin with a lexical perspective. Virtually any word or family of words can be examined, provided it is adequately documented in the corpus being used. Concordancing will generally cast light both on the meanings of the word in question, and on the contexts in which it is used. Minugh (1997) illustrates how CD-ROM collections of contemporary newspapers can be concordanced to help learners understand neologisms which are absent from dictionaries; Aitchison and Lewis (1995; Aitchison 1997) examine the use of the neologism *wimp* in such a corpus, showing how its meaning and derogatory connotations can be inferred - wimps are weak, effeminate males (of whom President Bush senior appears the historical archetype). Another fruitful area of study is lexical polysemy: learners can be given concordances of a word and asked to identify its various senses and the contextual patternings associated with each sense -

for instance the nominal and verbal uses of *lead* (Tribble and Jones 1990), or the different senses of *stripper* (Kettemann 1995b). Even if the word is a familiar one, such work may expand knowledge of its metaphorical uses, and of the patterns with which these are associated: in chapter 3, Partington illustrates the extraordinary range of uses of the word *black*, from *black spot* to *black hole*.

As far as grammatical features are concerned, matters are rather less straightforward. Concordances of some features can be generated by searching for grammatical words or phrases (such as *should* or *am/be/been/ being/is/was/were to*: Johns 1991a, 1996), or for word- or phrase-patterns (such as the plural possessive **s'* or the complementation pattern *to *ing*: the asterisk stands for any sequence of characters in a word). The difficulty is that not all grammatical features are unambiguously signalled by their surface forms: Tribble and Jones (1990) note how much easier it is to retrieve passives from a German corpus, where they are marked by forms of *werden*, than in English, where *be* has many other uses. Where a feature has no distinctive orthographic form, it may still be possible to locate instances by searching for other forms which often co-occur with it - for instance, by looking for *said* to find instances of reported speech, or for capitalized *Hardly* and *Not only* to find instances of subject-verb inversion in affirmative sentences. But for some grammatical features it can be virtually impossible to locate instances in these ways. For instance, relative clauses which lack relative pronouns (as in *people this book is of little interest to*) have no distinctive feature in their surface form which can be searched for, unless such structures have been explicitly indicated by codes or *tags* added to the corpus. (This is one of the main reasons why research corpora tend to be *annotated*, each word in the corpus being flanked by a tag indicating its part-of-speech category and/or its syntactic role: Garside et al. 1997; cfr. Partington, this volume, chapter 2: 3.2)

These problems highlight two central issues that must be considered when interrogating any corpus. First, the *precision* of the query, that is, the extent to which the search retrieves *only* instances of the feature(s) of interest. If we are interested in passives, a search for forms of *be* will be very imprecise, and to obtain a concordance showing only passive constructions we will have to manually delete the large number of citations which are, for our purposes, spurious. Second, the *recall* of the query - that is, the extent to which it retrieves *all* the instances of the feature(s) of interest. If we are looking for conditional clauses, a search for *if* may provide tolerable precision (though we will have to delete cases of indirect speech, such as *I asked him if*), but recall will be at best partial, since our search will ignore conditional clauses with *unless*, or with subject-verb inversion (*should it rain/were it to rain/had it rained* etc.).

Given the difficulty of achieving adequate precision and recall, pedagogic proposals for descriptive work using corpora have tended to focus only on those grammatical features whose morphological and/or lexical correlates are systematic and distinctive. For similar reasons, semantic and pragmatic features have for the most part been ignored: there is no way we can search a corpus to find all the requests, all the propositions linked by causative relations, or all the references to past time, unless the corpus has been explicitly annotated to mark instances of these features. It is however possible to investigate specific forms which frequently have certain meanings and functions (if necessary, examining a larger context than is available in a KWIC display): instances illustrated in this volume include the use of general nouns as cohesive devices, and discourse markers in speech (Partington, chapter 3: 6; Zorzi, chapter 4).

In addition to examining individual linguistic features, corpora can be used to compare different ones. Most concordancing programs allow the user to specify a range of forms in a query, generating a single concordance combining instances of each. For instance, *Wordsmith Tools* (Scott 1996) allows the user to search either for alternative forms (e.g. *look/looked/looking/looks*), or for a pattern with respect to which alternatives to be ignored can be specified (e.g. *look** but not *lookalike*). Alternatively, a separate concordance can be generated for each form. These techniques offer a means of contrasting "confusable words" (Carpenter 1993), such as *interested* and *interesting* (Murison-Bowie 1993a), *see* and *watch* (Kettemann 1995b), *over* and *above* (Tribble and Jones 1990), *filled* and *full* (Flowerdew 1996), *rather* and *somewhat* (Partington, this volume, chapter 3: 3). Grammatical structures which have distinctive formal characteristics can also be contrasted: *will* and *going to* (Clear 2000); present perfect constructions with *for* and *since* (Jordan 1993; Kettemann 1995b, 1997); defining and non-defining relative clauses introduced by *(,) who* and *(,) which* (Murison-Bowie 1993a).

If a corpus can be divided into subcorpora, or if specialized corpora from different domains or genres are available, these can be used to compare the use of a particular feature in different types of text. This can provide a way of illustrating, for example, the different uses and frequencies in speech and writing of words such as *well* and *like*, or of contracted verb forms; the different senses of *interest* in arts and in business sections of newspapers (Murison-Bowie 1996); or the senses and relative frequencies of *sure* and *certain* in formal and informal prose (Biber, Conrad and Reppen 1994). Where both specialized and large heterogeneous corpora are available, uses identified in the former can be compared with uses in the latter in order to see if these are restricted to a particular text-type, where they may constitute technical terms, or whether they have a wider range. Gavioli (this volume, chapter 5: 3.2, 4.1) illustrates these procedures with respect to classified 'lonely hearts' advertisements, comparing uses in these with ones in the correspondence columns of a newspaper agony aunt and in the written texts of the BNC. In some cases, features used differently in different corpora can be identified computationally: *Wordsmith Tools* (Scott 1996) includes a "Keywords" programme which compares the lexical content of two corpora, and lists the words or phrases which are significantly more frequent in one than in the other, and, of these, those words which tend to occur in the same texts (Scott 2000).

2.2   Procedures of description: data-driven learning

Johns (1991a, 1991b, 1994, 1997) has coined the term "data-driven learning" (DDL) to describe the procedures by which concordances of particular language features can be analyzed by learners to infer and test descriptive generalizations concerning their use.[1] He argues that these procedures are of two main types: inductive and deductive. In the inductive type, learners infer generalizations from concordance data, discovering facts about the language for themselves by identifying patternings and coming up with hypotheses which will account for them, through successive operations of observation, classification, and generalization (Johns 1991a: 4). It has been widely argued that 'discovery learning' of this kind is particularly effective for the acquisition of grammar and vocabulary (see e.g. Hudson 1992; Batstone 1994; Singleton 1997), leading learners to notice patterns in the input (Schmidt 1990; N. Ellis 1996), stimulating deeper processing (Craik and Lockhart 1972), and improving subsequent retention (Joe 1998). Not only the process but also the contents of discovery learning may be particularly valuable: Johns (1991a: 5) argues that learners' discoveries are often more accurate and/or practical than the descriptions given by teachers or textbooks - accurate, in the sense that traditional descriptions may fail to match the reality of actual data; practical, in the sense that learners may find their own generalizations to be more readily applicable than ones formulated by experts, whose conceptual frameworks they may not share.

Johns' second type of procedure is deductive. In this case, learners apply previously-acquired generalizations in order to classify concordance data, testing the 'rules' they have learned, and thereby consolidating and/or

```
1   t year, Foreman will fight Gerry Cooney, a long since discredited Irish-American contender who has be
2   arges, said yesterday he had spent the 14 years since dropping out of active priesthood raising money
3   simists were predicting a heavy Polish win. <p> Since five of the Polonian team play for the national
4   hours. <p> Irene Schwidurski missed all those, since for many years she has refused to observe the m
5   put it to me very subtly but very bluntly that since Great Britain was going to be in the final anyw
```

Figure 3. Which lines illustrate the temporal, and which the causal sense of *since*?

```
1   rm of responsibility: "They have been in charge ___ five of the last six years but will not agree th
2   r half an hour. Kirwan has had Achilles trouble ___ he arrived in Wales a week ago, yet, having play
3   awesome reputation which the work has acquired ___ its first performance over 160 years ago places
4   y of the vilification he claims to have endured ___ moving in on the club and Martin Edwards, the ch
5   ion, one of the richest in France, has run Nice ___ nearly a quarter of a century. His father did th
```

Figure 4. In which lines is the blanked out word *for*, and in which *since*?

```
1    repayment obligations. Paying back some dollars 12bn since
2    Twain's tremor caused very little damage and has long since
3     who came to Britain from Pakistan in 1982, has lived for
4    1947. <p> Only one fresh piece of evidence has emerged since

A.   five years in Huddersfield, West Yorkshire, with Alison Mit
B.   1985 has squeezed domestic growth. <p> At the annual confer
C.   Monday, when the family were given a few personal effects
D.   ceded its title to the great earthquake of 1906, when fires
```

Figure 5. Which continuation matches each numbered line?

refining their knowledge. Johns (1991b, 1994, 1997) outlines a variety of deductive activities, based on grouping concordance lines, filling in blanked out elements, and matching jumbled halves of lines. These activities are summarily illustrated in Figures 3-5, which focus on the uses of *for* and *since*. As well as providing opportunities for applying linguistic generalizations, activities of these kinds provide a controlled means of developing the ability to observe and classify recurrent features in concordance data, which is, as we have seen, also essential to inductive work.

The distinction between inductive and deductive activities using corpus data is however one of emphasis rather than absolute. As Murison-Bowie (1996) notes, arriving at a satisfactory generalization from raw data involves not just inducing it but also testing it deductively to check that it works; equally, applying a previously-given generalization will often involve refining and restructuring it in order to maximize its accuracy and practicality, in that

> much of what might be understood intuitively as rules are [*sic*] not supported by the evidence, and much of what can be observed is not commonly described by existing rules.
> (Murison-Bowie 1996: 185)

Thus, if a corpus is used to test generalizations provided by a teacher or textbook, the evidence may well partly disconfirm these, so that alternative or additional hypotheses will need to be formulated inductively. In the literature, we find a number of inadequate textbook generalizations proposed for investigation using corpus data: the rule that distinguishes *going to* and *will* as future forms (Clear 2000); the 'backshift' rule for tense in reported speech (Kettemann 1995b); rules of tense sequencing in conditional sentences (Mindt 1997; Partington 1998). If the learner searches for occurrences of *going to* and *will/'ll*, of reported speech verbs such as *said*, or of *if/whether*, s/he will probably find a fair number of citations that fail to fit the textbook rule. Recognizing the latter's limits, s/he may seek to modify and improve it. Even where the data does in fact fit a previous generalization, applying the latter to a concordance is likely to lead to greater articulation, with the creation of a series of more detailed schemata which describe subsets of the data more practically. Thus Aston (1995b) illustrates how concordance data not only confirms the 'rule' that *since*, in its temporal sense, refers to a moment in time, but also highlights such recurrent phraseologies as *since then* and *ever since*, which may not be mentioned in textbook accounts. Similarly, a learner who starts with the dictionary's account of *hand over* before 'applying' it to the concordance in Figure 2 above may well end up refining the dictionary generalization, for instance by identifying the verb's preference for valuables as an object. In practice, virtually all descriptively-focussed work with concordances involves a mixture of induction and deduction, in proportions which depend on the focus of the activity and the structuring of the data. In this respect DDL fits with current views of language learning as a matter of progressive approximation and knowledge restructuring (Skehan 1998): the examples presented by Partington (this volume, chapter 3) and Zorzi (this volume, chapter 4) illustrate the procedures involved in further detail.

3. Expanding the DDL perspective

According to Kennedy (1992: cfr. the preface to this volume), one of the reasons why corpora have had relatively little impact on classroom language teaching is because the latter is currently more concerned with the processes than with the contents of learning. At first sight, Johns' data-driven approach, which has primarily been conceived as a means of showing how particular lexicogrammatical phenomena are used, does little to bridge this gap. Communicative language teaching (at any rate in its "strong" form: Howatt 1984) considers competence to develop not out of explicit knowledge, but out of the engagement of capacity to negotiate meaning. Contemporary 'task-based' syllabuses are drawn up in methodological terms, aiming to specify contexts for learning rather than contents to be learnt (Breen and Candlin 1980; Prabhu 1987) - even if recent years have seen renewed interest in form-focussed activities to complement this emphasis, as noted in the last section.

Corpora need not, however, simply be seen as sources of knowledge about the language. In the first place, as we have seen, data-driven learning is a way of developing metalinguistic and metacognitive awareness, enhancing learners' ability to notice regularities in data and to interpret them. In this respect DDL, as Johns has argued (1991a: 3), may help learners achieve greater independence. Such a view offers a much closer match with the focus on the learning process in current pedagogy, where the importance of developing autonomy has been stressed both from a motivational and an educational perspective (see e.g. Benson and Voller 1997). In the second place, the use of corpora does not necessarily imply a focus on language forms. Once we begin to move away from the model of corpus linguistics, with its emphasis on maximally-accurate language description, we find that there are a considerable number of ways in which corpus-based work can provide opportunities for negotiating meaning, which in their turn can also be seen as encouraging autonomy.

3.1 Corpora in a communicative context

First, data-driven learning can readily be situated in contexts which call for communication. As Bernardini has shown (2000a, c; this volume, chapter 9: 4.1), the analysis of concordances can be treated as a problem-solving or 'reasoning gap' task (Prabhu 1987), whose procedures and outcomes become the object of learners' reports and discussions. Just as the objective in a traditional communication task may be to establish a consensus on the best way from A to B on a fictional map, the objective of a DDL activity can be that of establishing a consensus as to how some feature of the language works - with the advantage that learners may well be more motivated to discover linguistic facts than textbook fictions. From this perspective, many of the techniques traditionally employed in communication tasks can be exploited in DDL: for instance, a long concordance can be divided up and the parts given to different learners or different groups to analyze, who can subsequently be asked to regroup and formulate joint analyses which bridge the information gap deriving from their different data inputs. The number of variables calling for negotiation in such tasks can be increased by allowing learners to choose the data, the corpus, and indeed the object of research. Bernardini (this volume, chapter 9: 4.1) argues that a corpus can be viewed as a virgin terrain for learners to explore at will, where they can discuss the progress of their journeys and recount their discoveries to each other.

Providing a communicative context for DDL work may also help learners improve their strategies for working with corpora. Johns has argued that data-driven learning places the learner in the position of a researcher (1991a: 2): tasks such as those just outlined create a research setting in which the teams or individuals involved can learn from each other in the process of investigating phenomena and discussing their methods and findings. To use corpora effectively in increasingly independent research, learners need technical, methodological, and conceptual knowledge and abilities. They need to be able to identify and formulate appropriate problems, to select appropriate corpora to interrogate, to design queries whose recall and precision are adequate to their purposes, and to manipulate and interpret the output so as to obtain usable and reliable answers. In Johns' examples of DDL, it is the teacher who selects and structures the data to be analyzed, and suggests the techniques to be used. Fully autonomous use, on the other hand, implies that learners should be able both to select and structure data and to apply appropriate techniques of analysis for themselves: how to best do so can be a major focus of communication when working with corpora.

The issue of learner control is discussed in several of the chapters in this volume, which suggest a number of ways in which it can be progressively increased, and thereby provide a range of grading criteria for corpus-based activities (cfr. 6.1 below). Partington (chapter 3) generally assumes a collaborative classroom framework - à la Johns - where teachers and learners discuss teacher-selected data in order to develop shared interpretations. This approach leaves relatively little space for learner initiative, but by giving them the opportunity to study alongside an expert, provides a good means of showing them what it may be possible to observe in, and conclude from, corpus data. Zorzi (chapter 4: 2.3) instead argues for the use of data where the teacher has no 'right answers' as to what should be found in the analysis. Learners are not simply asked to replicate the expert's work, but must instead reach, and assume responsibility for, their own conclusions. To this end she proposes that learners should work on features which are poorly described by textbooks, teachers, and reference materials, such as discourse markers in speech. Brodine (chapter 6: 5, 6.2) discusses whether teachers should pre-edit concordances, or present learners with 'raw' data from the corpus. She argues that dealing with raw data will develop learners' ability to cope with polysemy and ambiguity, a requisite not only for independent corpus work but also for their everyday reading. Other chapters instead look at what may be involved in independent corpus use, and the attitudes and skills required. Gavioli (chapter 5) proposes that small corpora of simple texts make it easier for learners to engage and conceptualize their interpretative skills, as well as to realize that "the results are only as good as the corpus" (Sinclair 1991a: 13). Zanettin (chapter 7) and Bertaccini and Aston (chapter 8) examine the position of the learner who interrogates a specialized corpus to solve specific problems of text understanding and production, underlining the extent to which such use requires creative interrogation techniques, and a willingness to disconfirm previous hypotheses. Bernardini (chapter 9) illustrates how a learner can explore a large corpus independently, working from an arbitrary starting point, and discusses the strategies this calls for. In these chapters the focus is thus as much on the interpretative and developmental processes as it is on the descriptive products of corpus-based research.

As possible stimuli for communication using corpora, we have so far only considered methods and outcomes relating to lexicogrammatical features, reflecting the emphasis within the DDL paradigm on forms and their uses rather than on meanings and their realizations. To some extent, this emphasis is a consequence of the nature of concordancing software, which allows the retrieval of specific forms - occurrences of particular character strings and combinations of strings. However, corpora can also provide opportunities for focussing on meanings in data, as we shall see in the next section.

4. Corpora and meaning

4.1 Incidental learning and serendipity

One consequence of DDL's focus on the teacher-directed study of specific forms is a lack of attention to incidental learning in corpus use. Anyone who actually interrogates a corpus for themselves will be immediately struck by the way in which virtually any query may throw up unexpected discoveries, perhaps having little to do with the problem being investigated - unfamiliar expressions, unknown cultural references, memorable instances, curious texts. Discussing work by Moon (1998) on the uses and variation of the formula *two Xs short of a Y*, Murison-Bowie (1996: 195) narrates his discovery of the for him unforgettable phrase *two marbles short of a Parthenon*. Aston (1995b) describes how examining a concordance of *dire* from a newspaper corpus led to his discovery of Dire Dawa, a town famed for its illicit commercial activities. The possibility of encountering and further exploring such curiosities seems one of the richest potentials of corpora for the language learner, who may acquire a wide variety of linguistic and/or cultural knowledge as a result of such incidental learning - incidental in the sense of being only indirectly linked to the original focus of interest (Aston 2000). Bernardini (this volume, chapter 9: 2.4) argues that learners should be encouraged to follow up curiosities in corpora, rather than limiting their attention to pre-determined problems. In this respect she takes issue with Johns' (1991a) view of learners as linguistic researchers, and instead suggests that they should be viewed as explorers, who can adopt a 'serendipity principle' with respect to the corpus, taking their own paths through it, as one discovery leads to another.

In illustration, let us return to the last line in the concordance in Figure 2 above, with its *When you hand over your housekeeping at the Sainsbury checkout*. What, some learners might ask, is *housekeeping*? And what is *Sainsbury*? They may manage to infer from the citation that Sainsbury is a shop of some kind, and that housekeeping is something valuable. Instead of turning to a dictionary or encyclopedia for further help, they can turn to the corpus to find further examples of these unfamiliar words, or to read more of the text from which this citation comes.

Following the first of these strategies, Figure 6 lists 20 randomly-selected occurrences of *Sainsbury* in the British National Corpus. This concordance makes it clear that Sainsbury is one of the leading British supermarket chains (and that reference to this chain is the most frequent use of the word). The corpus here acts as an encyclopedia, with the concordance constituting a text to be scanned for information about Sainsbury('s) - i.e. in a search for meaning.

Curiosity might also concern the text from which the original citation was taken. What is all this stuff about handing over the housekeeping in Sainsbury's? Again, this is a question about meaning, and to find the answer, we must get an idea what this text is, and what is going on in this part of it. This again requires reading, but this time of the original text, from which an extract follows:

> But do they make us pay over the odds? A new superstore chain says they do. Food Giant claims we're all spending far more than we need to when we shop at the well-known supermarkets. We could shop at one of their 19 superstores around the country and save a fortune. They point out that when you hand over your housekeeping at the Sainsbury checkout, more than seven percent of your money is pure profit for the store chain. Tesco make just under seven percent. Yet Food Giant only takes around four per cent profit. And they say that's plenty for a healthy business. If the chain proves popular you could soon have a Food Giant near you. They don't have to build their stores from scratch.
>
> (*Daily Mirror*, 1992)

Most concordance programs allow the user to view the entire text from which a particular citation is taken in a couple of keystrokes, providing almost limitless reading opportunities. Following up curiosities allows learners to select texts to read and to choose how to read them, as well as providing reasons for doing so - reasons which may be meaning rather than

```
1   ct entries will win a copy of the new Sainsbury's Pocket Guide to Wine. The top 30 entrants
2   .¦ Supermarket Round-up¦¦ BARGAINS at Sainsbury's this week include 50 party-size sausage ro
3   Kingfisher to 570p and 6p apiece off Sainsbury and Argyll to 574p and 426p.¦ Debt fears hit
4   econd largest supermarket chain after Sainsbury's - will cut prices on more than 1,000 items
5   d. 'We don't anticipate any increase," Sainsbury's said.^ TURNING THE SCREW: DIY stores will
6   uld possibly have at their disposal.¦ Sainsbury's, ranking 17 in The Times 1000 with 82 000
7   ironmental health director today.¦ At Sainsbury in Boreham yesterday morning head office spo
8   cer today as it tries to compete with Sainsbury as the UK's most profitable retailer.¦ Altho
9   dicated at the National Gallery, Lord Sainsbury said in his speech that, while he was very h
10  th the end of wartime rationing. Lord Sainsbury, (above) great grandson of the founder is ch
11  nized in the early eighties, first by Sainsbury and then by Tesco: both chains ran distingui
12  OSE/Vicar of Cirencester Voice over¦ Sainsbury's Homebase was one of three stores brought b
13  vercome obstacles holding up plans by Sainsbury's to build a supermarket on the Grange Road
14  h Authority.¦ She is the wife of Jeff Sainsbury, Tory leader on Cardiff City Council.¦ Forme
15  e best picture taken at Alton Towers' Sainsbury's days on Saturday July 31, and Sunday, Augu
16  agazine launch¦¦ The launch party for Sainsbury's the Magazine, held at Les ambassadeurs on
17  hen be phased in so that Homebase and Sainsbury's staff will be able to present a smart new
18  ward at the Savoy Hotel on April 14.¦ Sainsbury's FutureCooks was launched in 1990 and is no
19  g the (...) (PS000) Yeah (PS0HU) in Sainsbury's (...) (.) (PS000) Oh dear. (PS000) A wom
20  t these. (PS0JX) [reading] [from jar] Sainsbury's own conserve [].  (PS0JY) Absolutely.(.)
```

Figure 6. *Sainsbury* in the BNC (random 20 lines)

simply form-focussed in nature. What this text is about is supermarkets' profit margins - something which many of us have cause to be interested in.

Considering corpora as sources of material to be read, for information or indeed for pleasure, can lead us to a rather different view of corpus-based activities from the DDL approach. We may, for example, ask in what ways corpus-based activities can help develop learners' reading skills; how they can facilitate or deepen understanding of a specific text; or how they can facilitate understanding of a particular topic or subject domain, or of a particular genre or type of text.

4.2 Corpora and reading

The role of corpora in developing reading skills has received little attention in the literature. Contemporary approaches to the teaching of reading in a foreign language usually adopt a 'top-down' perspective, stressing prediction of local meanings on the basis of more global knowledge concerning the topic and the type of text, along with understandings of the text-so-far (Smith 1971). In contrast, Brodine (this volume, chapter 6: 2) underlines how interpreting concordance lines generally involves 'bottom-up' interpretation, with an attempt to derive wider textual meanings from an extremely limited local context. Faced with the first line in Figure 6,

> entries will win a copy of the new Sainsbury's Pocket Guide to Wine. The top 30 entrants

the reader has to infer from the local lexical clues (*entries, win, top, entrants*) that what is being described here is a competition - and one, moreover, with fairly small consolation prizes. There is growing evidence that bottom-up interpretative skills are fundamental for fluent reading (Eskey and Grabe 1988), and Brodine shows how concordance analysis can engage these, both by providing general practice and by allowing specific types of problems of bottom-up interpretation to be focussed on. One such problem, she argues, is lexicogrammatical ambiguity: even if the learner is aware of the various uses of polysemous items, s/he may nonetheless have difficulty in recognizing which is involved in a particular instance. Brodine shows how concordances of polysemous items can provide practice in this kind of bottom-up discrimination: learners can be asked to categorize concordance lines, deciding in each case whether *play* is a noun or a verb, whether an **ing* form is verbal (*He is working hard*), adjectival (*She is a working girl*) or nominal (*He hates working*), whether *if* introduces an indirect question or a conditional, whether *this* refers anaphorically or cataphorically, etc. A second kind of problem she examines concerns syntactic analysis, where learners can be asked to parse complex nominal groups or to identify the boundaries of embedded clauses using prepared concordances.

The possibility of reading extended contexts for individual concordance lines allows such work to be alternated or combined with more 'top-down' approaches. For instance, if the learner first uses a concordance line to derive bottom-up hypotheses as to aspects of the text's global meaning, these hypotheses can then be used to read a larger portion of the text on a top-down basis. Here is a longer extract from what we previously hypothesized was an announcement of a competition:

> *The prizes*
> The first prize is a magnificent week-long visit to New Zealand to discover the flavour of the wonderful wines of the southern hemisphere. The trip includes excursions to some of the top New Zealand wineries, such as Nobilo - the largest family-owned concern - Babich and Delegats. The winner will also have the chance to explore the unspoiled treasures of the country's North and South Islands. The prize includes flights, accommodation and the cost of a hire car for a week. The second prize is a visit to the German wine-making regions of the picturesque Rhine and Mosel valleys. And the third prize is £1,000 worth of Sainsbury's wine.
> *How to enter*
> Fill out the entry form on the right, including your answers, tie-breaker and your full name, address and telephone number. Please state which regional final you would be able to attend from the list below, and provide a second option in case it is not possible to accommodate you at your first choice of location.
> *The finals*
> The first 500 correct entries will win a copy of the new Sainsbury's Pocket Guide to Wine. The top 30 entrants for each region will be invited to attend a regional final on one of the dates previously given. This will be part of an informal open tasting evening held at a Sainsbury's store where visitors will be able to taste a range of wines. Regional finalists will be asked to answer questions about a selected number of wines at the tasting.

Gavioli (1997) illustrates how studying concordances of frequent words in a text can help learners predict the structure and content of that text prior to reading it as a whole, as well as to check their knowledge of its key lexis. In this volume (chapter 5: 4), she shows how similar techniques can be used to prepare learners to deal with collections of texts of a particular type, and hence to read or write texts of that type. Again, the emphasis in this approach is as much on the meanings expressed as on the forms used, with the analysis of concordances serving to enhance learners' understanding of particular texts, and to develop procedures for their interpretation (see section 5 below).

4.3 Concordancing and text analysis

Gavioli's work shows how concordance lines may stimulate curiosity about the texts from which they derive, and provide a source of hypotheses as to the meanings of these texts before reading them. The opposite approach is also possible, however, going not from the concordance to the text but from the text to the concordance, as a means of casting further light on the meaning of a text which has already been read.

Suggestions for applying corpus-based techniques to text analysis have drawn largely on work in stylistics, where frequency lists and concordances have long been used to investigate works of literary authors

rank	word	freq.	rank	word	freq.	rank	word	freq.
1	The	151	18	With	18	35	All	10
2	I	122	19	As	16	36	Could	10
3	And	63	20	Me	16	37	Eye	10
4	It	44	21	Been	15	38	Have	10
5	A	43	22	No	15	39	More	10
6	Of	42	23	Old	15	40	There	10
7	To	34	24	Upon	15	41	They	10
8	Was	34	25	You	15	42	This	10
9	In	32	26	At	14	43	How	9
10	My	30	27	Him	14	44	Man	9
11	Had	29	28	His	14	45	Now	9
12	But	24	29	Louder	13	46	Sound	9
13	That	24	30	Night	13	47	Still	9
14	He	21	31	Very	12	48	What	9
15	For	18	32	When	12	49	Knew	8
16	Not	18	33	Heard	11	50	Them	8
17	So	18	34	Heart	11			

Figure 7. The most common words in Poe's *The tell-tale heart*

1. Learning with corpora: an overview

```
1   For his gold I had no desire. I think it was his eye! Yes, it was this! One of his eyes resembled
2   s eyes resembled that of a vulture - a pale blue eye with a film over it. Whenever it fell upon me
3   life of the old man, and thus rid myself of the eye for ever. Now this is the point. You fancy me
4   uch that a single thin ray fell upon the vulture eye. And this I did for seven long nights, every
5   s, every night just at midnight, but I found the eye always closed, and so it was impossible to do
6   it was not the old man who vexed me but his Evil Eye. And every morning, when the day broke, I wen
7   t out from the crevice and fell upon the vulture eye. It was open, wide, wide open, and I grew fur
8   d how steadily I could maintain the ray upon the eye. Meantime the hellish tattoo of the heart inc
9   . There was no pulsation. He was stone dead. His eye would trouble me no more. If still you think
10  e boards so cleverly so cunningly, that no human eye - not even his - could have detected anything
```

Figure 8. *Eye* in Poe's *The tell-tale heart*

(see e.g. Burrows 1992). Thus Tribble and Jones (1990: 32) suggest that learners studying a story or novel examine concordances of the names of characters to see how they are described and developed; Kettemann (1995a, b) proposes comparing the collocates of *he* and *she* to see how male and female roles are configured. As Gavioli (1997) notes, a frequency list will often reveal words which are of particular interest in a text: for instance, Figure 7 shows the 50 most frequent words in a short story by Edgar Alan Poe, *The tell-tale heart*.

As in all texts, most of these words are grammatical, closed-set items: articles, pronouns, conjunctions, prepositions, quantifiers, auxiliary verbs, etc. The list does however also include a handful of open-set, lexical ones - *old, louder, night, heard, heart, eye, man, sound, still* and *knew*. Let us take just one of these, *eye*, which occurs ten times in the story, and generate a concordance for it. Figure 8 lists the citations in the order in which they appear in the text, where we can see how Poe repeatedly describes the old man's eye as something detached from its owner (lines 2-8), and which becomes human again only with his death (9-10).

The patterns which emerge from analyses of this kind can be particularly interesting with literary and other culturally significant texts: in a revealing example, Stubbs (1996) shows how concordances of *happy* in Baden-Powell's farewell letters to the Scouts and Guides highlight what today seems extreme sexism. But similar techniques can be applied to more mundane text-types, as Gavioli (this volume, chapter 5: 4.2) shows with respect to letters to an agony aunt.

In the examples just cited, the concordances simply show the occurrences within the particular text being studied. It is however also possible to compare these occurrences with those in other texts, revealing to what extent they are distinctive of the text in question. The "Keywords" program in Scott's *Wordsmith Tools* (1996) automates this process, generating a list of those words which are significantly more (or less) frequent in one text or set of texts than in another (cfr. 2.1 above). For instance, if we perform this operation with the text-so-far of the present chapter (excluding the concordance examples), and compare it with all the written texts of the British National Corpus, we obtain the lists in Figures 9 and 10.

The first list includes many of the key terms of this chapter, providing cues to its gist (Scott 2000). The second instead highlights the fact that this text is expository in nature, rather than, say, narrative (Biber 1988). Gavioli (this volume, chapter 5: 4) suggests that such techniques may also be useful for the comparison of texts produced by learners with

1. Learning with corpora: an overview

1	Corpora	8	Partington	15	Learner
2	Concordance	9	Hand	16	Sainsbury
3	Learners	10	Texts	17	Gavioli
4	Corpus	11	Ddl	18	Occurrences
5	Concordances	12	Language	19	Can
6	Text	13	Johns	20	Concordancing
7	Uses	14	Data		

Figure 9. The 20 most significantly frequent words in this paper so far[2]

1	Was	4	His	7	Were
2	I	5	Her		
3	He	6	You		

Figure 10. Significantly infrequent words in this paper so far

native-speaker texts of the same type, for instance as a writing aid (cfr. 4.4 below).

Not just the frequency of its lexis, but also the collocational and colligational patterns in a particular text can be compared with those found elsewhere. Louw (1993, 1997) suggests that learners' understanding and appreciation of a poem may be enhanced by comparing its collocations with those more generally found in written texts. One of his examples comes from W.B. Yeats' *Memory*:

> One had a lovely face,
> And two or three had charm,
> But charm and face were in vain
> Because the mountain grass
> Cannot but keep the form
> Where the mountain hare has lain.

A concordance of *were in vain* (line 3) generated from the Bank of English shows that its subjects include *my cries of anguish, her complaints, his/their/those efforts, heroics, sacrifices,* and *insults,* all of which imply deliberate conscious effort by an actor. In using this phrase in reference to "charm and face", Yeats can be heard as suggesting that female attractiveness is the fruit of deliberate seductive effort - arguably a fairly sexist sentiment (Louw 1997: 246). Again, such procedures are not only of value in analyzing literary texts: Bertaccini and Aston (this volume, chapter 8: 2) show how they can reveal the evaluative stance of the journalist in a newspaper text, by highlighting the cultural connotations of particular lexical choices.

To summarize, the use of concordancing in text analysis can highlight two types of phenomena, both leading to greater understanding of the text in question. First, as with the Poe example, it may reveal patternings within a text, providing an *intratextual* basis for attributing meaning to specific occurrences and to the text as a whole. Second, as with the Yeats example, it may reveal peculiarities (or normalities) of that text in comparison to others, providing an *intertextual* basis for attributing meanings to it. Insofar as it aims to enhance the understanding of specific texts, a text-analytic approach is clearly meaning- rather than form-focussed, and in this respect seems fully compatible with the tenets of communicative language pedagogy.

It is also worth noting that the use of concordancing for text analysis offers a wide range of opportunities for incidental learning and for developing reading skills (cfr. 4.1 and 4.2 above). Investigating one aspect of a text will often incidentally highlight other features of potential interest. Thus, looking at the use of *eye* in *The tell-tale heart* (Figure 8 above), we see how Poe abandons the possessive *his* in favour of the definite article *the*, returning to the former only with the death of the eye's owner. This raises the question as to whether Poe uses a similar dissociative strategy in reference to other body parts - for instance with *heart* (as the story title's definite article would suggest) - and invites a broader investigation of the story's use of possessives. It may also trigger a search for other corpus texts where *the eye* is found, and perhaps a reading of these.

From the perspective of reading skills, the use of concordancing in text analysis invites the interaction of bottom-up and top-down modes of processing. In an intratextual analysis such as the Poe example, interpreting a concordance involves top-down use of knowledge of the text to recognize where individual citations come from and to expand their bottom-up interpretation. Where intertextual analysis is involved, as in the Yeats example, the bottom-up interpretation of citations from other texts has to be matched against the user's top-down interpretation of the text being analyzed. This interaction of processing modes would appear able to stimulate more critical and reflective reading, developing the learner's interpretative ability as well as enhancing understanding of the specific text.

Learners may have to be trained to recognize the relevance of a text-analytic approach, which presupposes a view of meaning as produced in relation to a wider textual background, through analogy with (or deviation from) patternings in the same or in other texts (Hoey 1991, 1997). Activities of the kinds described in this section may help learners to appreciate the value of this perspective. While presented as activities controlled by the teacher, who selects the text to be analyzed and the features to be investigated, there is no reason why learners should not carry out such work independently, as a means of investigating texts that they themselves desire to understand or appreciate more fully. Bernardini (2000b; this volume, chapter 9: 3.4) illustrates how learners using corpora can first pass from a concordance line which has aroused their curiosity to a reading of the text from which it is taken, and can then go on to generate further concordances in order to study that text from an intra- or intertextual perspective, integrating form- and meaning-focussed work in full autonomy.

4.4   Corpora and writing

Louw's analysis of Yeats' *Memory* explores the meaning of a particular verse by comparing it with similar forms in a wider corpus. In such intertextual work, the corpus acts as a reference tool to aid understanding of the text being read, and by virtue of the number of citations available, may do so better than traditional reference materials.

For the purposes of such intertextual analysis, it is not necessary for the text being investigated to belong to the corpus, or even to be in electronic form. And rather than a text being read, it may also be one being written by the learner. In this volume Gavioli (chapter 5: 4), Zanettin (chapter 7: 3) and Bertaccini and Aston (chapter 8: 3) all show how learners can use corpora when writing or translating in order to check whether a hypothesized realization is likely to convey the meaning desired, and to identify possible alternatives. Such use again requires training, as shown by the cautionary tale in Owen (1996):

> Ah Peng, a research student from China, studying at a British university [...] His latest piece of work contains the following sentence: *Many more experimental studies require to be done before we can say that ...* The teacher [...] has red-pencilled this and added a couple of notes. First, he suggests replacing *require* with *need*. Second, he says that if Ah Peng insists on using *require* then he could try *Many more experimental studies are required before we can say that ...*
>
> (Owen 1996: 222-3)

Ah Peng's response is to look up *require* in the Cobuild corpus, where he finds

> lines like this: *decided that a large number of laws would require to be passed by a two-thirds majority*. In fact, he finds more than a dozen of these [...] Ah Peng greets the teacher next week with a triumphant gleam in his eye.
>
> (Owen 1996: 222-3)

This example clearly demonstrates one of the positive features of corpus use - that of giving students a basis for arguing with their teachers - but it also underlines the importance of adequate training to do so. Ah Peng has in fact failed to understand the role of the corpus as a reference tool, since he views it solely as a means to provide support for his own hypotheses. Had he selected and examined the data more carefully, he would have found there were many more cases in the Cobuild corpus where *need* or *are required* were used in contexts analogous to his own (Aston 1997b: 62). As both Zanettin (chapter 7: 5) and Bertaccini and Aston (chapter 8: 3.2) illustrate in this volume, using corpora as writing aids requires a willingness to abandon one's first hypotheses, always looking out for other forms and meanings which may be more adequately attested and contextually appropriate.

5. Specialized corpora and the analysis of particular text-types

With whatever purpose corpora are consulted, it is important to select the right corpus for the job. A large mixed corpus, such as the Bank of English or the British National Corpus, can throw considerable light on how an item is used in the language as a whole, and allow relatively broad distinctions to be made, for instance between uses in speech and in writing. However, when acquiring the language for specific purposes, the learner will often be more concerned with understanding how an item is used in texts of a particular type (Biber, Conrad and Reppen 1994). From the perspective of text analysis too, the intertextual background against which a specific occurrence makes sense will often be that of a particular text-type. Zanettin (this volume, chapter 7: 3) shows how a newspaper report on the Olympic games can be reliably interpreted by concordancing other texts of the same genre and from the same subject domain.

Most early work using corpora in pedagogy was based on small, specialized collections of texts (see Flowerdew 1996 for a review), and most of the papers in this volume describe work using relatively small corpora of this kind. These corpora are in their turn often divided into several yet more specialized subcorpora. Thus Partington (chapter 3) analyzes a 5-million word collection of newspaper articles, divided by domain into Home, Foreign, Sports, Business and Arts (following Murison-Bowie 1993b); Zorzi (chapter 4) employs a 500,000 word corpus of transcribed speech, divided according to genres ranging from face-to-face conversation to broadcast monologue (De Mauro et al. 1993); Brodine (chapter 6) uses a 1,000,000 word corpus of academic writing, divided into five subject domains (Murison-Bowie 1993c), along with a smaller corpus of texts contained in a student textbook. Other corpora examined are also smaller and more specialized: Zanettin (chapter 7) uses collections of English and Italian newspaper articles dealing with the 1992 Olympic games of 250,000 and 65,000 words respectively; Bertaccini and Aston (chapter 8) *ad hoc* collections of under 20,000 words drawn from newspaper CD-ROMs and the World Wide Web; Gavioli (chapter 5) focusses on a tiny 2000-word collection of classified 'lonely hearts' advertisements.

From a pedagogic perspective, small specialized corpora would appear to offer a number of practical advantages over large mixed ones (Aston 1997b). In the first place, they are relatively simple to compile. A set of sports reports can be downloaded from newspaper CD-ROMs; a collection of academic research papers in a particular area can be scanned from a library's journal holdings; texts dealing with a particular subject can be located on the Internet using one of the web search engines and downloaded. Teachers and learners can thus easily create their own small specialized corpora, either prior to embarking on work in a given domain (Maia 1997; Pearson 2000; cfr. Zanettin, this volume, chapter 7: 2), or upon encountering a particular problem during a task (Bertaccini and Aston, this volume, chapter 8).

In the second place, such corpora are often simpler to analyze. Insofar as all the texts are similar, concordance lines are more likely to present recurrent patternings, facilitating their comparison and interpretation. As their source is already known to be a given type of text, this enables a degree of top-down processing, making it easier to relate citations to the overall structure and goals of the text, as in normal reading practice. As an example, of the two concordances of the word *may* below, the first, in Figure 11, was randomly selected from the heterogeneous BNC, and the second, in Figure 12, from a specialized corpus of scientific research articles on hepatitis C (Gavioli 1999).

In the hepatitis concordance, it is relatively easy to divide the citations into two groups: those where *may* indicates a generally recognized

```
1     . Charges against him were dropped in May 1988 after a meeting between the Crown Prose
2    e from bone and antler, although wood may have been used more often than is now appare
3    tor obtaining payment, the High Court may, notwithstanding that one month has not expi
4    ontracts. Any legal restrictions that may have been imposed by the vendor or already h
5    n an inhibiting layer; too much water may leach them away altogether, though that is s
6    other compulsive behaviours and they may even deny that these other addictions are "r
7    operation, until behind its tender it may have a string of vehicles more than two hund
8    ht. It is believed that this incident may be connected with the riots yesterday in Dep
9    owing a bereavement. Ultimately, it may be affected by my present precarious work ci
10   group to prepare for a referendum. It may be held around September or just before the
```

Figure 11. *May* in the BNC

```
1    termittent in 4 cases. These findings may indicate that all HCV infections become chr
2    s c. False-negative hepatitis C tests may occur for some time after infection. Altern
3    exception (patient H, in whom alcohol may have actually been a more important etiolog
4    Even third generation tests for HBsAg may not detect donors with low levels of HBsAg
5    more than one NANB virus, i.e., there may be agent(s) other than HCV. Our results in
6    ther authors, however, found that CPH may also progress to cirrhosis (4,16,23,24). Th
7    B hepatitis in this study or, indeed, may have been entirely responsible for some of
8    ent with chronic persistent hepatitis may represent the only case of chronic non-A, n
9    like agents that do not produce HBsAg may play a role[8-12]. <p> Despite numerous cla
10   s to infection with hepatitis B virus may also favour exposure to non-A, non-B hepati
```

Figure 12. *May* in the hepatitis corpus

possibility (and might be replaced with *can*), and those where it indicates a hypothesis of the author's (and might be replaced with *could*: on the uses of modals in academic writing, see Thompson, forthcoming). The citations in the BNC concordance, on the other hand, pose greater difficulties, being less easily contextualizable and reflecting a wider range of uses: larger contexts and more examples would be necessary to categorize them adequately. In these respects the specialized corpus provides the learner with more manageable data, reducing the range of interpretative options and therefore the need for teacher control and guidance.

Thirdly, incidental learning is likely to be less dispersive. The citations in Figure 11 could lead to a vast range of mutually unrelated linguistic, encyclopaedic or cultural discoveries by the learner (cfr. 3.1 above; Bernardini, this volume, chapter 9: 3). Those in Figure 12, being confined to a single text-type, are likely to lead to discoveries which relate to this text-type, and which may consequently be of more immediate relevance to the learner. Zanettin illustrates how the reader or writer who refers to a specialized corpus can often encounter information by chance which subsequently turns out to be useful to the task in which s/he is engaged (chapter 7: 3.6).

Users of small, specialized corpora must however be aware of their limits. Before drawing conclusions about a particular text-type, it must be asked if the corpus provides a reasonably representative sample of that text-type (Biber 1993). Obviously, we cannot draw conclusions about *may* in scientific research papers from the examples in Figure 12, drawn as they are from a handful of articles dealing with a single medical topic. But this in no way impedes us from coming up with interesting hypotheses to then test against a larger quantity and a wider variety of data, as Gavioli illustrates (this volume, chapter 5: 3.2).

Many of the findings to emerge from analyses of specialized corpora may be surprising to learners who are used only to the broad generalizations of grammars and dictionaries. For instance, a student analysis of Zanettin's Olympic Games corpus revealed the tendency to indicate contestants' origin with post-modifying phrases ("Kieren Perkins of Australia") rather than nationality adjectives ("the Australian Kieren Perkins"), as they had previously hypothesized (chapter 7: 3.1). Gavioli observes how in lonely hearts advertisements, the subject of *must* is always the desired partner rather than the advertiser (chapter 5: 3.1). Such information can help familiarize learners with conventional patterns for reading purposes, and help them orient to them in their written production (Granger and Tribble 1998). At the same time, studying the conventions of a particular text-type may also help learners to recognize creative uses, and to be successfully creative themselves. Gavioli shows how lonely hearts ads may deviate from the recurrent patterns of the genre in order to achieve particularly striking effects, and proposes a follow-up activity where learners try to create 'creative' advertisements of their own which similarly play with convention (chapter 5: 4).

It should be stressed that specialized corpora can highlight the areas of meaning as well as the forms associated with a particular text-type. For instance, a domain-specific corpus can be used to learn about the concepts associated with that domain: Mparutsa et al. (1991) used concordances of expressions of causation in a geology corpus to help learners identify key geological processes. Gavioli (this volume, chapter 5) shows how her corpus of lonely hearts ads highlights descriptions of physical appearance, age, ethnicity, sexual orientation and leisure interests; Zanettin's corpus of newspaper reports on the Olympic Games (chapter 7: 2) might similarly be used to identify key roles, objects, events and tactics in particular sports. A genre-specific corpus, on the other hand, can be used to learn about that genre's rhetorical structuring: it may, for example, be possible to link particular uses to particular positions and functions within texts. Thus Aston (1997b) shows how learners writing a newspaper article can use a newspaper corpus to verify both whether the kind of information they have included is typically present, and whether it is structured in the same way. In her corpus of Hepatitis C research articles, Gavioli (1997) notes how the word *recently* predominantly occurs in introductions, particularly in the sentence-initial phrase *Until (very) recently* - a finding which can be interpreted in terms of Swales' (1990) observation that research article introductions need to establish a 'niche' for their work in terms of an unexplored problem in the field. Brodine (this volume, chapter 6: 5.3) proposes activities to investigate how 'problem-solution' patterns (Hoey 1983) are realized in academic writing, using a corpus of social science texts.

Insofar as they render the learner's task easier, specialized corpora make them particularly suitable as a tool to train learners in corpus use (cfr. 6.1 below). Conversely, however, they can also be seen as limiting the learner's opportunities. In the final paper in this volume, Bernardini (chapter 9: 5) argues that for the autonomous advanced learner, large heterogeneous corpora are more motivating than small specialized ones, since they open a greater variety of unpredictable avenues to be explored. It is also clearly useful for learners to be able to compare findings across different types of texts in order to develop their sensitivity to variation, as well as their competence in different registers. Bernardini shows how the British National Corpus, whose texts are classified according to such parameters as domain, mode (spoken, written, or written-to-be-spoken), and speaker/author characteristics (Burnard 1995), permits a wide range of comparisons between different broad categories of texts. Gavioli (chapter 5: 3.2) instead compares specialized corpora, examining personal descriptions in lonely hearts ads and in letters to a newspaper agony aunt: where both corpora share common features, she proposes that learners should expand the investigatation to the full range of BNC written texts to see if these generalizations can be broadened. This approach is similar to that used in stylistics and forensic linguistics (e.g. Mosteller and Wallace 1964; Coulthard 1993), which attempt to distinguish those uses which are specific to a particular text or set of texts from those which are more general (cfr. Partington, this volume, chapter 2: 2).

Ultimately, just as we have underlined the complementary nature of intratextual and intertextual approaches to text analysis (cfr. 4.3 above), we can see a similar complementarity of approaches to the analysis of text-types, based on the isolated study of specialized corpora on the one hand (what we might call 'intratypal' analysis), and on comparison with other specialized or more general corpora on the other (what we might call 'intertypal' analysis). Insofar as both approaches would appear to be of value, we are likely to want to prepare learners to work with a variety of corpora of varying sizes and degrees of specialization. Choosing appropriate corpora is thus a further area where learners will need to develop strategies and criteria if they are to carry out effective independent work.

6. Towards autonomy: the roles of teachers and learners

Perhaps the greatest attraction of corpora for language pedagogy is their potential for autonomous learning: as Leech has put it, "the main rationale of corpora in teaching is their immediate availability for students' use" (1997: 7). Where self-access facilities are available, such use can take place outside as well as inside the classroom, without the direct control of the teacher. The papers in this volume illustrate how it is possible for learners to take responsibility not only for analyzing corpus data, but also for formulating problems for investigation and strategies for solving them, selecting and even designing appropriate corpora for the purpose (Zanettin, chapter 7: 2; Bertaccini and Aston, chapter 8).

Such independent use of corpora has a number of implications for the roles of teachers and learners. As Aston (1995b) points out, corpora can remove much of the need for the teacher to act as an authority concerning the language, since they can provide more reliable information than teacher intuition, and in this respect they place the native and the non-native speaker teacher on an equal footing. The teacher's role is instead that of a facilitator (Johns 1991a), helping learners to identify and perform activities which match their particular objectives and learning styles, and to understand the potentials and limits of different corpora from this perspective. Since a corpus "enables the learner/student to explore, to investigate, to generalize, to test hypotheses; but it does not itself initiate or direct the path of learning" (Leech 1997: 5), learners need to acquire criteria and methods which will enable them to choose and follow suitable learning paths.

To do so effectively, it may be necessary for both teachers and learners to modify many of their presuppositions concerning the nature of language and the nature of language learning. They will need to realize that language use is not simply a matter of employing universally applicable rules; they will need to realize that generalizations from evidence are rarely definitive, but a matter of progressive approximation; and they will need to realize that partial, limited generalizations may be more useful than ones which are broader in scope but harder to apply. As the chapters in this volume underline, these requirements imply a pedagogic emphasis on the processes of corpus-based work as much as on particular products as findings, with a selection of activities which can increasingly engage learners' interpretative capacity.

An approach which is 'process-focussed' in this respect would seem able to resolve the conflict noted by Kennedy (1992: 364) between the use of corpora and the priorities of communicative language teaching (cfr. the preface to this volume). The latter's emphasis on the learner and the learning process can be fully respected by work which prioritizes the development of learners' ability to use corpora independently. In the paper which closes this volume, Bernardini (chapter 9) illustrates the enormous potential of such use for the culturally and linguistically sophisticated learner. In contrast, Hadley (1998; forthcoming) describes the terror of beginners and false beginners faced with concordance printouts "full of English words", whose initial reaction was however slowly overcome thanks to the motivational effect of 'authentic' data, and the realization that they could learn from concordance analysis. These two cases represent the extremes between which the teacher must help learners find paths, by slowly relinquishing control over the data with which they are presented, and the tasks which they are asked to carry out. The papers in this volume offer suggestions, but no pretence as to definitive solutions, as to how this mediation can be effected.

6.1 Controlling the data, controlling the task

One way the difficulty of the data to which the learner is exposed can be limited is by careful selection of the corpus or subcorpus to be used. It may, for example, be possible to use corpora which are linguistically simple (Gavioli, this volume, chapter 5: 3), or indeed simplified (Murison-Bowie 1996) - though the latter, as 'non-authentic' texts, may be less motivating for learners as well as less reliable in providing indications of actual use. Alternatively, it may be possible to use corpora composed of texts with which learners are already familiar (Willis 1998; Barlow and Burdine 1998; Seidlhofer 2000; cfr. Brodine, this volume, chapter 6), or which are predictable inasmuch as they are taken from well-known domains and/or genres (Partington, this volume, chapter 3). In any case it is likely that corpora which are homogeneous, where all the texts are of the same type, will pose fewer difficulties than heterogeneous ones (cfr. section 5 above).

Another way in which the difficulty of data can be reduced is by selecting and editing concordances, so as to exclude citations which pose particular problems of interpretation. This will generally require manual intervention on the teacher's part, even if in theory, as Leech notes,

> it should be possible to develop a program which selects, from a corpus, sample sentences which fulfil certain criteria, such as brevity, complexity, the presence or absence of certain lexical or syntactic categories, and so on.
> (Leech 1997: 13)

Not only the difficulty of the data, but also that of the task may be controlled. Ways of reducing difficulty from this perspective include:

- Choosing tasks which do not pose undue problems of precision and recall in interrogating the corpus. As noted in 2.1 above, it is easiest to find occurrences of a use where the latter has clear, unambiguous formal correlates. It is, for example, easier to find occurrences of *already* than of *yet* as temporal adverbs, since the former does not have other uses. (Such difficulties can of course be avoided completely if the teacher pre-edits the concordances for learners to analyze: cfr. Zorzi, this volume, chapter 4; Brodine, chapter 6.)
- Choosing tasks which require little manipulation of the output in order to categorize and sort citations, remove irrelevant citations, etc. The teacher can restrict the amount of data, remove in advance any citations which may be misleading, and indeed pre-categorize and

pre-sort these so as to group similar instances (Zorzi, this volume, chapter 4: 3.1).
- Choosing tasks which do not require all the data to be classified and interpreted. It is clearly easier to find a few citations in a concordance which match (or fail to match) a particular pattern than it is to list all those which do so - for instance, in a concordance of *chair*, to see if there are any cases where this does *not* denote a physical object.
- Choosing tasks which require relatively superficial interpretation of the data. For instance, it is easier to divide a concordance of *hand* (Figure 1 above) into nominal and verbal uses than into literal and metaphorical ones, and to identify recurrent collocations rather than recurrent semantic or pragmatic patterns.
- Choosing tasks which allow learners to help and support each other. For instance, learners can be asked to work together on a set of data, or they can be given different data relating to the same problem. In such cases not only may two heads be better than one, but the opportunity is created to use the language in communicative interaction (cfr. 3.1 above).
- Choosing tasks whose more complex aspects can be delegated to more able students. It may, for instance, be possible to ask students who are proficient computer users to help others with the technical aspects of software use, or those of greater linguistic ability to pre-edit concordances for the rest of the class.

In selecting and grading appropriate tasks, the teacher's role becomes that of organizing what Resnick (1989) has termed a "cognitive apprenticeship", by offering learners ever-increasing opportunities to take control of increasingly complex and varied aspects of corpus use. This will involve not only teaching learners to use concordancing software, where "the process of getting to grips with the software invariably shades into getting to grips with the techniques of linguistic analysis" (Leech 1997: 9), but above all developing a 'corpus mentality' - showing learners how corpora provide sources, of varying reliability and ease of use, of all kinds of different information about the culture and the language, about specific texts and kinds of texts, and at the same time offer all kinds of possibilities to engage in spoken and written communication. It is the experience and belief of the contributors to this volume that the uses of corpora in pedagogy need not be pre-determined by the teacher, but can be negotiated with learners in a shared process of learning about language and about language learning, and about corpora and their uses.

7. Conclusions

The arguments presented in this chapter in favour of the use of corpora in language pedagogy have been primarily theoretical. It has been argued that such use can be fully compatible with the tenets of contemporary communicative language teaching, and that it can provide learners with types of knowledge and help them develop types of abilities which may be less readily available using other resources. This volume provides a wide variety of practical examples to illustrate these claims. As yet, however, there is little in the way of empirical evidence to show that corpus use improves particular aspects of competence or successfully engages capacity more effectively than other teaching and learning materials. For instance, it remains to be shown that data-driven discovery learning is a more effective means of developing competence than traditional rule-teaching and deductive practice, or how these two approaches can best be combined (though see Robinson 1996; Cobb 1997); similarly, it remains to be shown that access to corpora results in significantly improved understanding or production of texts (though see Bowker 1998). Nor has empirical work yet been conducted to compare the value of corpus-based work for different kinds of learners.

In the absence of such evidence, it would, as Widdowson (2000) notes, be foolish to depict corpus use as a panacea for language pedagogy. This volume seeks to show that corpora can provide opportunities for learning in many areas, and can do so in ways which are motivating, and which complement and integrate other resources. If we accept Corder's (1986) argument that the two necessary conditions for language learning are motivation and opportunity for language use, then corpora would appear to be tools which many teachers and learners should consider adding to their range of pedagogic options, particularly as more corpora and more user-friendly software become available in an overall context of increasing computer literacy.

Notes

1. Johns maintains a web page on data-driven learning, including a bibliography, at http://web.bham.ac.uk/johnstf

2. *Wordsmith Tools* allows significance to be calculated with either chi-squared or log-likelihood tests: to generate the lists in Figures 9 and 10 the latter has been used ($p < 0.000001$).

2 CORPORA AND THEIR USES IN LANGUAGE RESEARCH

Alan Partington

1. Introduction

This chapter provides a brief overview of some of the principal corpora of electronic texts and of the uses to which they have been put in language research. Most attention will be paid to those uses involving the description of particular aspects of contemporary English. The subsequent chapter will illustrate how language teachers and learners can construct and use corpora in similar manners, even with limited technical resources, to investigate particular aspects of a language for themselves.

W. Nelson Francis, the co-compiler of one of the earliest and most widely used computerized corpora, created at Brown University, defines a corpus in functional terms, as "a collection of texts assumed to be representative of a given language, dialect, or other subset of a language, to be used for linguistic analysis" (1982: 7). Some of the main fields in which such analyses have been carried out are:

- style and authorship studies, generally aiming to identify distinctive characteristics of a particular author's writings;
- contemporary linguistic studies, describing aspects of a language, dialect, genre or other sub-language, in its written and/or spoken form;
- comparisons of different languages or varieties, including:
  - two or more separate languages (translation studies);
  - two or more dialects or regional varieties (e.g. British English vs. American English);
  - two or more historical states of a language (diachronic studies);
  - two or more uses of a language (registers, genres, sectorial languages, etc.);
- lexicography, especially dictionary production;
- language teaching research, in the area of syllabus and materials design (to find out which aspects of syntax, lexis, discourse, etc. should be given priority), and in that of methodology (with the aim of exploiting corpora more or less directly in the classroom: see Aston, this volume, chapter 1).

There are, of course, overlaps between these areas, and research often has implications in several of them.

Most analyses use quantitative methods, exploiting the twin concepts of frequency - which relates to past observation - and probability - which relates to future predictability. If something is seen to happen frequently in a representative collection of texts, then it is significant precisely because this regularity can be used as the basis for predicting how other, as yet unanalyzed, texts will behave, and, in the end, for hypothesizing a description of how the entire universe of discourse under study - whether a language, a register, a dialect or a particular type of text - is organized.

The two main tools of corpus analysis are frequency lists and concordances. At its simplest, a frequency list is just a list of items - usually single words - showing the number of times each occurs in a body of texts. The significance of a particular frequency can be estimated in a variety of manners, for instance by calculating its z-score, that it to say, the deviance of its frequency from the mean frequency of all the items in the corpus. A second type of list consists of a given item's collocates (i.e. those items which appear close to it in a text), showing the frequency with which each occurs within a given distance from the item in question. A commonly-used statistic to assess the significance of collocational frequency is the mutual information index, which compares collocational frequency with the frequency with which the items in question appear in the corpus as a whole. Thus the word *order* may occur with *the* much more frequently than, say, the word *restore*, but since this latter is much less frequent than *the* in the corpus as a whole, it may well be the case that the combination *restore* with *order* is more significant (see Clear 1993 and Stubbs 1995 for discussions of measures of collocational significance).

The frequencies of words or collocates in one body of text can also be compared with those of another, and differences ranked according to their significance. In these ways, it is possible to characterize linguistic features in terms of their frequency and of their distinctiveness within texts, and texts in terms of the distinctive features which characterize them.

A concordance is a list of extracts retrieved from a corpus, each of which contains the item being studied (the keyword, which may be a word, word pattern or sequence) along with the immediate co-text to its left and right. The most commonly-used type of concordance, called a KWIC (KeyWord In Context) concordance, shows just one line for each extract, with the keyword in the centre of the line. But most concordance programs also allow the user to view a larger co-text, and in many cases to browse through the entire text from which a particular extract is taken. A concordance thus allows the user to look for eventual patterns in the co-text, which may offer clues to the meaning and usage of the keyword itself.

2. Style and authorship studies

Frequency lists and concordances were compiled for literary and stylistic studies well before the advent of computers. However, the computer's capacity to store and process text has given enormous impetus to this kind of work. A good example is Spevack's Shakespeare concordance collection (1972), which contains concordances for all the 29,066 different word forms contained in the plays and sonnets, and which he used to specify Shakespeare's "core vocabulary". In cases of disputed authorship, different texts can be compared statistically in order to see whether they share the same characteristics: Coulthard (1993, 1994) used a corpus of general English and a collection of police reports to evaluate the accused's confession in a celebrated murder case. He found that the structure <Subject + *then* + verb>, which appeared regularly in the confession ("Chris then jumped over and I followed", "Chris then climbed up the drainpipe"), was very unusual in the general English corpus, but much more common in police reports - the implication being that the confession had been, at the very least, guided.

3. General language corpora

3.1 Representing the written and spoken repertoire

When we are dealing with the language of a single author, a corpus can include the whole of the universe of discourse under study - for instance, the entire Shakespearean canon. But where the universe under study is the language of a people, or one of its domains of use (such as police reports), a corpus can at most provide a sample which is more or less representative of it.

Francis and Kucera, compilers of the first computerized corpus at Brown University, intended it to represent contemporary written American English (Kucera and Francis 1967; Francis and Kucera 1979). Realizing it would only be a tiny sample of the universe they wished to investigate, they invited a group of experts to collectively decide

> the size of the corpus (1,000,000 words), the number of texts (500, of 2000 words each), the universe (material in English, by American writers, first published in 1961), the subdivisions (15 genres, 9 of 'informative prose' and

> 6 of 'imaginative prose') and by a fascinating process of individual vote and average consensus, how many samples from each genre (ranging from 6 in science fiction to 80 in learned and scientific).
>
> (W.N. Francis 1982: 16)

Their professed aims included statistical analysis of word frequencies in English, and discovery of "the true facts" about English grammar (W.N. Francis 1982). They were aware of difficulties on both fronts. Carroll et al. (1971) calculated that to include all the estimated 600,000 word types in English, a corpus of 500,000,000 word tokens would be needed, given the massive skewing of vocabulary frequencies in natural language. In any corpus the most frequent 1% of types account for about 75% of the tokens, whereas words occurring only once (*hapax legomena*) make up around 40-50% of its types, but less than 1% of its tokens. Only the most common few hundred words in the language are reliably documented in a corpus the size of Brown.[1]

Francis and Kucera were also aware of opposition to the idea that a corpus could be used to discover grammatical facts. For the Chomskyan school, the aim of linguistics was to study competence - the ideal speaker's knowledge of a language - by means of introspection, whereas Francis' team had decided to concern itself with performance - looking at real speakers' actual language production. On hearing of the Brown project, a fellow linguist told Francis he was wasting his time. A native speaker, he maintained, could think of far more examples of a particular grammatical structure in ten minutes than a corpus could provide. Subsequent history has however shown that the wealth of authentic examples provided by corpora can highlight patterns which are invisible to unassisted introspection.[2]

Francis and Kucera were also concerned to make the Brown corpus public, in order to save other researchers the labour of compiling their own collections of text and to supply a standard body of data which would permit comparative studies. In this respect their work has been an unqualified success, as bibliographies of the field testify (Altenberg 1986, 1991a, 1995):

> a Swedish scholar has used it to make counts of letter frequencies in printed English; a philosopher in Hong Kong is studying collocations of the word *good*; a scholar in Jerusalem is studying word families; and my own students have used it in many studies, including the English modal auxiliaries and the progressive aspect of English verbs.
>
> (W.N. Francis 1982: 8)

Researchers at the Universities of Lancaster, Oslo and Bergen compiled a 'sister corpus' of British English, christened the LOB corpus (Johansson et al. 1978). Like Brown, this consists of 2,000 text samples, each 500 words long, making a total of a million words, and it shares approximately the same genre divisions. It has been widely used to study British English and also to compare it with American, as represented in Brown (see 5.1 below).

Both Brown and LOB contain only written texts. Until recently, the most widely used corpus of spoken English was the London-Lund Corpus (LLC). About 400,000 words in length, this consists of material from the Survey of English Usage, originally compiled manually with the aim of describing the grammatical repertoire of educated adult native speakers of British English (Svartvik and Quirk 1980), and used in compiling the *Comprehensive Grammar of the English Language* (Quirk et al. 1985). LLC contains a variety of different spoken text types, from spontaneous conversation to more scripted speech such as prepared public oration.

A comparison of LLC with Brown and LOB reveals interesting differences. For instance, the most frequent word in LLC is *I*, whereas in the two written corpora it is *the*. However, there is a difference between the unscripted and the scripted spoken text types. *I* is the most frequent word in the LLC conversations, but in the LLC scripted speech the commonest word is *the*, with *I* in only fifth position (in LOB *I* is in 17th place, in Brown, 20th). *You* is the fifth most common word in the LLC conversations, but only 32nd and 33rd in LOB and Brown. A number of verbs which occur frequently in LLC are not even in the top hundred items in LOB and Brown, e.g. *know* (15th in conversation, 28th in scripted speech), *think* (25th and 30th), *see* (45th and 60th), *get* (64th and 76th), *say* (88th and 92nd) (Hofland and Johansson 1982).

Growth in computing power has seen a corresponding growth in corpus size. More recently constructed corpora include the British National Corpus (BNC), a collection of 90 million words of written and 10 million words of spoken British English; the Longman-Lancaster Corpus (30 million words of written British and American English); the Cancode Corpus of Spoken English (5 million words). A somewhat different kind of corpus is the Bank of English (the development of the Birmingham-Cobuild Collection, often referred to as the 'Cobuild corpus'), which increases from year to year as new texts are added to it, and has grown from 20 million words in 1987 to over 300 million today. The costs of developing these corpora have largely been borne by dictionary publishers, who have used them as a resource for lexicography (see section 6 below), but many are now available for teaching and research purposes at relatively low cost.[3]

3.2 Adding information to corpora

Some kinds of information cannot easily be retrieved from a corpus in its 'raw', unedited form. Most of the corpora mentioned in this section have therefore been annotated in various ways to facilitate analysis. The most widespread form of annotation, part-of-speech tagging, involves adding to every word in the corpus a tag indicating which word class it belongs to, such as noun, proper noun, finite verb, adjective, determiner, and so on. Most part-of-speech tagging is carried out automatically by software programs which have been taught to recognize the likely class to which a word might belong in a certain context. One of its principal motivations is to obtain more precise frequency lists, since tagging makes it easier to distinguish between homographs, or different words written in the same manner (e.g. *post* as a noun meaning 'pole' or as a verb meaning 'send'). Tagging may also aid lemmatization, that is the grouping together of different forms of the same word (e.g. *lie, lying, lay, lain*), by enabling us to exclude such homographs as the nouns *lie* and *lay*.

Part-of-speech tagging also facilitates syntactic queries, allowing the researcher to locate such combinations as adverb pairs (*quite clearly, rather well*, etc.) or verb pairs (*make do, help finish*, etc.). But perhaps the most important reason for tagging is to enable the corpus to be handled by a parsing system, which attempts to analyze the syntactic structure of each sentence. Parsing opens the way to systematic study of the frequency of particular constructions and of their co-occurrence with other constructions or with particular lexical items. The kind of analysis which results will, of course, depend on the rules or statistical procedures which the parser adopts. While some small corpora, such as the Susanne corpus (a subset of the LOB corpus: Sampson 1995), have been fully parsed manually, automatic parsers, such as the Constraint Grammar system applied to the Bank of English (Karlsson 1994), have so far provided only limited analyses: Karlsson's system assigns to each word in the corpus a tag specifying its syntactic function (object, adverbial, finite main verb, etc.), but does not identify higher structural units such as clauses. The importance of tagging for descriptive purposes is largely proportional to corpus size: when working with relatively small corpora, researchers may simply be able to rely on their own discrimination to identify those examples which match specific patterns.

A good overall introduction to corpus annotation can be found in Garside et al. (1997).

4. The description of contemporary English

4.1 Lexis

Lexical research using corpora has been primarily interested in the frequencies of words and word senses and their collocational behaviour, that is, their patterns of combination with other words. Sinclair notes how collocations "can be dramatic and interesting because unexpected, or they can be important in the lexical structure of the language because of being frequently repeated" (1991a: 170). Thus phrases such as "forestfuls of grief" (Larkin) or "a grief ago" (Dylan Thomas) are dramatic because unusual collocations of *grief*, while *overcome with grief*, *come to grief*, and *Good grief!* are more clichéd because more usual.

In an interesting example of such research, Biber, Conrad and Reppen (1994) find that the most common use of *certain* is not that which usually springs to mind:

> An informal survey found that native speakers most commonly associate *certain* with the condition of certainty [...] In contrast, *certain* is much more commonly used to mark a referent as named but not clearly described or known, as in *a certain kind*, *in certain types*, *to a certain extent*, *there are certain aspects*.
>
> (Biber, Conrad and Reppen 1994: 178)

They go on to argue the importance of collocational studies for register analysis (to identify distinctive features of particular registers: see 5.4 below), for lexicography (to include register-specific information in dictionary entries) and for language teaching (to improve syllabus design, especially in ESP: see Aston, this volume, chapter 1: 2; Brodine, chapter 6). For instance, comparing the use of *certain* in the social science and the fiction texts in the Longman-Lancaster corpus, they note that

> *certain* marking 'certainty' is significantly more common in Fiction than in Social Science, while most occurrences of *certain* in Social Science mark referents as named but not clearly described (and thus in some sense not certain!)
>
> (Biber, Conrad and Reppen 1994: 179)

4.2 Syntax

Studies like Biber, Conrad and Reppen's show that regularities in collocational behaviour may be particular to the individual item, even to a particular sense of a particular item, not to mention to a particular register. In this respect, every word seems to have its own particular set of syntactic structures. Before the advent of corpora, grammarians tended to "assume that the study of grammar had strict limits, and lexis, on the whole lies outside them" (G. Francis 1993: 142), a view which was also widespread in language teaching:

> Our approach to language teaching, then, is structural. The words we choose to present for use in the structures are only of secondary importance, because once the patterns of English are mastered, it is relatively easy to learn new words to fit into the patterns.
> (Broughton 1968: 14)

Corpus linguistics, on the other hand, has stressed the interdependence of lexis and syntax:

> syntactic structures and lexical items (or strings of lexical items) are co-selected, and [...] it is impossible to look at one independently of the other. Particular syntactic structures tend to co-occur with particular lexical items, and - on the other side of the coin - lexical items seem to occur in a limited range of structures.
> (G. Francis 1993: 147)

As an example, Francis examines the word *possible*. This item "has a wide range of environments which make it unique among adjectives" (1993: 147). It appears in the pattern <*the* + superlative adjective + *possible* + head noun>, as in *the highest possible level, the worst possible outcome*. It also appears, combined with *as*, after a wide range of adjectives, adverbs and quantifiers: *as early as possible, as often as possible, as soon as possible*. Other frequent patterns include *where/wherever possible, when/whenever possible, if possible*. This range of environments is grammatically unique. But *possible* is by no means unusual in this respect:

> If we take any one of a huge range of the more frequent words in English, and examine its citations *en masse*, it will emerge that it, too, has a unique grammatical profile, which certainly cannot be encapsulated by calling the word in question an adjective or a noun or a preposition.
> (G. Francis 1993: 147)

Lists of collocations can highlight not only the grammatical differences between lexical items and senses but also previously unsuspected similarities. A number of studies have investigated what Quirk et al. (1985: 8.104ff) call "amplifying intensifiers", which they subdivide into "maximizers" (*absolutely, altogether, completely, entirely, extremely, fully, perfectly, quite, thoroughly, totally, utterly,* etc.) and "boosters" (a more open set of items, including *badly, bitterly, deeply, enormously, greatly, heartily, intensely, severely, strongly* and *terribly*). According to Quirk et al, maximizers "denote the upper end of the scale", insofar as the semantic quality indicated by the modified item is present to an absolute degree (*quite drunk, entirely clueless*). Boosters, on the other hand, simply denote "a high degree, a high point on the scale". However, in a study of the London-Lund spoken corpus, Altenberg (1991b) argues that the real difference lies in their collocates. Maximizers modify 'non-scalar' items like *perfect, unique, impossible, worthless*, etc., whose meaning already contains the idea of an absolute degree (they are not usually used in comparative and superlative forms: LDOCE 1987: 454-5). Boosters, on the other hand, modify 'scalar' items like *small, happy, cold*, etc., which can have many different degrees.

Such simple divisions may, however, be unreliable. Partington (1991) found that in the Cobuild corpus, 50% of the non-scalar adjectives listed by the Cobuild Grammar ('classifying adjectives': Cobuild 1990) are modified at least once by at least one adverb which Quirk et al. list as a booster. Similarly, the adjectives modified by items listed as maximizers include a number normally classified as scalar (e.g. *entirely new, absolutely quiet, perfectly simple*). These examples all contradict the expectation of maximizer with non-scalar and booster with scalar. Going on to compare the collocates of different intensifiers, Partington found that among Quirk et al.'s maximizers, *completely, entirely, totally* and *utterly* all had a tendency to collocate with items from two particular semantic fields, that of "absence of a quality" (*exempt, incapable, irrelevant, lost, meaningless, unaware, uneducated*, etc.) and that of "change of state" (*altered, changed, destroyed, different, new, rebuilt, transformed*, etc.). Most of these collocates were only found with these intensifiers, which appear to form a single group in terms of their combinatory potential.

Other intensifiers, on the other hand, had highly individual collocates. *Absolutely*, for instance, showed practically no collocational overlap with other items listed as maximizers, being the only one to modify adjectives expressing a very strong attitude or opinion (*delighted, enchanting, essential, marvellous, preposterous, shocking, wonderful*, etc.). In this respect *absolutely* appears to belong to a grammatical category of its own. The implications of findings like these for the design of grammars for language teaching and learning are discussed by Hunston and Francis (1998, 2000).

4.3 Discourse and text

Corpora have also benefitted the study of features of discourse which have a primarily pragmatic function. Tognini-Bonelli (1993a, 1993b) studied the use of items such as *real, actual* and *actually* in the Cobuild corpus. She showed how *real* can be used to signal the existence of an alternative concept or entity which is left unexpressed and dismissed as being unreal or unimportant, as in "the real losers in the election will be ..." - no other losers find a mention in the surrounding text. *Actual* and *actually* instead point to how text producers see (or wish receivers to believe they see) the discourse they are producing.

Other studies have investigated features of spoken discourse: pauses (Stenström 1990a), repeats and other non-fluencies (Stenström and Svartvik 1994), hedges, back-channel responses and softeners (Altenberg 1990). Altenberg found that items in these last three categories made up 9.4% of all word-class tokens in a 50,000 word portion of the London-Lund corpus, making them more frequent than prepositions, adverbs, determiners, conjunctions or adjectives. Zorzi (this volume, chapter 4) shows how the study of spoken discourse markers in corpus data can provide insights for language teachers and learners which are lacking from grammars and textbooks.

5. Comparing regions, languages, times and sublanguages

5.1 Comparing regional varieties

A large number of studies have compared corpora consisting of different language varieties. One particularly imaginative study by Leech and Fallon (1992) analyzed differences between the LOB and Brown corpora in the hope that this might shed light on differences between British and American culture in the early Sixties. Some of their findings were fairly predictable - *tea* occurs more frequently in LOB. But others were less so: words relating to the legal, military and business fields were all more common in Brown, as well as words relating to travel - perhaps reflecting the greater distances to be covered in America. As for grammatical differences, *if, but,* and, in general, indicators of possibility and uncertainty were all more frequent in LOB. The authors comment that these findings

> add up to a suggestion - no more than that - that the LOB Corpus shows conformity with one British stereotype, of the wishy-washy Briton who lacks firmness and decisiveness, seeing two sides to every question, and shades of grey instead of black and white.
>
> (Leech and Fallon 1992: 44)

Comparison of different varieties of English should be enormously aided by the completion of the International Corpus of English, which involves teams of researchers in twenty countries, including East Africa, Hong Kong, India, Nigeria and Singapore. Each is assembling a one-million-word corpus of the English used in their geographical area, following a design similar to that of Brown and LOB (Greenbaum 1991, 1992). Each corpus will be tagged and parsed.[4]

5.2 Comparing languages: corpora and translation studies

Fundamental to translation is the concept of *equivalence* - linguistic (the form of a message is equivalent in two languages), cognitive or semantic (the information content of a message is equivalent in two languages), and pragmatic (the significance of a message is the same for the target community as for the source community). Corpora containing sets of texts in different languages can be used as sources of linguistic, semantic and pragmatic information to aid the translation process:

> If the idea is not simply to reproduce the formal structures of the source text but also to give some thought, and sometimes priority, to how similar meanings and functions are typically expressed in the target language, then the need to study authentic instances of similar discourse in the two languages becomes obvious.
>
> (Baker 1993: 236)

Clearly, the more similar the sets of texts in two languages, the more useful they will tend to be.

There are various different types of 'equivalent corpora'. Translated or bilingual parallel corpora consist of two sets of texts, one the translation of the other. The best known example of this type is the Canadian *Hansard*, the written record of the proceedings of the Canadian Parliament which is prepared in both French and English. When computerized, parallel corpora can be aligned so that, for any textual string in the corpus, both the source sentence and its translation can be retrieved and displayed. Such corpora are widely used for compiling multilingual terminology databases and for developing machine translation software. A different type of equivalent corpus consists of two sets of texts selected using the same criteria, but which are not translations of each other. An example is the PIXI corpus (Gavioli and Mansfield 1990), which consists of transcripts of service encounters in Italian and in British bookshops. Zanettin (1994; this volume, chapter 7) describes ways of designing small-scale equivalent corpora of written texts, and gives suggestions for their pedagogical use.

5.3 Investigating language change

Corpus linguistics seems to be bringing about a partial reconciliation between synchronic and diachronic linguistics, which had until recently tended to go their separate ways. A synchronic approach tells linguists *how* the bits and pieces of a language fit together, but a diachronic approach can help them to understand *why*, revealing the forces and processes - social changes, and the needs and desires of speakers - which shape the development of a language and put the pieces there in the first place. The ARCHER corpus (Biber, Finegan et al. 1994), which contains texts from 1650 to the present day from various social and professional fields, has been used to analyze the development of scientific research writing in English (Atkinson 1992, 1996). The Helsinki Corpus (Kytö and Rissanen 1990; Kytö 1991), which contains texts from the Old English period up to Early Modern English from various regions of Britain, has been used to analyze the spread of linguistic changes over the country.[5]

While some changes appear socially motivated, others appear to reflect general linguistic tendencies. Mair (1995) compares the use of the verb *help* in the LOB corpus (consisting of texts published in 1961), and in a new corpus compiled using the same criteria in 1991.[6] He finds that the verb *help* is now being used more frequently without a following *to* (*help buy* rather than *help to buy*), i.e. as a modal verb meaning "facilitate or contribute to doing something" rather than as a lexical verb meaning "give aid to someone". Partington (1993) has traced similar changes in the function of a number of intensifying adverbs (*absolutely*, *perfectly*, *entirely*, *utterly*, *highly*, etc.). Comparing historical citations in the *Oxford English Dictionary* (OED 1989) with contemporary data from the Cobuild corpus, he notes how these words have been progressively delexicalized, their function changing from lexical to modal and finally to purely intensifying. Their collocational behaviour seems to reflect this shift: for example, *very*, once a modal with a truth-declaring function, now combines very widely indeed, and it is also the intensifier with the least independent lexical content. Delexicalization and widening of collocation are probably both part of the same phenomenon: once an intensifier begins to collocate with more and more modifiers, it seems to automatically lose part of its independent lexical content.

5.4 Comparing text-types

Many corpora are designed to contain a variety of text-types, thus allowing these types to be compared. The best known work in this area is probably that of Biber (1988), who used cluster-analysis techniques to compare the various text-types contained in the LOB and London-Lund corpora. On the basis of an analysis of some 67 linguistic features in a sample of 481 texts, he identified differences on six 'dimensions' relating to their communicative function (involved vs. informational production, narrative vs. non-narrative concerns, explicit vs situation-dependent reference, overt expression of persuasion, abstract vs. non-abstract information, on-line informational elaboration). Biber characterizes each dimension, or more precisely, each of its opposite poles, by a set of co-occurring features. For example, frequent use of *that* deletion, second person pronouns, and present tense verbs are among the indicators of 'involved production', while a high type-token ratio and long sentences are among those of 'informational production'. Biber suggests that registers can be seen as configurations of positions on his six dimensions: thus casual conversation is involved (low on information) and non-abstract, whereas scientific exposition is the opposite in these respects. This means that any text can be assigned to a particular register by analyzing its features and plotting its position along these dimensions, and that maps of the differences and similarities between registers can be compiled, even to the point of visualizing how close or far apart these are in multi-dimensional 'space'.

One conclusion which can be drawn from Biber's work is that no single register can be identified as 'general English'. Biber, Conrad and Reppen (1994) note how EFL textbooks often maintain the fiction that they are written in general, albeit simplified, English, whereas they are in fact in an 'EFL textbook' register. While this fiction may be useful with beginners, they argue that intermediate and advanced students must be exposed to authentic texts if they are to acquire specific registers and to develop an awareness of the ways in which texts differ according to their functions. Corpus analysis provides a means of identifying the features characterizing particular registers, and hence of selecting appropriate texts to use in teaching (Aston 1997a).

6. Lexicography

Probably the greatest impact that corpus linguistics has had on English language teaching is in the design of learners' dictionaries. Sinclair (1987b) lists the principal tasks of the lexicographer as:

- collection of material;
- selection of entries;
- construction and arrangement of the entries;

- selection of examples;
- design of definitions.

Of these, all but the last have been influenced by the advent of corpora.

The collection of material, traditionally a haphazard combination of noting interesting occurrences and of introspection, is now being based on the systematic analysis of large representative corpora. The first edition of the Cobuild dictionary (Cobuild 1987) used a 20-million-word corpus of contemporary English (mainly written), and a smaller one taken from EFL textbooks (Renouf 1987a: 16-18): the second edition (Cobuild 1995) drew on 200 million words from the Bank of English. LDOCE (1995) and OALD (1995) both exploited the 100-million-word British National Corpus, and CIDE (1995) drew on the similarly-sized Cambridge Language Survey.

The selection of entries is largely dictated by frequency of appearance in the corpus, although a word not in the corpus may find its way into the dictionary "if it appeared in another EFL dictionary or was a very colloquial usage that just happened never to have been used in the corpus texts" (Krishnamurthy 1987: 74).

The construction of entries is based on the analysis of concordances for every form of each entry. These can provide grammatical information (for example a regular noun which has no s-form occurrences can reasonably be assumed to be uncountable), and can highlight collocational regularities. Concordance lines can be grouped and counted according to the different senses of the word, allowing the latter to be arranged in order of frequency.

The selection and ordering of examples is also facilitated by concordance analysis, though different dictionaries adopt different approaches in this area. CIDE (making use of its international corpus) includes examples from as many varieties of the language as possible. In Cobuild,

> The first example selected for any word or sense of a word was intended to show typical usage in terms of syntactic behaviour or collocation. Subsequent examples registered syntactic patterns, further collocations, etc.
> (Krishnamurthy 1987: 76)

Cobuild also aims not to alter examples taken from the corpus in any way, while other dictionaries modify them for ease of understanding. LDOCE generally provides invented or modified examples first, following these by authentic ones. In any case, the wealth of corpus examples enables dictionary compilers to have a more accurate picture of the usage, frequency and, as it were, the 'social weight' of a word or word sense. A good deal of pragmatic information is also beginning to be included in dictionaries, explaining not just what a word means and when it is used, but also what it is used to do.

7. Corpora and language pedagogy

Besides the creation of learner dictionaries and grammars, corpora have had a variety of other applications in language teaching. They have been used both to help decide what to teach, in syllabus design, and as an aid to teaching it. Willis and Willis (1988) used frequency lists and concordances from the Cobuild corpus to specify the contents of a 'lexical' syllabus aiming to teach "the common uses of common words" (Sinclair and Renouf 1988). Other researchers have constructed corpora from specific domains for the purposes of ESP syllabus design. Flowerdew (1993) used the frequencies of words and structures in a collection of Biology lectures to determine the English to be taught to science undergraduates, having found these to be radically different from those in a large general corpus. Similarly, Stubbs and Gerbig (1993) used a corpus of geography textbooks to show how notions such as change, causation and agency are handled in particular ways, some typical of geographical language and some perhaps of 'textbook English', but which in any case deserve to be brought to learners' attention.

Other researchers have used corpora as a basis for classroom materials and activities. Some of the proposals in this area involve the analysis of corpus data by teachers in order to

> (i) determine the most frequent patterns in a particular domain; (ii) enrich their own knowledge of the language, perhaps in response to questions asked in the classroom; (iii) provide 'authentic data' examples; and (iv) generate teaching materials.
>
> (Barlow 1996a: 30)

Others instead involve the learner in the analysis:

> teachers may also wish to have their students explore corpus materials directly, either in following a path of investigation determined by the teacher (so that the students come to understand a particular pattern of usage such as *say* versus *tell*, or the collocations of *bright*), or in exploring an issue in a more open-ended way.
>
> (Barlow 1996a: 30)

The case studies provided in the next chapter illustrate how it is possible for teachers to use 'home-made' corpora to meet these various goals, developing and refining syllabuses and materials, enriching their own knowledge and understanding of the language, and giving learners the opportunity to explore data as a means of developing their own understanding of the language and their study skills.

Notes

1. This regularity in the distribution of lexical types was first noted by Zipf (1935):

    The commonest word in English - *the* - has approximately twice the frequency of the next two, *of* and *and* [...] The frequency drops sharply and fairly steadily, so that the nineteenth most frequent word, *be*, has less than ten per cent of the frequency of *the*, and the eighty-fourth word, *two*, has less than five per cent.
    (Sinclair 1991a: 18)

2. Intuitive introspection does of course play a role in corpus linguistics, but it is not the primary data source. As Leech (1991: 74) comments:

    Recent corpus users have accepted that corpora, in supplying first-hand textual data, cannot be meaningfully analyzed without the intuition and interpretative skills of the analyst, using knowledge of the language (*qua* native speaker or proficient non-native speaker) and knowledge about the language (*qua* linguist). In other words, corpus use is seen as a question of corpus plus intuition, rather than of corpus or intuition.

    A dispute between Owen (1993) and Francis and Sinclair (1994) highlights this point. Owen argues that corpus grammarians eschew intuition, which "in theory plays no part in the compilation process since categories will emerge from the data", but that they "in practice take a few short cuts" (1993: 179). Francis and Sinclair answer that the interaction of data and intuition is central to corpus-based work, since "when someone's intuition does not line up with the corpus evidence, there is a problem to be resolved" (1994: 191).

3. Brown, LOB, London-Lund and a number of other small corpora have been included on a CD-ROM published by ICAME (International Computer Archive of Medieval and Modern English: http://www.hit.uib.no/icame/cd). The full BNC can be consulted or purchased over the Internet, while a 2-million word sample of the corpus is available on CD-ROM (see

http://info.ox.ac.uk/bnc). Cobuild provides a look-up service to part of the Bank of English over the Internet (http://titania.cobuild.collins.co.uk). Access to the CANCODE corpus may be granted for specific research purposes by Cambridge University Press (http://www.cup.cam.ac.uk).

4. The first of the ICE corpora, that of British English, is available on CD-ROM (http://www.ucl.ac.uk/english-usage/ice/index.htm).

5. The Helsinki corpus is included on the ICAME CD-ROM (see note 3 above).

6. Mair compiled 1991 versions of both LOB and Brown, known as Flob and Frown, which are included on the ICAME CD-ROM (see note 3 above).

3 CORPUS-BASED DESCRIPTION IN TEACHING AND LEARNING

Alan Partington

1. Resources and procedures

This chapter provides a number of examples illustrating the role of corpora as research tools, using concordances to uncover detailed information on the collocational behaviour of particular linguistic items. Such enquiries may be relevant to language teaching and learning in a number of ways. First of all, teachers can use these techniques to increase their own knowledge of a particular language area, refining the often fairly general information available from dictionaries, grammars, textbooks, etc. Second, corpus data can be used as teaching material, being presented to learners either directly or, when more convenient, in a pre-edited form (see the pioneering work in this area of Johns 1991b and Higgins 1991). Finally, learners can be trained to use corpora to carry out investigations into language use for themselves. To do so, they need to know not only how to operate the technology, but also what sort of investigations can profitably be carried out. The examples in this chapter are meant to illustrate some of the kinds of studies which may be feasible from one or other of these three perspectives. They investigate various types of meaning - denotational, connotational, syntactic, idiomatic and textual.

All the investigations described were carried out using *MicroConcord* (Scott and Johns 1993) to prepare concordances from a collection of five million words of written text. *MicroConcord* comes with two corpora: a million words from *The Independent* newspaper (*Corpus A:* Murison-Bowie 1993b) and another million words of academic writing from various fields (*Corpus B:* Murison-Bowie 1993c). It is relatively easy to compile similar corpora (from CD-ROMs or the Internet: see Zanettin, this volume, chapter 7: 2), and for the purpose of these studies, a further three million words from *The Independent* for 1992 were added to the *MicroConcord Corpus A* texts. In some cases, only this enlarged newspaper corpus was used, for others, the academic texts of *Corpus B* were also exploited.

Newspaper texts are not representative of the English language as a whole, but provided we do not overgeneralize our findings, they seem a reasonable basis for many investigations. All language production belongs to one genre or another, and the English language is a collection of such genres, none of which can be considered 'general English' (see Partington, this volume, chapter 2: 5.4). Newspaper articles are the most widely read of long text types - almost every educated adult has considerable experience of them - and are of interest to a wide variety of learners. They also vary considerably, not only according to topic (the texts in the corpus were grouped into home, foreign, arts, business and sports sections), but also because they are prepared in different ways (Bell 1991). Many hard news articles (including front page news, sports match commentaries, news flashes, etc.) are produced in a very short time, under constraints which may mean that they have certain features in common with spoken language (Cowie 1992). Opinion articles, soft news human interest stories, and pieces on general culture may take quite a time to complete and only be used when space allows, a fact again reflected in the language they contain.

2. The value of context

A corpus is not always the best place to look if you simply want to know the definition of a word. Dictionaries and encyclopaedias are designed to describe conceptual or denotational meanings, arranging the different senses of a word in some kind of order. Corpus examples give only contextual clues, from which it is not always easy to reconstruct the conceptual meaning of a word precisely, since speakers and writers tend to take it for granted that the hearer or reader will have a good idea of the conceptual meaning of most words used.

This point can be illustrated by looking at terms from a technical register, that of business English. Not everyone knows precisely what *equities* are, and the concordance below (showing complete sentences, sorted by the word following *equities*) hardly supplies a clear picture:

1   It will invest about 80 per cent of its funds in blue chip UK **equities**.
2   [...] to achieve the rapid development of a paperless settlement, payments and registration system for domestic **equities**.
3   'France has not seen many large equity issues recently," said Fred Bombrum, French **equities** analyst at stockbroker Hoare Govett.
4   **Equities** and government stocks fell back.
5   [...] the authorities were orchestrating a base rate rise and the stock market is now providing stark illustration of how **equities** and climbing interest rates do not mix.
6   However, the upside potential for the shares considering the current climate for **equities** are insufficient to offset the risks for small investors.

7   Sterling, helped conveniently by the Bank of England, was relatively steady, and **equities** closed 19 points up.
8   **EQUITIES** displayed traces of their old confidence yesterday with the FT-SE share index recapturing 4.6 points
9   Turnover in UK **equities** has seen an increase of almost 50 per cent over the past year,
10 European Markets: **Equities** lose the earnings edge to cash
11 Brokers suggested that in the new climate of anxiety brought on by the steep fall in **equities**, ministers would have to reassure investors by pricing the issue lower and offering higher returns.
12 For them it is more a question of investing in **equities** or not.
13 **Equities** recovered from a sharp early setback yesterday.
14 Despite sterling travails, however, British money market rates fell as traders became convinced that the fragility of **equities** ruled out another interest rate rise.
15 But the weakness of **equities** showed that it is a nervous respite.
16 But the bearish view was not universally held and Nicholas Knight, the UK **equities** strategist at Nomura, said: 'The market may go lower but the time to buy is now.
17 While **equities** suffered Government stocks boomed, scoring gains of up to £212.
18 What the market appeared to be saying was that, with **equities** weak, the recent rise in base rates to 15 per cent was the limit.
19 These concerns in turn took their toll of **equities**, which in any case are increasingly being supported by institutional cashflow.
20 The evidence of deep concern, if not panic, was the universal reaction to go short of sterling and **equities** yesterday, and interest rate futures gave little sign of a remission.

The authors of these texts are writing for readers familiar with business English, which excludes the majority of native as well as non-native speakers of the language. What the latter need is a definition like the one to be found in LDOCE (1987):

> **equity** *n [usu. pl.] tech* an ordinary SHARE (= one of the equal parts into which the ownership of a company is divided), on which no fixed amount of interest is paid.

Without this conceptual information, the reader of the concordance tends to miss whatever clues there actually are. For example, in citation 8 the reference to the FT share index might be a clue to the fact that an equity is a type of share, but how can one be sure?

But once the user has this conceptual knowledge, the concordance can flesh it out with information on both the linguistic and socio-cultural uses of the item. Even in the few citations above, we discover some of the things equities can do. They can *suffer* (17), *fall* (11) or *fall back* (4), but they can also *recover* (13). They *close* (7) at a certain value. They *display confidence* (8) or they can be *fragile* or *weak* (14, 15, 18). They come in *issues* (3, 11) and they give *returns* (11). The concordance gives far more information on the use of the word than a dictionary can do, and might be used by learners to help choose the appropriate expression for a particular linguistic environment. Even in an encyclopaedia much of this information would be hard to come by.

3. Choosing the right synonym

Studies of second language acquisition and of learner strategies have shown that synonymy plays an important role in language learning. New vocabulary is often acquired by analogy, with words being remembered as similar in meaning to previously acquired items (Rudska et al. 1982, 1985; Carter 1987: 170-3), and 'definition through synonym' is a prominent feature of many dictionaries. Learners frequently feel the need to find alternative words to express particular concepts: Harvey and Yuill (1997) found that searches for synonyms accounted for over 10% of dictionary consultations during a writing task. Given the rarity of absolute synonymy, however, learners also need to know which of the synonyms they have found is the most suitable for a given context. Harvey and Yuill found that, in over 36% of synonym searches, learners failed to find the information they were looking for. No other type of dictionary search - which included looking for syntactic, semantic, collocational and register information - met with such a low level of success.

Using concordance data to compare the contexts of synonyms may help learners decide in what circumstances they are interchangeable. If we look up the nouns *couple* and *pair* in three recent dictionaries (LDOCE 1995, CIDE 1995 and Cobuild 1995), we are told that one of the principal uses of *couple* is to refer to two people who "are married or having a sexual or romantic relationship" (LDOCE), and that *couple* is not always strictly two items, but can mean any small number. All three dictionaries state that *pair* is used with items which are normally used together, such as *a pair of trousers* and *a pair of scissors* which are made in two parts and then joined, and that it can also be used of people who "have a relationship or are doing something together" (CIDE). All give plenty of examples.

Concordances of these words, however, provide a wealth of further information. For instance, a concordance of *couple* in the newspaper corpus highlights its use to express time (*the next couple of days, in a couple of years, a couple of years back, over the last couple of months, over the past couple of decades, over the last couple of centuries*) and distance (*just a couple of kilometres out of West Germany, a couple of miles down the road, a couple of inches lower, a couple of hundred yards from the entrance*). It is also used frequently in sports language to refer to events of the same type: *a couple of fixtures/penalties/tackles/passes/rounds/chances/holes/shots/points*. All these examples involve use of *a couple* followed by *of*, a phraseology which is in contrast very rare in reference to people who 'live or spend time together'. *A pair of*, on the other hand, often refers to people (*a pair of pickpockets*), as well as items of clothing (*a pair of slippers/mittens/gloves/shoes/underpants/boots/tights/stays*) or body-parts (*hands, feet, ears, ankles* and *heels* - the latter in the expression *showing a clean pair of heels*). Other occurrences include *a pair of diamonds/old tennis rackets/aces/skyscrapers*. In all these cases, *a pair* would seem to suggest that the items go together in some way. People who form a pair seem to do so because they cooperate together - often in a sports team (*the pair added 92 runs for the third wicket*). There is also evidence that *pair* can have a derogatory sense, as in *make a right pair, you will* (implying a pair of idiots, or something similar).

Concordance data is particularly useful to discriminate semi-grammatical synonyms of this kind. Further examples might be the adverbs *rather* and *somewhat*, which belong to a group which Quirk et al. (1985) call "downtoners", since they moderate, or tone down, the adjective or verb they modify. Such items are notoriously difficult for dictionaries to deal with because they do not have a clear denotational meaning (unlike, say, *elephant* or *cautiously*), but can only really be described in terms of what they do to the phrases they find themselves in. Cobuild (1987) defines the two words differently - *rather* is 'to a certain, limited, or slight extent', whereas *somewhat* is 'to a fairly large extent or degree' - but then lists *somewhat* as a synonym of *rather* (but not vice-versa). LDOCE (1987) is more consistent, defining *rather* as 'to some degree' and *somewhat* as 'by some degree or amount', but then gives *rather* as a synonym of *somewhat*, but not vice-versa (the opposite of Cobuild). What neither dictionary explains, but concordances highlight, is that *somewhat* belongs to a more formal register than *rather*. First of all, it is much less frequent in the corpus, suggesting that its use is more restricted. Secondly, it collocates with 'difficult' adjectives and adverbs - *circuitous, disingenuously, fatuous, foolhardy*, *fusty*, etc, while *rather* appears with many more common-or-garden words. The inference 'do not use *somewhat* with words like *good*, *bad*, *happy*, *sad*' may be a useful one for learners.

There is, of course, no reason why only two words should be compared using these methods. One could usefully extend a study of *rather* and *somewhat* to *fairly* and *quite* (though in the case of the latter, it would be necessary to divide its occurrences as a downtoner from those as an intensifier). A good starting point for such investigations is Carpenter's (1993) collection of 'confusable words', which lists differences in the use of near-synonyms in the Bank of English.

4. Investigating connotation

Connotative meaning is not specific to language, but is shared by visual art, music and even smell. Consequently, it has been considered "incidental to language rather than an essential part of it" (Leech 1974: 15), and connotations are treated by traditional semantics as distinct from the 'core meanings' of words (Backhouse 1992: 297). However, knowledge of the connotative meaning of words is a vital part of communicative competence, and the non-native learner needs to acquire this sort of knowledge in order to avoid potential misunderstanding, social clumsiness or worse: as Stubbs (1996: 195) points out, "connotation is just as important as referential meaning, and often more so [...] It's not what we say, but the way that we say it". Frequently, their connotative meaning can be understood by studying the contexts in which particular words are used in corpus data.

Linguistic connotations are of at least three types. First, markers of particular varieties have what Backhouse (1992) calls "social" or "situational" connotations. The class, regional origin, age, sex, and relationship of speakers may all be connoted by particular lexico-grammatical choices. For example, the expression *absolutely awful* is readily identifiable as belonging to an upper-middle class variety in British English. Particular choices can also connote register: *beefy* is more colloquial than *robust*, and the selection by a speaker of one rather than the other reflects the formality of the register being used.

Second, connotations may be cultural. Leech (1974: 15) points out how the word *woman* has in the past been burdened with such attributes as 'frail', 'prone to tears', 'cowardly' and 'irrational', along with more positive qualities such as 'gentle', 'compassionate' and 'sensitive'. Such connotations are clearly liable to modification as social values change.

Thirdly, connotations may imply an evaluation by the speaker, expressing a favourable or unfavourable attitude to what they describe.

Backhouse's "I am firm, you are stubborn, he is pig-headed" (1992: 297) is a particularly clear example of the way in which synonymous adjectives may differ in their connotations. In this case, the connotation seems part of the core meaning of the word: *pig-headed* is used precisely because it connotes disapproval. The sole purpose of the term *venerable* is to put (male) old age in a good light; that of *callow* to express disapproval of youth. Where connotation is so intrinsic to a word, it is often a question of luck whether it will be revealed by corpus data, since like conceptual meanings, connotations of this kind are often taken for granted. In other cases, however, the connotation seems less intrinsic to the item in question, but a product of association with typical collocates, in a phenomenon Sinclair has termed 'semantic prosody'.[1] He notes how the verb *set in*, for example, seems regularly associated with unpleasant events in concordance data:

> The most striking feature of this phrasal verb is the nature of the subjects. In general they refer to unpleasant states of affairs. Only three refer to the weather; a few are neutral, such as *reaction* and *trend*. The main vocabulary is *rot* (3), *decay, ill-will, decadence, impoverishment, infection, prejudice, vicious (circle), rigor mortis, numbness, bitterness, mannerism, anticlimax, anarchy, disillusion, disillusionment, slump*. Not one of these is desirable or attractive.
>
> (Sinclair 1987b: 155-6)

The result of this habitual bad company is that *set in* cannot, in normal circumstances, refer to a desirable process. Louw (1993) suggests that any exception is usually with ironic intent. He quotes an example from David Lodge's novel, *Small World*:

> The modern conference resembles the pilgrimage of medieval Christendom in that it allows the participants to indulge themselves in all the pleasures and diversions of travel while apparently *bent on* self-improvement.

Corpus data shows that *bent on* usually collocates with undesirable objectives - *destroying, harrying, mayhem*, and the like. In upsetting this semantic prosody by making it collocate with the evidently desirable *self-improvement*, Lodge is here searching for an ironic effect.

Speakers and writers can of course diverge from a semantic prosody by accident. In these cases we may detect a difference between what the addresser is apparently saying and what they really believe. Louw cites the example of a British visitor to an African university, who declared "it is symptomatic of the University [...] which has such a high reputation that there are fifteen links between departments in the university here and equivalent departments [...] in Britain" (1993: 169). Corpus data shows that the semantic prosody of *symptomatic* is heavily unfavourable, suggesting that the speaker (who was presumably not being deliberately ironic) did not privately think so highly of the University in question.

In the past, dictionaries have not been able to deal satisfactorily with semantic prosodies, because these tend to remain hidden from the lexicographer's 'naked eye', emerging only as patterns in large numbers of examples. For instance, older dictionaries are generally silent about the derogatory connotations of the verb *peddle*. OALD (1989) gives its sense as "to sell goods in small quantities", with the metaphorical meaning of "advocate or promote (ideas, a philosophy, a way of life)". This definition-by-synonym misses the point that *peddle* (and *pedlar/peddler*) are used metaphorically precisely in order to avoid the positive connotations of *advocate* or *promote*, words which bestow a touch of *gravitas* on the ideas being mooted. The use of *peddle* implies disagreement and even hostility - telling the reader as much about the opinions and beliefs of the text producer as about the actual topic:

1   For nearly a week, the **widely-peddled** notion that straight people were safe from AIDS lay shattered.
2   I am surprised that senior Opposition politicians can find nothing better to do with their time than to **peddle** mischievous insinuations which simply distract attention from the important issues of the day.
3   What consolation will the **pedlars** of these cynically-manufactured crowd-pleasers have when
4   Sometimes he touched an unexpected note of wry, self-deprecating irony. '... one of the problems that I face, as someone who **peddles** hope, is the presumption against one's credibility and integrity.' Someone who **peddles** hope? He wasn't confessing cynicism so much as modestly doing himself down, after the English fashion.

Today's corpus-based dictionaries include more explicit indications of this unfavourable prosody. Cobuild (1995) remarks that *peddle* is "used showing disapproval"; CIDE (1995) that it is "esp. disapproving". OALD (1995), while making no reference to these connotations in its definition, provides examples which exhibit it in highly unfavourable environments: *peddling malicious gossip*, *peddling his crazy ideas*.

The semantic prosodies of *set in* and *peddle* are highly regular. Other words may have less noticeable connotations, which are present only in certain senses, or in certain registers. When the prosody of an item is not univocal, corpus data may show up tendencies, and highlight exceptions.

We may take as an example the word *dealings*, which none of the dictionaries just mentioned indicate as having particular connotations.

The most common use of *dealings* in the newspaper corpus is as a technical word denoting transactions on the Stock Exchange. Leaving aside this meaning, we find that its prosody is otherwise unfavourable. This is less explicitly indicated than in the case of *set up* or *peddle*: in 58 examples, there are only three modifiers of *dealings* which express negative value judgements (*shady*, *illegal*, and *behind-the-scenes*). It is the wider context which shows that *dealings* are unattractive or dishonest:

1   Behind the mask we may discern traits of craftiness in his business **dealings**,
2   the council intends to take a dim view of private dentists not behaving ethically in their commercial **dealings**.
3   rugby union is a 'profession' which dwells partly in the half-light of whispers and backroom **dealings** and partly in the daylight

Thus we find that people *deny*, *decline* or *refuse to discuss* their dealings, in the case of *investigation into*, *inquiry into*, *revelations about*, *allegations about*, or *exposé of* them. The phrase *dealings with* is also common, and those with whom dealings are done are pretty unsavoury (*Hizbollah, the Mafia, extremists, an unscrupulous Press*) - it is found in reports of judicial cases where someone is suspected of criminal association. Indeed it seems possible to imply that someone's affairs are shady simply by labelling them as dealings, and by the same token, that a person or group is unpleasant or criminal by talking of dealings with them. Since the taint or accusation is implicit, this claim is hard to prove, but consider:

1   but as more revelations have become known about her immediate family's **dealings** with the Mafia
2   his Democratic opponents [...] last week gave a scathing speech on the administration's pre-1990 **dealings** with Iraq

Writers who use *dealings* thus tell us something about their own attitudes, or else try to tamper with ours in a subtle fashion. If a newspaper tells us that someone became a millionaire through business transactions, we are likely to perceive him differently than if he got rich through property dealings (another example in the corpus).

In conclusion, we might look closely at the only case where *dealings* is modified by a favourable adjective:

> The Japanese leader's aim in his talks today with Jacques Delors, the Commission President, and John Major, the current chairman of the

European Council, must be to use the mutual admiration between Japan and Britain to foster more cordial **dealings** between his country and the rest of the Community. A Japanese spokesman yesterday denied that there was anything more to the Thatcher meeting than a wish to stay in touch with a respected former prime minister. But he added: 'We expect to develop our relations with the EC based on our good relations with the UK.'

Here the use of the words *foster* and *cordial* suggests that all is sweetness and light. By contrast, the appearance of the following *dealings* seems to imply that the real relationship between Japan and Europe is less straightforward. The suspicion of diplomatic subterfuge is confirmed by the next sentence's hint at secret negotiations with Baroness Thatcher.

Semantic prosodies are particularly difficult to predict where different uses of an item have different behaviours: thus *build up confidence* (transitive) is favourable, while *resistance builds up* (intransitive) is unfavourable (Louw 1993: 171). It may therefore be worthwhile to look at texts which are likely to exploit prosodic effects - newspaper reports, political speeches, advertising, etc. - to identify potential candidates, and then check these hypotheses against corpus data. One promising area is that of verbs (we have already mentioned *set in*, *be bent on*, and *peddle*), where an interesting exercise could be to compare the semantic prosodies of verbs which have similar conceptual meanings, such as *persist* and *persevere*. Another is that of intensifiers, where, for instance, Louw's (1993) claim that *utterly* has an unfavourable prosody invites comparison with other intensifying adverbs; and it would also be interesting to examine *utter*, and other intensifying adjectives, to see whether these share the prosodies of their adverbial forms.

5.   Investigating idiom and metaphor

Several of the examples examined in the last section involve idiomatic and metaphorical uses. Corpora can provide an extremely useful resource for investigating idioms and metaphors of various types. Figure 1 shows a selected 45 of the 1033 occurrences of *black* in the newspaper corpus, sorted by the following word.

Not all of these idiomatic uses of *black* are to be found in learners' dictionaries. CIDE (1995), for example, has definitions for *black comedy*, *black eye*, *black hole*, *black market*, *black look*, *black-out* and *black sheep*. We find many more in an encyclopaedic dictionary such as Webster (1989), but the concordance includes several further combinations. It also shows many ways of using these combinations that dictionaries do not consider.

3. Corpus-based description in teaching and learning

```
1   til recently it was only known from an early black and white photograph. <p> There was also
2   and otters, Cunliffe's has only a cat: it's    black and white, it's called Jess and it rides
3   Microvitec will make and sell Electrohome's    black and white screens in the UK and Electroho
4   the first pieces about relationships between  black and white people, in the West End when it
5   more relaxed relationship between white and   black and a greater understanding for different
6   d was 'one of the world's few areas of moral  black and white". So his Contras behave like ho
7   ielder, for pounds 37,500. PLAYERS will wear  black armbands out of respect for the victims o
8   Zealanders, appropriately garbed in funereal  black, arrive next week to scatter the ashes. <
9   urth game, then Speelman varied, capturing a  black bishop with a knight instead of his pawn.
10  ified dirt on the Democratic Party but for a  black book containing names of prostitutes and
11  mystery, the consequence of a complete news   black-out by the authorities on the circumstanc
12  rom the end by Kurt Sherlock, the former All- Black centre, brought New Zealand the first vic
13  lack politician. He is a graduate not of the  black churches and the civil rights movement, b
14  dy famous got it?' and Marchant even finds a  black comedy in the competition between chariti
15  treets, hello GoodFellas) the Mafia. Another  black comedy of sorts, The Big Shave (1967, 6 m
16  n the show the fact that Henry was the first  black comic to get his own television series in
17  te, has already received permission from the  Black Country Development Corporation for mixed
18  All Whites, incidentally, have their own All  Black date in a fortnight. <p> Quins need Paul
19  etting. <p> Just a fortnight previously on a  black day for rugby, Gareth Chilcott, the Bath
20  stall the day the club, which remains in the  black despite an annual shortfall of income aga
21  f Trade and Industry collected a spectacular  black eye after a late-night altercation outsid
22  evident enjoyment of parties, the mysterious  black eye acquired on the doorstep of one of Lo
23  the ends of the earth with her dresses, her   black eyes, her violin and her folly. What save
24  a competitor. PFS expects to be back in the   black for the full year. <p> Prem, LEP's new te
25  their layers of protective deceit, exposing   black hearts and guilty desires. Just like goin
26  n picture. Money may have disappeared down a  black hole (the budget was dollars 40m accordin
27  urs. For example, we learn how the notion of  black hole radiance - arguably Hawking's greate
28  ranti will want to be sure there are no more  black holes lurking in the company's books. And
29  's Cartier Million. <p> Things cannot all be  black, however. Sangster recently purchased a 1
30  > With dangerous sacrifices threatening, and  black knights cantering around his king, Karpov
31  t run?: Once he was a programme maker with a  black leather coat and a mission. Then he maste
```

33 mpton Wanderers ....2 THERE were nothing but **black** looks at the **Black** Country derby yesterda
34 dose to wipe out fortunes accumulated on the **black** market and through high-priced co-operati
35 nds 1,000, worth over 100,000 roubles on the **black** market, as part of a forthcoming deal and
36 rnment cars, diesel is only available on the **black** market. <p> For the past few weeks Presid
37 ationally slow, magnificently recorded, is a **black** mass indeed, somehow the more decadent, t
38 ms launch veered towards the Rock, a looming **black** mass. An officer on the bridge cut back t
39 the world to prepare for a possible rerun of **Black** Monday, the day in 1987 when stock market
40 sh the index fell 249.6 points to 2,052.3 on **Black** Monday. It then continued to decline, fal
41 at happened to Virginia? Everyone, white and **black**, save the very rich and the very poor, be
42 uerrillas to Dawson's Field, Jordan, and the **Black** September guerrilla uprising. He was also
43 Despite this the market treats Evans like a **black** sheep with a severe attack of Chancellori
44 n police custody after a brawl with Mosley's **Black** Shirts. In the Lords he was often the voi
45 ould have been new to most viewers, white or **black**. The comedy made a steady, surreptitious

Figure 1. 45 selected occurrences of *black* in the newspaper corpus, sorted by the following word

1 refore distortions of the Schwarzschild **black hole** solution in the interaction region, and co
2 For example, we learn how the notion of **black hole** radiance - arguably Hawking's greatest dis
3 ties. These include the 'big bang" and '**black hole**" types of singularity which closely corres
4 e the Schwarzschild exterior inside the **black hole**. <p> In addition, he has suggested some po
5 most energetic known cosmic explosions: **black holes** or quasars. But there are no such objects
6 will want to be sure there are no more **black holes** lurking in the company's books. And many
7 bids for fear that there may be further **black holes** in Ferranti's balance sheet. <p> They als
8 ture. Money may have disappeared down a **black hole** (the budget was dollars 40m according to H
9 enjoys getting up at 4.30 to go down a **black hole**? It makes me appreciate doing this for a l

Figure 2. *Black hole/holes* in the newspaper corpus

For example, the phrase *black and white* is the normal combination to refer to physical colour (some languages prefer 'white and black'), especially when opposed to 'colour' in photography (line 1) or video (3). However, when the reference is to skin colour, either *black and/or white* (4) or *white and/or black* (5, 41, 45) are used. We also discover the idiomatic *moral black and white* (6).

Black can be used as an abbreviating adjective standing for 'pertaining to black people' as in *black churches* (line 13). This is also its meaning in *black comic* (16). In this case, a non-native who had found *black comedy* in the dictionary (see also 14-15), might imagine that a black comic was one who practised such humour. However, a glance at the wider context for this line makes it clear that the expression refers to a comic who is black, the only meaning of this collocation in the corpus.

Lines 7 and 8 show that *black* sometimes has something to do with funerals and sad remembrance. From here it is a short step to understanding that *a black day* (19) marks an unhappy one. By the same token, if *things cannot all be black* (29), there must be some rays of hope around.

CIDE (1995) defines *a black eye* as "the result of the eye being hit, when the skin around the eye becomes bruised". However, it does not contain the information that in the plural, the collocation *black eyes* (23) is unlikely to mean that both eyes are bruised, but instead refers to their natural dark colouring.

Black hole has a number of possible meanings. Figure 2 shows a concordance of all the occurrences of *black hole/holes* in the corpus. The most frequent referent of *black hole* is an astrophysical phenomenon, defined by OALD (1995) as a "region in space from which no matter or radiation can escape" (lines 1-5). There is also a metaphorical use (6-8), meaning something into which money disappears without trace. Finally, (9) expresses a further literal sense, in which a black hole is simply a hole in the earth - a mine.

The same contrast between a fixed metaphorical collocation and, as it were, an 'accidental' literal one is to be found in lines 37 and 38 of the concordance of *black* (Figure 1), both of which contain *black mass*. In line 37 it refers to "a ceremony in which the Devil is worshipped instead of the Christian God" (CIDE 1995), whereas in line 38 it simply means a mass of something which is black in colour (actually a dark-coloured boat). The concordance of *black* also contains references to particular entities and events that are part of the shared cultural knowledge of the newspaper's readership. These include the *Black Country* (a region of England, north of Birmingham: 17, 33), the *All-Black* centre (referring to the New Zealand national rugby team: 12), Mosley's *Black Shirts* (the British fascist group of the 1930s: 44). Some relate to aspects of current affairs - uses which no dictionary is likely to include. However, such contemporary references are sometimes explained in the adjacent text, as it is not always taken for granted that the reader will recognize them. Thus line 39 tells us that *Black Monday* (which occurs eight times in the entire corpus) was the day in 1987 when stock markets collapsed.

Other words with a wide range of idiomatic and metaphorical uses might be investigated in the same way - other colours, parts of the body (*hand*, *head*, *eye*, etc.), or names of common animals and foodstuffs, for example. Like that of *black*, concordances of these words may need editing before being presented to learners, both in order to reduce their size, and because they may contain a high proportion of literal uses. It will also be useful to have a dictionary - if possible an encyclopaedic one - at hand. A teacher's predictions about what learners know and do not know, or what they wish to know, are not always accurate, as I realized when using the concordance of *black* with a class of mother-tongue Italians. The line which aroused most curiosity, not to say amusement, was that containing the phrase *black bishop* (line 9). The Italian name for the chess piece means 'standard bearer', and the idea of clerics being in the thick of battle, albeit of a chess variety, delighted them. This provoked a desire to know the English names for other chess pieces, most of which they discovered by examining this and other texts in the corpus which contained the word *chess*.

6. Reference in texts: general nouns

Even though most concordance programs allow the user to retrieve larger contexts than single lines and sentences, relatively little work in corpus linguistics has analyzed patterns in extended text. This section illustrates how concordancing can be used to examine cohesive links in discourse, focussing on the use of general nouns.

Halliday and Hasan (1976) describe general nouns as:

> a small set of nouns having generalized reference within the major noun classes, those such as 'human noun', 'place noun', 'fact noun' and the like. Examples are:
> - *people, person, man, woman, child, boy, girl* (human)
> - *creature* (non-human animate)
> - *thing, object* (inanimate concrete count)
> - *stuff* (inanimate concrete mass)

> - *business, affair, matter* (inanimate object)
> - *move* (action)
> - *place* (place)
> - *question, idea* (fact)
>
> These items [...] play a significant part in verbal interaction, and are also an important source of cohesion in the spoken language.
>
> (Halliday and Hasan 1976: 274)

Insofar as they refer to features of the context, these nouns are part of the system of deixis in English. Some usually have clear specific referents (for example the human general nouns, and also *creature*, *object* and *place*). Others may refer to longer stretches of discourse:

> This experience tended to confirm him in his view that Switzerland's decision to remain neutral was a **matter** more of luck than of judgement
>
> (Cobuild: *The Times*)

> [...] how he reckoned he didn't think they'd get one million pounds for him because he's obviously gone down in value since his stay at Forest and **stuff** like this [...]
>
> (Cobuild: Spoken corpus)

Some references may be so vast or vague that it is not possible to relate them to any particular part of the surrounding text:

> In each, three children bickered in the back. In the passenger seat of one, a worrying father dreaded the whole **thing**, while his placid wife drove on
>
> (Cobuild: *The Times*)

In fact, *thing* seems used here precisely in order to avoid being too specific.

It would perhaps be better to talk of 'general noun phrases' rather than general nouns, since the latter are usually accompanied by an article, demonstrative, or adjunct (such as *stuff like this*). Halliday and Hasan claim that:

> a general noun in cohesive function is almost always accompanied by the reference item *the*. This *the* is anaphoric, and the effect is that the whole complex '*the* + general noun' functions like an anaphoric reference item.
>
> (Halliday and Hasan 1976: 275)

However a glance at some general nouns in the Cobuild corpus shows that quite a number of instances are in phrases with the indefinite *a* and *such*:

> [...] they abandoned the felling of tropical trees to get at the plants established in their branchings, but burned a forest to ensure a monopoly in orchids. **Such things** hit you in the pit of the stomach [...]
> (Cobuild: General)

and that a general noun can also introduce cataphoric reference:

> The big **thing** at the moment is supply chain control.
> (Cobuild: General)

Here we shall examine the use of a relatively common indefinite general noun phrase, *a move*.

The KWIC concordance in Figure 3 lists all the occurrences in the newspaper corpus, sorted by the words and punctuation preceding *a move*: larger contexts are given as necessary in the discussion that follows. This sorting of the examples shows that *a move* occurs in three positions: clause-initial (following punctuation), after *in*, and after *such*. When the wider context is examined, it is clear that in most cases *a move* is anaphoric. The exception is *in a move* (lines 25-31), where it is cataphoric - that is to say, the course of action it refers to is about to be described. Of particular interest is the combination *in a move to*, which appears to be a tactic for information compression, perhaps typical of journalism. It allows the writer to state very concisely the intention behind the move before giving details of the move itself. In other combinations, *in a move* permits the writer to give his/her opinion of the possible outcome of the move, in a similar brief fashion: *in a move that could* (27), *in a move they may later regret* (30), *in a move which bids fair to* (31).

The most frequent position is clause-initial. Here, *a move* is followed by a participle or relative clause (as with *in a move*, the relative clause often contains a modal or is reduced to a participle). This usually has a function of conditional prediction - 'if a particular course of action were to be taken, such a move would or could have the following consequences'. However a number of examples have less to do with the practical result of an action than with its reception. In these cases, *a move* collocates with items expressing opinion or attitude, such as *favoured* (2), *welcome* (21), *unwelcome* (16), *disgust* (17). A focus on the move's reception seems particularly common when *a move* is followed by a participle: here we find *regarded* (19), *favoured* (2) and *welcomed* (12) (in each case followed by *by*). These seem to be typical collocations, used by journalists to describe what someone else thinks of a course of action (or what the journalist claims they think).[2]

3. Corpus-based description in teaching and learning

```
1   stead repay KLM out of operating profits -     a move analysts said would further endebt the air
2   ld be a creditors' scheme of arrangement -     a move favoured by the council associations - whi
3   find a way to return to mortgage lending -     a move likely to require the support of another f
4   alled for an outright ban on such pursuit,     a move ruled out by top police officers who said
5   would be a cut in personal income taxes -      a move that many companies have been calling for.
6   er into a Las Vegas-style gambling venue -     a move that would require a change in Californian
7   vote for extremist religious ideologies -      a move which could prove counter-productive. <p>
8   SNP conference in Perth later this month -     a move which will not help Labour's claim to be
9   nding rates by as much as one full point -     a move which could prompt a rise in UK base rates
10  to order the closure of Bosnia's airspace,     a move intended to protect mainly Muslim civilian
11  taken from anywhere in the penalty area',      a move designed to encourage attacking play.
12  for blacks in South Africa's urban areas,      a move welcomed by Nthato Motlana, chairman of
13  l Asian republics or to migrate to Russia,     a move that could trigger large-scale economic di
14  bino boss, was planned in the same office,     a move that is said to have catapulted Mr Gotti i
15  tiations over next year's legal aid rates,     a move that seems likely to fuel industrial actio
16  law would have to be ratified by Britain,      a move that would be deeply unwelcome in Buenos A
17  ks first of launching the ball into space,     a move that would have brought a bellow of disgus
18  included in the Retail Price Index (RPI),      a move that would lower the apparent inflation ra
19  ainst cash restraint on GPs' drug budgets,     a move regarded by Mr Clarke as a 'breakthrough"
20  t Peking now says it will check each case,     a move expected to slow repatriation to a trickle
21  ated His Majesty's Sagbutts and Cornetts),     a move which is welcome among amateur choirs, but
22  ng minority was barred from the elections,     a move which one senior Moscow official said was
23  abour's tax and spending plans in January,     a move which succeeded in stopping Labour from g
24  e demographic predominance of the Muslims,     a move which their leaders and their Syrian backe
25  (First Edition) HONG KONG (AP) - In           a move highlighting China's power over Hong Kong,
```

```
26  ss to depositors if BCCI were to close. In a move that appeared to distance it from Price Wa
27  rge Bush in the White House this week, in a move that could break the deadlock in the negot
28  ency is reshuffling its management. <p> In a move to tighten control of a far-reaching empir
29  to Basildon Bond stationery group DRG, in a move to rally support against the £697m bid fro
30  891026 </dt> <hl> Rushes </hl> <st> <p> IN A move which bids fair to relegate the phrase 'ta
31  d of the deaf and blind charity, Sense. In a move which they may later regret, Jayne Torvill
32  he British Medical Association backed such a move 18 months ago, but only a handful of hosp
33  first choreographer in the US to make such a move. Among the 13 musicals she choreographed w
34  right for Denmark itself to push for such a move, but, of course, it would make our positio
35  wspapers, too many editors.' Besides, such a move for Mr and Mrs Evans was not practical at
36  ero quota on ivory remains in place.' Such a move, he added, would allow the countries conce
37  minister must recognise the folly of such a move. Not only would Britain be shooting itself
38  p of strict monetarists would support such a move. They appear to believe sterling entered t
39  used against Israel in the Gulf war. Such a move will no doubt alarm the military analysts,
40  nge policy and call for a referendum. Such a move would represent a U-turn. Neil Kinnock tol
41  snia themselves. Most observers agree such a move would be an almost certain recipe for furt
43  t might be reasonable to devalue. But such a move would be taken after the UK's counter-infl
44  's stake up to 29.9 per cent - though such a move would require the approval of Jaguar share
45  se of all that's happened," she says, such a move would have to come one step at a time. 'Al
46  ation from doctors and hospitals. <p> Such a move would mean a fundamental change in how inf
47  than to the Tories, the net effect of such a move would be to cut Labour's majority (or inc
```

Figure 3. *a move* in the newspaper corpus

3. Corpus-based description in teaching and learning

The examples in the second group (26-31) all contain *in a move to* or *in a move that/which*, invariably with a cataphoric function. While *in a move to* - at least in these examples - introduces information about the purpose of the move (*to rally support*: 29, or *to tighten control of a far-reaching empire*: 28), *in a move that/which* introduces other effects it might have, perhaps unintentionally. In either case, the purpose or result is stated before the description of the move itself, as the following wider contexts show:

30   IN A move which bids fair to relegate the phrase 'taking coals to Newcastle" to the lexicographical dustbin, the makers of a new dollars 15 million film have decided to build a slum in Calcutta.
31   In a move which they may later regret, Jayne Torvill and Christopher Dean have lent their name to a challenge cup for the team who raises the most money for charity.

The examples in the final group (32-47) involve the combination *such a move*. This is clearly anaphoric. Again we may note the use of modals: in eight of the sixteen occurrences it is followed by *would*, and in another by *will no doubt*. Curiously, however, there are none of the more tentative expressions (*could, may, seems likely to*) found in the other groups. *Such a move* seems to appear where someone has reservations about it, or where it has limited or negative value for someone:

26   [...] the net effect of **such a move** would be to cut Labour's majority [...]
30   [...] **such a move** for Mr and Mrs. Evans was not practical [...]
33   [...] **such a move** would have to come one step at a time [...]
34   **Such a move** will no doubt alarm the military analysts [...]
35   [...] must recognise the folly of **such a move**.

These examples suggest that the connotations of *such a move* are that the move is so dramatic that it needs thinking hard about - a hypothesis supported by the only case in the corpus where *such a move* appears with a pre-modifying adjective:

Mansell is unlikely to make *such a drastic move* and he will be racing until the end of the season.

Overall, the corpus evidence suggests that *a move* has a variety of uses, some anaphoric, some cataphoric, which focus on different aspects of the move itself and vary in their connotations. Other general nouns from Halliday and Hasan's list, cited at the beginning of this section, might be studied in the same manner. In the light of the last example above, one interesting area of research might be the use of pre-modifying adjectives to express the writer's attitude to the general noun's referent, and the way in which such phrases take on particular semantic prosodies. For instance, a search in the newspaper corpus for *the old* found many general noun phrases (*the old adage/argument/approach/attitudes/notion/fears* etc.) where *old* indicates distance from or disapproval of the referent. In reference to people, on the other hand, *the old* appears to be a humorous way of expressing quite the converse; *the old trouper/Bogeyman/codger/ warhorse* all suggest closeness or sympathy. Other investigations might involve comparing different text types, for instance to see whether *a move* has the same uses outside journalism.

7. Further investigations: syntax

Many studies of syntax have been carried out using corpus data, and syntax is one of the best documented areas of work using corpora in language pedagogy. Jordan (1993), for instance, describes learner projects for research in such areas as the use of *for* and *since* with the present perfect (cfr. Aston, this volume, chapter 2: 2.2); Johns (1991b) demonstrates how corpus-based worksheets can help them understand *that* clauses. Elsewhere I have described a student study of *if* clauses (Partington 1998), where learners discovered that the sequence of tenses in the two parts of an *if* sentence is far more complicated than generally depicted in textbooks. They also found significant differences in the kinds of *if* clauses employed in different text-types.

Similar analyses can be performed on syntactic phenomena marked by other particular words or phrases. As well as *if*, other conditional and pseudo-conditional markers might be investigated (*provided that*, *unless*, *as long as*, *no matter how/when/what*, *whenever*, *supposing*, etc.), and other subordinators with a particular syntax (*despite*, *until*, *in case*, etc.). An obvious area is that of the syntactic environments of particular verbs - learners are often unsure what preposition to use following such verbs as *accuse*, *blame*, *criticize*, etc., which verbs require a gerund, which the infinitive (with or without *to*), and which a finite verb clause. Learners' grammars and dictionaries provide some indications on these matters, but concordances can provide much more information, since they supply more examples and can highlight relatively subtle tendencies. For instance, CIDE (1995) gives examples for *persist* which contain *persist in*, taking a gerund, and *persist with* before a normal noun phrase. The 87 occurrences of *persist* from the corpus paint a more complex picture. *Persist in* is found with noun phrases as well as gerunds (*Lautrec persisted in his commitment to scenes from everyday life*), whereas *persist with* is only found before a noun phrase. In both cases, the subject is almost always personal - somebody is persisting in or with a course of action. Other constructions are found when the subject of the verb is impersonal or abstract (*fears, doubts, rumours, the notion, the feeling*): *persist* may be followed by prepositions such as *about* and *over* (*fears persisted over the UK trade deficit*), by *that* and a finite clause (*the notion has persisted that Conservatism is not an ideology*), and by *for/until/after/over* and a temporal expression (*it may persist for many weeks*).

Verb plus verb constructions are a further area which may repay examination. A concordance of the verb *afford* highlights how, when the context is money (or anything else which someone might 'permit themselves'), it is accompanied by a possibility modal (*can, couldn't, wasn't able to*, etc.) - the verb really has the form 'be able to afford'. Without a probability modal, it is a different verb altogether, meaning 'provide'. A concordance of the verb *dare* shows that it generally occurs in negative or interrogative contexts. The exceptions are fixed expressions like *I dare say* and *I dare you (to)*.

In all these cases, concordances can provide teachers and learners with data to help them go beyond, or more clearly understand, the syntactic distinctions made in grammars and textbooks. The greatest problems are, in fact, likely to arise from an excess of information, and the need to restrict it for pedagogic purposes, a question examined by Gavioli (this volume, chapter 5: 1).

8. Conclusions

This chapter has aimed to show how teachers and learners can use small- to medium-sized corpora to explore different kinds of meaning - denotational, connotational, metaphorical and cultural - on the levels of lexical, syntactic, and textual organization. It has emphasized how collocational patterns - sometimes described as a meaning type in their own right (Leech 1974: 20) - shed light on these other kinds of meaning, which are largely a function and a result of the way linguistic units are combined.

While the investigations described were all motivated by pedagogic concerns, they relate to language teaching and learning in different ways. Some were carried out directly in the classroom with learners. Others served to provide the teacher with data on points which were felt to deserve pedagogic attention. All tried to 'test' the statements found in traditional resources, such as grammars and dictionaries, supplementing the information these provide.

There are, of course, limits to the information that can be obtained from corpora like those used here. One limit has to do with size: rare words occur too infrequently in a small corpus to be studied with any confidence. And although a good number of collocates are found for the more frequent items, any single collocation usually has very few occurrences. This means that it is rarely possible to study the combinatory behaviour of collocations themselves. Conversely, concordances of frequent words may need careful sorting and editing to avoid information overload, and most learners will need some kind of initial training to be able to read them profitably (see Gavioli, this volume, chapter 5: 3).

A further limit derives from the fact that the corpora used here are restricted to a single type of texts, of which they are debatably representative. While playing a significant role in the culture, newspaper texts are not a cross-section of the universe of English discourse, nor is a collection taken from two years of one newspaper a cross-section of the universe of British journalism. The findings of investigations like these should not, therefore, be generalized from without caution. This is, of course, ultimately true for all studies based on data observation: as stressed elsewhere in this volume (Partington, chapter 2), corpus-based research involves observing samples of language production in order to predict how the language may behave elsewhere. In this sense, studies such as those described here have no 'findings'; they merely offer predictions to be tested against further data. Like all language learners, the corpus user develops predictions from limited experience, predictions which have to be continually tested and revised in the light of new experiences of the language in use.

Notes

1. The term 'prosody' is borrowed from Firth (in Palmer 1968), who uses it to refer to phonological colouring which spreads beyond segmental boundaries. Semantic prosody refers to the spreading of connotational colouring beyond single word boundaries.

2. The data also suggests that while newspapers talk as frequently about moves yet to occur as ones already completed, different phraseologies may be employed in the two cases. Relative clauses with *would* or *could* seem more typical of incomplete moves, while participles seem more frequent when moves are complete (even if there are some participles - *favoured* (Figure 3, line 2) and *ruled out* (line 4) - which imply that the move has yet to be taken).

4 THE PEDAGOGIC USE OF SPOKEN CORPORA: LEARNING DISCOURSE MARKERS IN ITALIAN

Daniela Zorzi

1. Introduction

The increasing availability of electronic corpora of transcribed speech has given new impetus to the description of spoken language, in particular of face-to-face interaction. Research has focussed both on interactional structure (e.g. Stenström 1994, who uses data from the London-Lund corpus; Aijmer 1996, who integrates the London-Lund data with examples from the Birmingham Corpus of Spoken English) and on its lexico-grammatical characteristics (e.g. Carter and McCarthy 1995; McCarthy and Carter 1995; McCarthy 1998; who use data from the CANCODE corpus to underline differences between spoken and written language). This research can be considered of pedagogic relevance insofar as a greater understanding of the workings of the spoken language - a pedagogic 'grammar of speech' which identifies items and patterns typical of particular spoken genres - may help develop learners' oral comprehension and production skills.

However theoretically convincing, this premise poses two practical problems if we are to come up with actual pedagogic applications:

- how to teach these items and patterns in such a way as to sensitize learners to contextually-determined variation in their use;
- how to develop learners' awareness of the meaning and use of features for which systematic descriptions are not yet available.

Research has shown that the choice between apparently similar items and patterns in speech often depends on complex contextual factors. Gardner (1998) shows how different receipt tokens (*mhm*, *mm*, *yeah*) indicate different types of hearer participation in a story-telling; Aston (1995a) relates differences in the thanking routines used to close service encounters to differences in the way in which the encounter had previously developed. For most features of speech, we possess even more limited and partial descriptions, and this renders a traditional pedagogic approach, based on presentation of a language 'point', practice exercises, and opportunities for its situationalized production, largely inappropriate. Instead, it suggests that we should treat features of the spoken language as an area of research for teachers and learners alike.

In language teaching, corpora and concordancing have mainly been used in two different ways: as research tools in the preparation of reference materials such as dictionaries, grammars, and in some cases textbooks; and by giving learners direct access to corpora and concordances, so that they can explore them as researchers (cfr. Aston, this volume, chapter 1: 3.1). This second perspective involves giving learners indications of research procedures which they can carry out on their own, so that they become aware of regularities of use (Johns 1991b; Jordan 1993; Gavioli 1996, 1997; Aston 1995b). Corpora of transcribed speech provide one possible basis for tasks of observation and analysis which "involve learners in investing energy and attention in order to discover something about the language for themselves" (Tomlinson 1998: ix). Such tasks fall into the category of linguistic awareness activities (Van Lier 1995; 1996), emphasizing the importance of learners "gradually developing their own awareness of how language is used through discoveries that they make themselves" (Tomlinson 1998: x). In particular these tasks will favour consciousness-raising, "subtly highlighting relevant aspects of the input without any overt explanation" (Sharwood Smith 1994: 178), and trying to develop the learner's capacity to notice and focus on such features (Schmidt 1994).

In this chapter I suggest ways in which spoken corpus data can be used to assist learners in this progressive process of discovery, helping them to acquire learning strategies that are broadly applicable to unsystematic features of the language, and which enable them to reduce the range of possible meanings of such features by exploiting contextual clues. Specifically, I shall focus on how learners of Italian as an L2 can be helped to attribute meaning to various discourse markers in speech, through guided observation of the contexts in which they occur.[1]

2. Discourse markers and second language teaching

2.1 Discourse markers in speech

Discourse markers have been described as "sequentially dependent elements which bracket units of talk" (Schiffrin 1987: 31) which are "external to the propositional content, being an expression of modal attitudes and/or discursive interaction" (Bazzanella 1994: 146), and which make utterances relevant by introducing, underlining, and arguing the speaker's expressive content (Moeschler 1988). From a strictly lexical standpoint, they include conjunctions (*but*), interjections (*oh*),[2] verb forms (*see*), and adverbs (*well*); they can be used alone, in combination (*well then*), or in series (*oh well, but then see*). While a wide variety of definitions and taxonomies of discourse markers have been proposed within different theoretical frameworks - speech act theory (e.g. van Dijk 1979), relevance theory (e.g. Moeschler 1988; Aijmer 1996), discourse analysis (e.g. Schiffrin 1987; Fraser 1990; Stenström 1994; Bazzanella 1990, 1995) - the definition I shall adopt here comes from this last field:

> Discourse markers are those items which, having lost part of their original lexical meaning, take on other meanings which serve to highlight the structuring of the discourse, connect sentential, intersentential and extrasentential elements, and show how the utterance fits into an interpersonal dimension, emphasizing the interactive structure of the conversation.
>
> (Bazzanella 1995: 225)

This definition takes into account the two functions of markers on which most researchers appear to agree:

- *the interactive function.* Discourse markers "underline, in the sequencing of turns, the joint construction of the message and the development of the interaction" (Bazzanella 1994: 151);
- *the metatextual function.* Discourse markers organize the argumentative structure of text by indicating main points, changes in topic, reformulations and digressions.

Corpus linguistics has underlined the frequency of discourse markers in speech:

> The extent of the importance of discourse items such as hedges, responses and softeners [...] in spoken English is shown by Altenberg (1990) who, in a study of a 50,000-word sample of the London-Lund corpus found that they made up 9.4% of all word class tokens and were more frequent than prepositions, adverbs, determiners, conjunctions or adjectives. Because discourse items are not handled well in most dictionaries and grammars, they are not part of traditional language teaching, with consequent effects on the naturalness of learners' English.
>
> (Kennedy 1992: 357)

McCarthy and Carter (1997) contrast the fifty most frequent items in a spoken corpus of 100,000 words (CANCODE) and in a similarly-sized written corpus of newspaper texts. Only their spoken list includes *oh*, *so*, *right*, *well*, and *really*, or indeed *know* and *think*, which frequently occur in multi-word expressions generally classed as discourse markers (*you know*, *I think*: Schiffrin 1987; Stenström, 1990b).

2.2 Discourse markers in pedagogy

The centrality of discourse markers is well known to those who teach the spoken language:

> One of the difficulties that language teachers face with features such as discourse markers is how does one 'teach' such features in a natural way, not only given that they are almost subconscious items for speakers, but also given that they seem to be so central to natural discourse?
> (McCarthy and Carter 1994: 68)

Broadly speaking, two main approaches to teaching them have been employed. One is to start from a list of functions (e.g. 'indicate doubt or puzzlement') which can be activated with various forms (*maybe*, *really*, *oh*, etc.). The other is to start from a list of forms, each of which can activate a number of functions.

In the first approach, the focus is on building up learners' conversational skills, meaning by this abilities such as holding the floor, yielding a turn, drawing in other speakers, hesitating, bidding to speak, and the like. Corresponding to each of these abilities, learners are given a list of gambits[3] which they first encounter and identify in oral texts and/or transcriptions, and then practice using for themselves in more or less guided manners. Argondizzo (1995) suggests a number of activities of this kind: for instance, the teacher writes on the blackboard a list of hesitation devices, or expressions which can be used to bring in another speaker, and constructs role plays for learners to use them in. Or, after analyzing authentic encounters, learners try to insert such conversational features into the scripted dialogues in their textbook. Such controlled practice activities may be followed by 'spontaneous' incidental use in other tasks:

> While initially it may be necessary and worthwhile to spend some teaching-time specifically on gambits, for the most part they should be practised incidentally, i.e. incorporated into models for other role-play situations.
> (Edmondson and House 1981: 84)

A similar line is often taken by work focussing on the development of oral comprehension of certain text types, which underlines the importance of markers for understanding the structure of the discourse and the attitudes of speakers towards what they are saying, and in constructing an interpersonal dimension with the hearer.

In the second approach, on the other hand, the focus is on the markers themselves, variously listed as particles, lexical items, interjections, fillers, and so on. Acknowledging their contribution to the sense of the discourse, they are presented to learners along with their possible meanings, often grouped according to their grammatical category. An interesting example - albeit focussing on linguistic description rather than language teaching - is provided by Stenström (1994), who uses Sinclair and Coulthard's (1975) exchange model of discourse analysis to describe oral interaction in the London-Lund corpus (Svartvik and Quirk 1980). In a section entitled "Interactional signals and discourse markers" she gives an alphabetical list of the 30 most common lexical items in this category (*actually*, *ah*, *now*, *OK*, *right*, *well*, etc.), and singles out three examples (*right*, *now*, *anyway*) for study. On the basis of their position in the turn and the place of that turn in the exchange, she concludes, "Generalizing somewhat, *right* looks backward, *now* looks forward, while *anyway* looks both ways" (Stenström 1994: 64). While recognizing that these items cannot always be assigned to clear-cut functional categories, she completes her analysis with a table matching certain functions (appeal, acknowledge, evaluate, uptake, answer, frame, stall) with certain lexical items (*you know*, *mhm*, *right*, *really*, etc.), showing for instance that the 'stall' function is expressed by *really* and by *well*, and that *well* can also function as 'uptake'. The section ends with an exercise presenting a text from the London-Lund corpus with the discourse markers blanked out; the problem is to fill in the blanks using the items listed below the text. While her main aim is to provide students of linguistics with opportunities to practice the descriptive model proposed, it is clear that Stenström's approach could also be adopted for language teaching purposes.

The main drawback to both these approaches - whether based on lists of functions or lists of markers - is that they fail to consider how the selection of a particular marker may be determined by the context - by the way the encounter has developed and is projected to develop. If the expression selected - out of all those which seem similar - ultimately depends on the particular discourse context, lists of these kinds can only be of limited pedagogic use. Apart from the fact that their classifications are often questionable (many are based on analyses of written dialogues, or of remembered and invented examples, rather than of transcribed spontaneous speech), the very act of listing involves a process of decontextualization. If discourse markers convey meanings which are in addition to or in replacement of their literal meaning, and these meanings are dependent on the context, relating to the development of the ongoing interaction, it is methodologically misguided to present them in simple form/function relationships. To do so risks presenting as a generalizable 'rule of use' what is actually only one possible behavioural norm. As Stame notes:

> The high frequency of markers in speech leads in some cases to the identification of a 'weak function', oriented generically towards control of the discourse and to maintenance of the conversation. This function resembles that described by Schiffrin (1987: 321) in relation to markers whose specific communicative contribution is weakened by their use for very general and diverse discourse purposes. *Even in such cases, however, the use of one particular marker rather than another would not appear to be a matter of chance or free variation.*
>
> (Stame 1994: 207; my emphasis)

If the meaning of a discourse marker is dependent on its context, then the guided explication of such contexts may be helpful to learners. Concordances from corpora of transcribed speech can provide a series of such contexts, showing a set of occurrences of a given marker with contextualizations which may range from a single line to the whole text. Concordances also facilitate analysis by highlighting features of the immediate context such as the item's position within the turn and its recurrent collocates.

2.3 Teaching discourse markers in Italian as a foreign language

In what still appears to be the only detailed discussion of discourse markers in the context of teaching Italian as a foreign language, Brighetti and Licari (1987) stress the pedagogic importance of these devices - generally relegated to an indeterminate category of 'fillers' - as "contributing decisively to the speaker's assumption of particular strategic positions with respect to the hearer, according to the nature of the communicative situation" (1987: 62). Their study calls into question approaches based on form-function matchings such as those discussed above, showing how reductive these generally are. Their proposals revolve around four points:

- It is both possible and useful to make a systematic inventory of the most frequently used markers in everyday language;
- Such an inventory is essential for the design of more effective syllabuses and materials;
- From a methodological viewpoint, teachers should have access to a

pre-pedagogical analysis of each marker, carried out prior to the development of specific teaching materials, to provide a systematic basis for awareness work with learners;
- Such work should be based on the observation of authentic materials, rather than materials constructed for language teaching purposes.

Brighetti and Licari illustrate their notion of pre-pedagogical analysis with a description of the uses and functions of *magari*. This is a broadly-used, relatively vague marker which signals the speaker's stance towards the probability of an event/state of affairs and its desirability, and which at the same time weighs, through various modes of negotiation with the interlocutor, desirability against probability (in this respect its translations might range from 'maybe' to 'hopefully').[4] Foreigners tend to find it difficult to use:

> coming into contact with the Italian of everyday use after having studied from books outside Italy, this is one of the words most likely to strike you, as it crops up again and again.
> (*Cassell's colloquial Italian* 1980: 82)

Brighetti and Licari show that both the definitions in Italian dictionaries and the translations with 'perhaps' or 'if only' proposed by *Cassell's colloquial Italian* are at best reductive and partial. Without wishing to detract from their analysis, with its numerous examples (for which they unfortunately do not provide sources), I would argue that:

a) The use of a corpus of naturally-occurring speech can enhance available descriptions by providing information not found elsewhere. To cite just one example, a simple frequency count in the LIP corpus of spoken Italian (De Mauro et al. 1993),[5] reveals that out of 284 cases of *magari*, only one involves a desiderative use in a syntactically complete form (*magari* + imperfect subjunctive: 'if only I were'), and in only four do we find a desiderative *magari* used holophrastically:

(1) LIP MD18. *Television quiz programme sponsored by a brand of coffee. If E guesses correctly she wins 80 million lire. [*magari *stands for '*magari vincessi*' (if only I was to win)].*
A: signora sono ottanta milioni ma lei sa cosa sono ottanta milioni eh?? *(signora eighty million now you know what eighty million is?)*
E: magari *(if only)*
A: pensi che piacere che le da' questo caffe' [...] *(think how much you like this coffee)*

In all the remaining cases, *magari* is either used to indicate uncertainty of various kinds, as in (2), or to mitigate the force of a proposal, making it less brusque (3):

(2) LIP NE11. *Television sale of anti-cellulite products.*
 […] puo' esser causata **magari** da un fattore ormonale puo' essere causata perche' magari avete avuto una gravidanza da poco […] *(it may be caused perhaps by some hormone factor, it may be caused because perhaps you have just had a pregnancy)*

(3) LIP MB4. *Informal conversation between B and F. B has forgotten to ring a friend.*
 F: va be' **magari** chiamala adesso *(well you could always ring her now)*
 B: si' infatti adesso la chiamo *(yes actually now I will)*

In a similarly-sized corpus of written texts taken from the Italian financial daily *Sole-24 ore*, we find only 34 instances of *magari*, of which only one, in direct speech, is desiderative. This comparison suggests that *magari* is far more frequent in speech than in writing (Zorzi 1996), and that it is far more frequently used as an indicator of possibility than of desirability. None of this information is to be found in dictionaries or grammars, or, for that matter, in Brighetti and Licari's account.

b) Direct access by learners to corpus data can supplement or replace pre-pedagogical analysis for or by the teacher. Taylor (1991), Mparutsa et al. (1991) and others have stressed that direct, interactive use of corpora by students can counterbalance their otherwise uncritical subjection to the authority of the textbook, and cultivate curiosity and a research perspective towards learning. Discourse markers are a potentially interesting research topic from this perspective because there is little authority to appeal to, given that textbooks and reference works provide so little information. Learners' investigations can be done alongside the teacher, who for once does not have all the answers.

c) Procedures acquired in trying to attribute meaning to markers through corpus exploration can be applied to other features of the language which are similarly unsystematic. By observing the occurrences of a particular marker or markers, treated as *samples* of raw data and not, as in Brighetti and Licari's account, as selected *examples* of an *a priori* categorization, unexpected regularities may emerge (for the sample/example distinction, see Gavioli, this volume, chapter 5: 2.3). These may lead to the

4. The pedagogic use of spoken corpora

formulation of new hypotheses, which can in turn be tested against further data, in a potentially open-ended research process.

3. Teaching a research perspective with a spoken corpus

To summarize the previous section, the learner who wants to understand the meaning of a discourse marker in a given context has traditionally had the following resources to choose from:

- dictionaries and grammar books, which present only some uses of markers (mostly based on written sources), and which are not sensitive to the way their meaning varies according to context;
- teaching materials listing functions and some of the markers associated with them, or listing markers and some of their possible functions;
- scholarly articles which describe the use of particular markers. These are however rare, and have had little influence on teaching materials to date. They are also unlikely to be accessible to learners.

This section considers how learners can be made aware of (and trained to recognize) the meanings of markers by consulting a spoken corpus. It shows how they can extend and problematize the meagre information provided elsewhere, and how they can learn to restrict the range of possible meanings of a given instance. All the proposals for pedagogic applications use data from the LIP corpus (De Mauro et al. 1993: cfr. notes 5 and 6).

3.1 What data should learners be given?

If learners have direct access to a spoken corpus and a concordancing program, they can work with these online, compiling and manipulating concordances of occurrences of particular discourse markers and examining the individual texts from which these are taken. If, on the other hand, learners can only be given printouts of concordances compiled by the teacher (Johns 1991b), three basic choices have to be made:

- whether to include all the occurrences in the corpus, or only an initial or random sample;
- whether to include all the uses of the form in question, or only those cases where it functions as a discourse marker, pre-editing the concordance to remove 'irrelevant' lines;
- whether to sort the concordance lines according to some pre-determined criterion.

As an example, let us consider the marker *dai*. This is a delexicalized verb form, also used as an interjection or linker, corresponding to the exclamatory imperative of the verb *dare* ('to give'). If we examine its treatment in authoritative reference works, we find that "the imperative is used outside its primary context, but without losing its force of appeal" (Serianni 1988), while Battaglia (1966) classifies it with exclamations, specifying that it "invites someone to act promptly or to hurry up, or expresses annoyance or exasperation". *Dai* is additionally a homograph of the 2nd person singular present indicative form of *dare*, and of a preposition + article contraction (*da + i*) meaning 'from/by the'.

According to the nature of the concordance data with which we present learners, different research procedures will be called for.

3.1.1 *All occurrences*

If learners are required to deal with all the occurrences, or with a concordance arbitrarily shortened to - say - 50 lines, their first step is an editing process. The concordance in Figure 1, which shows 12 randomly selected instances of *dai* in the LIP corpus, includes a heterogeneous mixture of uses. In line 7 *dai* is a lexical verb, and in lines 5, 9, 11 and 12, it is a preposition + article.[6]

To identify the uses of *dai* as a discourse marker, the learner has to use other linguistic knowledge to exclude these homographs, for instance by recognizing the passive verbs which precede *dai* as a preposition + article introducing the agent (*essere stato convinto*: 11; *e' ammesso*: 12).

3.1.2 *Selected occurrences*

If learners are given a pre-edited concordance, limited to occurrences of *dai* as a discourse marker, they can immediately experiment with sorting the instances in various ways (either online, or cutting up printouts) to explore what appear to be systematic regularities in its use. For example, in the concordance in Figure 2, we can see that lines 4, 6, 7 and 8 contain the forms *va be'* ('all right') or *va bene* ('okay') immediately before or after *dai*.

Finding this regularity in such a small amount of data does not allow us to infer that *va bene* is a typical collocate of *dai*: this is merely a hypothesis, which needs at the very least to be tested against the whole corpus (*va bene* actually co-occurs with only 13 of the 132 instances of *dai* as a discourse marker). But when our main concern is teaching rather than description, it matters less that the learner should necessarily discover 'new' lexicogrammatical information, or even that the information should

4. *The pedagogic use of spoken corpora*

```
1   nte ahah ecco questa qua e' aperta # da aprire dai Cacco mettilo tu lo zero B: dai dai ecco D:
2   e' come se io paragonassi il vomito alla merda dai B: [RIDE] C: scusa siamo sempre in quell'am
3   F: ah ok B: ma_ l'Anna con fidanzo F: non so dai digli di portarlo_ <???> B: ma infatti_ aha
4   e ora arrivi? A: alle otto sono li' B: va bene dai A: si' B: <?> A: ciao
5   zo mondo_ dietro a cui l'abbiamo detto vengono dai paesi a cui noi mandiamo i soldi # i finanz
6   il Lancers e' piu' buono? B: piu' buono? A: si' dai questo non e' B: no e' buono il vino rosso
7   punti eccetera e -pi- perche' non pigli e gli dai un'occhiata e mi dici che come fare_? D:
8   va be' co' Lucia e lei con tuo cugino # va be' dai vieni A: si' B: allora se ti vedo_ bene alt
9   antenna e' che puo' ricevere un segnale che va dai quaranta ai novecento megahertz quindi o ab
10  one di H: spinose I: la luna A: be' no spinose dai su' le zone come si chiamano il nome delle
11  use dira' di essere stato convinto ad accusare dai genitori del Giappone che ritenevano esse V
12  endono possibile ma soprattutto non e' ammesso dai fatti dalla realta' # # se quindi attacchia
```

Figure 1. *dai* in the LIP corpus (random selection)

```
1   ta # da aprire dai Cacco mettilo tu lo zero B: dai dai ecco D: non e' quello e' quell' altro A:
2   oe' recitava C: o quello allora era bravissimo dai cioe' era una cosa talmente A: figurati se c
3   lettera in cui si diceva B: si' si' A: allora dai non scherziamo B: quindi va be' A: non dobbi
4   va be' co' Lucia e lei con tuo cugino # va be' dai vieni A: si' B: allora se ti vedo_ bene altr
5   re mi sembra un po' da_ B: no pero' e' bellino dai secondo me e' meritato tra l' altro doveva v
6   h guarda_ B: si' A: guarda te_ un giallo bello dai B: va be' A: scegli un giallo bello B: va be
7   pegni co_' e so' vengo un po' tardi B: va bene dai a che ora arrivi? A: alle otto sono li' B: v
8   e ora arrivi? A: alle otto sono li' B: va bene dai A: si' B: <?> A: ciao
```

Figure 2. Pre-edited concordance (*dai* as a discourse marker)

```
1           B: no_ <??> [interruzione] A: mh B: va bene dai A: va bo' B: ci sentiamo domani A: va bo' B:
2   ci vediamo martedi' B: si' ci vediamo martedi' dai A: che e' il tuo compleanno B: il mio comple
3   vo preparare B: ci vediamo in settimana allora dai A: eh? B: no_ ci vediamo in settimana [inter
4   h guarda_ B: si' A: guarda te_ un giallo bello dai B: va be' A: scegli un giallo bello B: va be
5   te a mangiare con noi A: no_ adesso siamo qua_ dai B: va be' faccio un salto dai se faccio pres
6       le zone sono A: le zone sono # equatoriale B: dai dille bene vai bene sai A: equatoriale C: li
7     tipo di A: <F> [esprimente_disappunto] B: dai facciamo una cosa Piero sposami e mantienimi
8       Sardegna a trovarmi A: ma dai in Sardegna? B: dai prendi l'aereo io ti vengo a prendere A: [in
9       equatoriale A: e_ tropici <?> C: tropicale B: dai va bene stai dicendo bene C: tropicale B:
10  ah va be' A: allora vi posso raccontare di_ C: dai raccontaci A: allora son partita cosi' la ma
```

Figure 3. Edited and sorted concordance of *dai* to call attention to position in sentence and turn

```
1     primo giorno di scuola comunque lo farei C: ma dai il primo giorno se ci pensi te lo ricordi il
2   ggesse Massimo A: no ma Massimo li legge B: ma dai legge A: no no Massimo li legge e me li ripe
3   sempio li ho lavati in lavatrice e basta C: ma dai li lavi in lavatrice ma dai_ A: cazzo dici?
4   venerea? B: [RIDE] C: ho preso l'Aikido B: ma dai perche' proprio una malattia venerea? C: eh
5       in mano anche <?> mi pare no? [silenzio] A: ma dai ## pero'_ non puoi far la lotta <?> sono m
6   come ci balli? C: a piedi a piedi scalzi B: ma dai sandro C: con la testa appoggia
7       cia morire sua sorella_ lascia m<orire> A: ma dai son palle tu<tte>     il cardinale lo il card
```

Figure 4. *dai* collocating with *ma* ('but')

4. The pedagogic use of spoken corpora 97

be true of the universe as a whole. The main point is the procedure (the formulation and testing of hypotheses) as a way of promoting learning, in which partial generalizations of this kind arguably play a fundamental role (Aston 1995b).

3.1.3 *Sorted occurrences*
If learners start from a concordance of occurrences which has been not only pre-edited but also pre-sorted in such a way as to make certain regularities more evident, it is the teacher who has formulated the hypothesis and effectively chosen the data as 'examples' to support it. The concordance in Figure 3 has been edited and sorted so as to call attention to the fact that the marker *dai* may occur at the end of a turn (lines 1-5) or at the beginning (lines 6-10).

Concordances can also be edited and sorted so as to call attention to frequent collocations.[7] The concordance in Figure 4 shows *dai* collocating with *ma* ('but'), which adds an adversative meaning. In these cases *ma dai* is always turn-initial, and expresses disagreement with the interlocutor.

3.1.4 *Criteria for choice*
The form in which concordance data is provided thus influences the kinds of operations which learners need to carry out. With a concordance of raw data, they must start by limiting and identifying the feature to analyze, and in doing so, must draw on other knowledge of the language system. With a concordance that has been edited to eliminate all but a certain type of use of the item in question, learners can be asked to sort the data so as to highlight such features as turn-position or recurrent collocates. With a concordance which has been pre-sorted to call attention to a particular feature, a recognition process is invoked on data which have in a sense been simplified so as to highlight the phenomenon in question (of the two previous concordances, the first focuses on the position of *dai* in the turn; the second, on its collocation with *ma*).

These three options just illustrated clearly involve very different operations. Following this order - first dealing with raw data, then selected data, then sorted data - seems likely to be the most fruitful procedure for the learner who is ready to handle independent research. The reverse order, starting with data which has been pre-edited and sorted to facilitate recognition of certain regularities, may be more suitable for those learners who are not yet familiar with corpora and concordances.

3.2 How can we help learners identify regularities?

Simply providing learners with concordances (even where edited and sorted) does not necessarily entail that they will be able to infer the meanings of the items under consideration. It will probably be necessary to help them to see significant regularities in the way such context-sensitive items as markers function in talk, developing pedagogic procedures to guide the process of observation. Before approaching this problem in the L2, it may be helpful for learners to realize that in the L1, too, discourse markers contribute to the construction of meaning.

Carrying out an activity using the L1 as preparation for a similar task in the L2 allows them to draw on their native-speaker intuitions and command of the items involved. As well as familiarizing them with the tools (corpora and concordancing software/printouts), it may make learners aware of the range of variables to be considered when attributing meaning - the frequency of the item in the corpus, its position within the turn, its collocations, whether or not the item could be replaced with others, and so on. It may also make them aware of how much variability there is in the way such features as markers are used. For example, the following activity summarized from Hatch (1992: 269ff), which was originally designed to sensitize ESL teachers to the uses of *just*, also seems suitable for learners in their L1:

- *Present a hypothesis*. Hulquist (1985), analyzing a radio broadcast in which listeners call in for medical advice, noted that the doctor used *just* more frequently when giving advice to women than to men. After considering a number of variables, Hulquist relates the use of *just* to 'sympathetic involvement'.
- *Present other points of view*. In other contexts, *just* seems to mark a contrast, with the expectation of something more or something different, playing down what is currently happening.
- *Present the item in relation to another* (e.g. *really*). Students examine the uses of both items in a new situation type.
- *List contextualized examples*. Fragments or sentences including *just* and *really* from a spoken corpus.
- *Compare other data*. Students examine *just* and *really* in other spoken data.
- *Critique the original hypothesis*. Students discuss the limits of the initial hypothesis, and formulate alternatives.

To follow up this activity, Hatch makes various proposals for independent work. This may involve a similar research task on other discourse items - for example, learners might examine the occurrences of *in brief, in my opinion, to my way of thinking*, and try to explain the differences in their use on the basis of their intuitions, a corpus, and/or other data (e.g. their own or other learners' productions). Once learners have become familiar with the tools and some of the research procedures involved, several other subsequent steps are possible.

3.2.1 *Repetition*
Propose a procedure similar to the one used with the L1 data, this time choosing an L2 marker. For example, look at contexts of use of *guarda/ guardi*. Like *dai, guarda* ('look') is a delexicalized imperative, but as well as the confidential *tu* form, we also find instances of the more formal 3rd-person form, *guardi*. Like other delexicalized verbal markers such as *vedi* ('see'), *senti* ('listen'), and *sai* ('you know'), it has the function of calling the interlocutor's attention to a proposed change in topic or shift in emphasis, and is generally found in an initial position: *guarda/guardi* "functions as an appeal which steers interpretation of what follows in the direction desired by the speaker" (Manili 1986: 168).

Propose a hypothesis as to the use of the marker. Examining examples from "contemporary fiction, informal everyday spoken dialogue and recorded texts", Manili claims that *guardi* is much more frequent than *guarda*, both as an opening signal and as a mitigating device (1986: 174ff).

Provide a small corpus, or have the learner construct a subcorpus from a larger one (cfr. Zanettin, this volume, chapter 7: 2). For instance, to test Manili's hypothesis, take the first 20 dialogues from the LIP corpus in which the speakers address each other with *tu* and the first 20 in which they use the 3rd-person *lei*, and compare the frequencies of the two forms. In this case, Manili's hypothesis is not confirmed: *guarda* is much more frequent than *guardi* as an opener, and the mitigating function is little in evidence. It is found only where *guarda/guardi* collocates with *comunque* ('however'), *allora* ('then'/'so'), *poi* ('then') or other explicit mitigating devices such as remedial laughter (Gavioli 1995). Much more frequently, *guarda/guardi* collocates with *no* ('no') or *ma* ('but'), and signals the speaker's disagreement with something said previously. Other recurrent collocations involve repetition of the same word (*guarda guarda*) and use with the second person pronoun (*guarda te/tu*), both of which signal surprise, admiration or amazement.

Beyond the actual details of analysis, what is important here is that questioning a proposed interpretation helps the learner to observe the contexts in which an item occurs and to extend the available information about its use. In this case, it calls attention to two meanings of *guarda/guardi* which were absent from the initial hypothesis, those of disagreement/objection and admiration/amazement.

3.2.2 *Checklists*

Give learners a checklist showing the contextual features that seem relevant for determining the meaning of a marker. This may either be a general list which is applicable to the analysis of any discourse marker (and perhaps other items), providing a preparatory basis for more specific independent research by the learner, or it may include specific features, based on the teacher's own previous research on the marker in question. It may require the learner to observe the position of the marker in the turn/exchange, the type of environment (e.g. whether characterized by agreement and approval, or by disagreement, adversatives or insults), recurrent collocates, etc. Thus a checklist based on an analysis of the 132 occurrences of *dai* as a discourse marker in the LIP corpus (cfr. 3.1 above) might include information such as the following:

- *Position within the turn.* Where *dai* is turn-final, note how many times the following turn begins with a marker of agreement, such as *sì* ('yes'), *va be'* ('all right'), *va bene* ('okay'), *sì va bene*, etc., or of disagreement, such as *ma* ('but'), *no*, etc. Where *dai* is turn-initial, note how many times it is followed by an imperative (*dai dimmi, vieni*) or by an exhortative subjunctive ('let's') (*dai, facciamo*).
- *Collocations.* Note what other markers *dai* collocates with. Observe whether it collocates more frequently with markers or with other items. Choose a recurrent collocation and observe its position in the turn.
- *Environments.* Within a span extending three words to the left and three to the right of *dai*, the most frequent collocates are *ma* (35), *no* (31), *che* (31), *dai* (30), and *non* (26). Some of these strongly suggest negative environments (*no, non*) or adversative ones (*ma*), while others (*che* and *dai*) are less clear in this respect. Observe the position within the turn of *dai* in each case. Then expand the concordancer's default one-line context (or use printed concordances showing a larger context) to test the hypothesis that *dai* generally occurs in contexts of disagreement.

Such a checklist gives detailed criteria for analysis while leaving the actual interpretation of single cases - the attribution of meaning - to the learner.

3.2.3 *Independent research*
Have learners work with the corpus online, without further guidance. This approach has the disadvantage of being time-consuming, but the advantage of being open-ended: wholly unforeseen information may emerge. How productive this approach may be depends on a number of factors: the size and characteristics of the corpus; learners' attitudes towards and interest in research of this kind; their proficiency in the language; their previous preparation in research procedures, e.g. whether or not they are aware of types of regularities to look for. Learners must not only have the necessary time and motivation to carry out the research, but they must also have been adequately trained to do it (cfr. Gavioli, this volume, chapter 5).

The corpus must not generate an unmanageable number of occurrences. Aston (1997c) reports that when learners work on concordances providing a large number of instances, they tend to abandon investigation as soon as they have found a few cases to confirm their initial hypothesis, disregarding further possible analyses. In consequence they frequently fail to see more extensive regularities, or make unsupported generalizations.

Learners also seem to do better with a homogeneous corpus, or one whose criteria of construction are known (Aston, this volume, chapter 1: 5). For example, to understand the constraints on the use of *ma dai* (see 3.1 above), it helps to be able to see that in the LIP corpus, it only occurs in those texts classified as "two-way communicative exchanges with unregulated turn-taking" - i.e. informal two-party conversation. In asymmetrical encounters (oral examinations, interviews, classroom interaction) in which speech rights are assigned *a priori*, and which are therefore rather more formal and predictable, *ma dai* never occurs, arguably because it belongs to a colloquial register.

3.3 How can we integrate concordance-based research into classroom tasks?

Research procedures such as those outlined can be combined to form part of wider, integrated tasks. For example, learners can be given a transcript of an authentic dialogue from which some of the markers have been omitted or blanked out, and then listed separately. They then use the corpus as a source of information on each of these items in order to fill in the gaps, before comparing their choices with the original. Any discrepancies can become the object of further research, in order to discover whether their choices can be considered valid alternatives, or whether they alter the sense of the dialogue. This activity differs from that proposed by Stenström (1994) (described in 2.2 above), insofar as the learner has direct access to the corpus as a resource, not just to a pre-pedagogical analysis carried out by the teacher or materials writer.

An intermediate solution is that described by Johns (1997), who proposes a preparatory phase of controlled concordance analysis before starting less-controlled exercises. Distinguishing between 'show mode' and 'quiz mode' use of concordances, he suggests that before being asked to fill in the blanks in a text or set of concordance lines, learners should be shown pre-edited concordances of the items they will subsequently be required to use. This preparatory phase may also involve activities which guide learners to see certain patterns or to focus their attention on particular occurrences. Johns reports that learners who had not been through this phase were more likely to make errors, tending to fill in the gaps in a text on the basis of only one line of context. They also tended to rapidly lose interest in concordancing. The phase of familiarization should concern not only procedures for identifying regularities (on which I have primarily focussed in this section), but also the specific linguistic features under investigation (see Partington, this volume, chapter 3, for examples).

3.4 From concordances to texts

The proposals so far made in this chapter involve using concordances to highlight the recurrent collocations and positions of discourse markers, with the aim of helping learners to attribute meanings to them. As noted previously, the meaning of a discourse marker largely seems to depend on its position within a sequence of talk, or to use Hoey's terms (1997, 2000), its colligational features. Only local features of colligation may however be evident from a single concordance line: consequently it may be useful to go beyond this local context to that of a larger sequence of talk, or indeed to the entire interaction.

Let us return to the example of *dai* (cfr. 3.1 above). Our analysis of the immediate context has allowed us to formulate the hypothesis that *dai* appears in situations of disagreement. Observing wider contexts allows us to test this hypothesis, and - should it be confirmed - to articulate the notion of disagreement more fully. It becomes possible, for instance, to distinguish between disagreement with the proposition expressed by another participant (where *dai* acts as an invitation to modify this proposition) and disagreement with another participant's behaviour (where *dai* is used to solicit a change in attitude).

In example (4), speakers A and B differ in their views on an Italian newspaper for which B once worked. A says that everyone says it's a good paper, which B can't believe, adding that it has no influence in political circles. Along with *dai* we find other items which suggest disagreement - *no*, *non*; *ma* ('but'), *eppure* ('yet'); expletives:

(4) LIP MB7
A: dico bah pero' un bel giornale il Carlino eh? *(I say but a good paper the Carlino yeah?)*
B: chi lo dice_? *(says who?)*
A: tutti *(everyone)*
B: tutti chi_? *(who's everyone?)*
A: tut<ti> a Milano <?> e' importante *(everyone in Milan <?> is important)*
B: no_ non *(no no)*
A: <?>
B: non ci credo **dai** *(I don't believe it)*
A: eppure ti dico di si' *(yet I tell you yes)*
B: ma chi scusa chi? *(but who sorry who?)*
A: ma che <?> a qualunque *(but what <?> at every)*
B: ma se non contiamo una sega_ *(but if we don't count a wank)*
A: a qualunque livello e in qualunque ambiente viene considerato un giornale_ grosso importante_ di grande tradizione_ *(at every level and in every circle it's considered a big important paper with a great tradition)*

In example (5), on the other hand, the disagreement concerns behaviour. In this phone conversation A invites B to drop round, but B makes it clear he has no desire to go out, and his *dai* solicits A not to insist with the invitation:

(5) MB52
A: vienimi a trovare [linea_disturbata] *(come and see me [noise on line])*
B: devo farmi tutto devo farmi anche la barba tutto dovrei farmi *(I have to do everything I still have to shave everything I have to do)*
A: ho capito *(I see)*
B: ah # andare in giro cosi' sono_ # mica tanto presentabile *(ah going around like this I'm not exactly fit to see)*
A: conciato male *(bit of a wreck)*
B: no be' ci ho la barba lunga insomma **dai** *(no well I've just got a beard)*
A: mh va bene # # niente come non detto *(mm all right doesn't matter forget it)*

Dai, therefore, invites another participant to modify what they have said or done. In the first of these examples, the interlocutor maintains their initial position (*yet I tell you yes*), whereas in the second they modify it (*all right doesn't matter forget it*).

Rather than the details of the analysis, the point to be stressed is again the procedure involved. To assess whether *dai* really occurs in contexts of disagreement, the learner tries using disagreement as a frame within which to interpret wider stretches of these texts, searching for other signals which might confirm this interpretation of their general sense. In Cazden's (1984) terms, this involves a shift from a prevalently 'opaque' approach, where linguistic features are the object of observation, to a more 'transparent' one, where the primary focus is on meaning. An interaction between these two perspectives, it has been argued, is key to the continuing development of communicative competence:

> Our linguistic skills are such that peripheral attention to words, utterances and sentences is sufficient to allow us to focus on the meanings. However, when something goes wrong, either with the language, or with our ability to make sense of it, then our focal attention would be required to address the language directly in order to sort out the problems. In reaching higher standards of language knowledge and use, it seems reasonable to assume that it will be inevitable, as well as necessary, from time to time, for language to become opaque so as to allow 'construction work' to be conducted to bring the language data and our interpretive skills closer together, or to coordinate expressive requirements and linguistic resources.
> (Van Lier 1996: 75)

4. Conclusions

This chapter has tried to show how applying particular research procedures to a spoken corpus can help learners see how features of the context restrict the possible meanings of polyfunctional items such as discourse markers. These contextual features include both *what* the marker appears with - that is, its collocates - and *where* it appears - that is, its position in the turn/exchange, as well as the type of interaction involved. The underlying assumption has been that:

> Students' learning of any element is likely to be facilitated and made more effective if the same three foci are kept in view: the properties of a formal pattern - both paradigmatic and syntagmatic ones; the semantic value(s) of that formal pattern; the context(s) in which the choice of the pattern is possible.
>
> (Hasan and Parrett 1994: 205)

Insofar as the aim is to enable learners to observe the formal properties of markers, to recognize their semantic values, and to identify contexts in which they can be appropriately used, the pedagogic potential of the concordancer would appear to lie in its ability to highlight one feature at a time - features of form, syntagmatic associations in terms of collocations and positions, paradigmatic replaceability in terms not only of formal classes but also of recurrent categories of pragmatic use.

From a more general pedagogic perspective, the value of corpus-based concordancing lies in the fact that it permits differentiated research procedures. I have stressed how the type and ordering of the data to which learners are exposed may imply different research modes, depending on whether or not the raw data has been previously transformed into teaching material by editing and sorting. Learners can be asked to recognize regularities previously identified by the teacher or other learners (cfr. Gavioli, this volume, chapter 5: 3.1), or they can identify them themselves, selecting an element to analyze and then seeking regularities in its use. By providing information on the characteristics of the corpus, suggestions as to procedures to imitate, and indications as to parameters to consider in the analysis, the teacher may enable learners to discover significant patterns in discourse for themselves.

Notes

1. One pedagogic proposal based on the observation of authentic data has been elaborated by Carter and McCarthy (1995) and McCarthy and Carter (1995), who envision a three-stage structure consisting of illustration (data observation), interaction (reflection and discussion on the features which emerge), and induction (creation of a generalization or rule to account for these features, which can in its turn be tested and redefined against further data). In this way, they argue,

    the patchy, confusing, and often inadequate treatment of the grammar of spoken language in published resources, may turn out to be a cue for imaginative discovery and problem solving work in the grammar class.
    (Carter and McCarthy 1995: 155)

    When we turn, however, to examine the best-known application of their approach (Carter and McCarthy 1997), we find that they simply present the learner with examples of various speech genres taken from the CANCODE corpus, with a line-by-line commentary highlighting particular features (elliptical forms, discourse markers, set phrases, hedges, etc.) which leaves little space for "imaginative discovery and problem-solving work" by the learner.

2. Interjections include phonosymbols, or

> phonic sequences which are not necessarily doubly articulated, forming markers which (a) have no lexical meaning, but may have one or more holophrastic meanings; and (b) have forms which may deviate from the phonological system of the language.
>
> (Voghera 1993: 108)

3. Keller (1979) proposes lists of gambits containing various kinds of expressions (lexical phrases, discourse markers, well-formed sentences) that serve interaction by signalling openings, closings, interruptions, topic changes and formulations, and the like.

4. Although - as the entire argument in this chapter illustrates - it is highly problematic to propose translations for these markers or the lexical items they are derived from, an attempt has been made in order to give a rough idea of their sense.

5. The LIP corpus (*Lessico di frequenza dell'Italiano Parlato*) consists of transcribed speech recorded in four cities: Milan, Florence, Naples, and Rome. It includes 500,000 orthographic words, divided into five sections of 100,000 words each:

   - two-way face-to-face communicative exchanges with free turn-taking (conversations at home, at work, on public transport, etc.);
   - two-way communicative exchanges with free turn-taking, not face-to-face (telephone calls, call-in radio and TV programmes, etc.);
   - two-way face-to-face communicative exchanges with restricted turn-taking (meetings, debates, interviews, oral examinations, classroom interrogations, etc.);
   - one-way communicative exchanges with the audience present (school and university lectures, papers given at conventions, political speeches, funeral orations, courtroom harangues);
   - one-way unscripted communicative exchanges with a remote audience (TV and radio programmes).

6. Transcription conventions used in extracts from the LIP corpus are as follows:

A:	beginning of new turn by speaker A
#	short pause
# #	long pause
word_	word lengthened
wo\<rd\>	word cut short: segment in angle brackets reconstructed
\<F\>	phonosymbol (see note 2 above)

4. The pedagogic use of spoken corpora

<?>   untranscribable speech: number of ? indicates length
[comment]   description of paralinguistic feature or non-verbal event

7. Some concordance programs (notably *MicroConcord*: Scott and Johns 1993) employ default sort orders which automatically list occurrences according to the first word to the right or left of the search string. In such cases it may be necessary to train learners to re-sort concordances in order of occurrence, or at least to experiment with other sort orders, in order to reduce the inherent bias towards a focus on adjacent left/right collocates.

5 THE LEARNER AS RESEARCHER: INTRODUCING CORPUS CONCORDANCING IN THE CLASSROOM

Laura Gavioli

1. Introduction

Corpora have been widely exploited in applied linguistics to provide learners with more reliable reference tools (e.g. Cobuild 1987, 1990, 1995), to rationalize syllabus design (e.g. Flowerdew 1993), and to prepare, or guide teachers to prepare, classroom materials (Willis and Willis 1988; Tribble and Jones 1990; for a review see Ma 1993). In all these cases the linguist, teacher or materials designer acts as a filter between the corpus and the learner. Another school of thought has however claimed that this mediation may not be necessary. Johns (1991a, 1994) has argued that learners can interact directly with corpora, taking on the role of linguistic researchers to formulate and test their own hypotheses about language behaviour. "Data-driven learning", as he calls it, enables the learner to "take part in building up his or her *own* profiles of meaning and uses" (Johns 1994: 297, emphasis in the original). Experiments have shown that interacting with corpora can stimulate learners' intuitions about language use and allow them to derive linguistic generalizations in an individual, autonomous way (Johns and King 1991).

Johns' approach shifts the primary function of corpora from describing to learning the language, and their place from the research laboratory to the classroom. This shift raises two main issues. The first is practical. Corpora typically contain millions of words of data, so as to maximize their reliability. Yet even 50,000 words - over 100 pages like this one - is a lot of material for learners, particularly at beginner or intermediate level. Without filtering the data, how can we make large quantities of material accessible to them? How can learners analyze corpora without getting lost? The second issue is theoretical. Even if we can teach learners methods for analyzing corpora, why should they use them? Are the results of their analyses likely to be worth the effort? In this paper I discuss possible answers to these questions. I illustrate a number of activities designed to familiarize learners with corpus analysis, and to develop their ability to perform it productively.[1] At the same time, I argue that a key function of such activities must be to make learners aware of the

5. The learner as researcher

assumptions on which data-driven research is based, and to realize its implications for their own language learning.

I first discuss the practical and theoretical issues involved in the use of corpora and concordances in greater detail (section 2). I then propose some activities designed to help learners use corpora to identify recurrent features of various types and to generalize from them - activities which lead gradually from 'easy' analyses focussing on patterns that recur in a particular text-type, to ones which raise more complex questions of generalizability across different kinds of text (section 3). I then discuss how analytical work aiming at the discovery of recurrent features and the construction of generalizations can help learners in producing texts of their own, not only by helping them to conform to conventional use, but also to exploit the language creatively (section 4). I conclude with a series of observations relating to the selection and grading of corpora and of corpus-based activities from the perspective proposed.

2. Issues in the analysis of corpus data

2.1 Observing and generalizing

The main instrument of corpus analysis is the concordancer. By listing the occurrences of a particular feature, concordances show the frequency of that feature in the corpus in question, and the frequency with which it co-occurs with other features. Concordances highlight those aspects of language use which show up as recurrent patterns in the corpus - in a word, as repetition. To identify these patterns requires particular methods of analysis. Concordance lines have to be grouped on the basis of shared features, and classified in more general terms which will account for their distribution. For instance, when analyzing a concordance of the word *blue*, it may be possible to notice the recurrence of phrases like *blue chip* or *out of the blue*, and to see whether these combinations seem typical of a particular domain or genre (such as *blue chip* in newspaper stock-market reports), or are more widespread (as seems the case with *out of the blue*). These processes of observation and generalization may seem banal, but can pose many difficulties to learners. Unlike traditional teaching materials, a concordance may not provide univocal support for a particular analysis, and learners, because they are not native speakers of the language, cannot confidently rely on their intuitions to guide and back up their observations and to suggest and reinforce explanatory generalizations.

Observing and generalizing from recurrent patterns in concordances may also require a rather different view of language use and of language learning from activities based on traditional teaching materials. Bolinger (1976) criticizes the idea that language is generated by applying rules to combine words and morphemes into sentences, noting that many rule-based combinations do not seem to occur in practice. Thus we say *a long time ago* and *a short time ago*, but only *long ago*, not *short ago*; we say *he looked at me suspiciously* and *he regarded me suspiciously*, but only *he looked at me*, not *he regarded me*. Bolinger suggests that we do not produce certain forms because we have no memory of them, "we have not heard it done" (1976: 4). Instead of using rules to combine words and morphemes, he suggests that we produce most utterances using multi-word chunks which we have stored as wholes, following what Sinclair (1991a) has more recently termed an "idiom principle". From this perspective, identifying and learning recurrent patterns and their typical contexts of use becomes central to the entire language learning process (Aston 1995b). Learners who view language use as a matter of combining words and morphemes may realize that many such combinations are odd to native speakers, but still fail to appreciate the importance of focussing their attention on larger chunks and recognizing and manipulating these.

2.2 The learner as researcher

Stressing how concordance data can stimulate users to induce their own generalizations, Johns (1991a, 1994) suggests that the learner should approach corpora as a researcher. Unlike dictionaries, grammars and textbooks, a concordance does not offer explanations; it merely provides data which it is up to the user to explain. Inductive work is not new in language pedagogy: the practice of many teachers and materials writers involves presenting a series of similar instances to help learners induce generalizations. Analyzing a concordance, however, is not necessarily the same thing as analyzing five or six sentences on the blackboard or in a textbook (cfr. Zorzi, this volume, chapter 4: 3.1).

- A concordance may contain many more instances. A search for the words *attractive*, *beautiful* and *pretty* in a 230,000-word corpus of letters to a newspaper agony aunt (see 3.2 below) found 21 occurrences of *attractive*, 12 of *beautiful* and 80 of *pretty* - hardly numbers to be managed rapidly by learners.
- A concordance will often show more than one pattern of use. In the case just mentioned, many of the occurrences of *pretty* were adverbial (*pretty good*, *pretty sure*) rather than adjectival. Careful reading and manual categorization of the concordance lines was then

5. The learner as researcher

```
1  ble to find suitable sites or have not complied with the ruling. <p> Recently residents of some of the
2  and other authorised practitioners who complied with a statutory code of conduct to charge for conveya
3  would be impossible for the husband to comply with or would cripple his business. <p> On joint assets
4  concern in Austria in May 1945 was to comply with the Yalta agreement ordering repatriation so that t
5  e Minister of Agriculture, 'failing to comply with natural justice". <p> Until yesterday morning, the
6  & Lyle (1986) ICR 371. <p> In order to comply with Community law, it was now necessary to agree the sa
7  te US given 'an assurance that it will comply with its obligations in relation to the use of the name"
8  ember of the represented class without complying with the requirements of the county court rules. <p>
```

Figure 1. *compli*/comply* with* in *MicroConcord Corpus A*

required in order to reveal that *pretty* only appeared as an adjective 14 times, making *attractive* the most frequent of the three adjectival forms (see the data in Appendix B).

- Even where a concordance only provides instances of a single pattern, considerable analysis may still be necessary to confirm this. The concordance in Figure 1 was generated to help learners investigate the use of *comply with*, following their teacher's intuitive explanation that it is used with personal subjects. In lines 2 and 3 it can be immediately seen that the subjects are people (*practitioners* and *the husband*), but in the other lines this is not apparent.[2] Looking at wider contexts reveals that in several of these other lines the subjects (underlined) are authorities or organizations - *many authorities* (1), *the Minister of Agriculture* (5), and *Deloitte US* (a branch of a multinational firm: 7). In other cases, the construction is impersonal, but a person or organization is still the implied subject - *the British Army* (4), *a named representative defendant* (8), and, we may guess, some governmental authority in (6).

1   But *many authorities* have either not been able to find suitable sites or have not **complied with** the ruling.

4   But the Cossacks had been fighting for the Germans and *the British Army*'s main concern in Austria in May 1945 was to **comply with** the Yalta agreement ordering repatriation

5   The nuns' request for a judicial review of the order to slaughter the flock had been based upon *John Gummer, the Minister of Agriculture*, 'failing to **comply with** natural justice".

6   In order to **comply with** Community law, it was now necessary to agree the same date of retirement for both sexes.

7   John Bullock, senior partner of Deloitte (UK), said: 'We have been unable to gain satisfactory assurances from Touche Ross." Neither had *Deloitte US* given 'an assurance that it will **comply with** its obligations in relation to the use of the name"

8   There was no reason to suppose that in proceedings under Order 5, rule 5, it was intended to enable *a named representative defendant* to claim against a member of the represented class without **complying with** the requirements of the county court rules.

Observing recurrences and inducing generalizations from a concordance may thus require specific skills. The data may have to be reduced to manageable quantities, and it may not be interpretable in terms of a single generalization. Even when it is, this generalization may only be revealed after all the lines have been classified. In the *comply with* concordance, learners initially classified subjects (explicit or implicit) as persons (*husband, practitioner*), authorities (*the Minister of Agriculture*), and companies (*Deloitte US*), and only subsequently ascribed them to the single more general category of 'people and organizations'.

2.3 Samples vs. examples

To clarify what is involved in interpreting corpus data, it seems useful to make a conceptual distinction between *samples* and *examples*. The instances which teachers write on the blackboard and which materials writers include in textbooks are generally chosen to illustrate some abstract formal or functional feature - the meaning of a word, a rule of grammar, a convention of use. All that is necessarily shared by the instances in a concordance, on the other hand, is a common orthographic form - the sequence of characters we have asked the computer to look for. The blackboard and textbook provide *examples*, in the sense that they are intended to exemplify a particular linguistic feature. The concordance instead provides *samples*, selected for the sole reason that they contain a particular combination of characters. While samples can of course be used as a source of examples, this transformation requires human intervention via analysis and selection.[3]

Even the texts in textbooks, authentic or otherwise, can generally be seen as examples which have been chosen to illustrate particular features of language in use (and to exclude features thought likely to be difficult or distracting). The texts constituting corpora, on the other hand, are generally included to provide samples of particular text-types, without any prior analysis of their linguistic characteristics (Atkins et al. 1992). Whether sentences or texts, examples are thus likely to suggest certain generalizations quite explicitly and unambiguously; samples, on the other hand, merely provide occurrences of varying tractability from which possible generalizations have to be worked out. If learners assume that corpus data will coherently illustrate a generalized principle of the type that they are accustomed to find provided by teachers and textbooks, treating them as examples rather than samples, they are likely to misunderstand and misuse them.

2.4 Recurrence and typicality

Since we cannot assume that a single generalization will necessarily account for all the data, analyzing a concordance involves looking for linguistic features which recur in at least some instances in the sample provided. Such features may be of many kinds, and may be more or less evident. We may find recurrent word combinations, or collocations (such as *chip* following *blue*, and *good* following *pretty*). We may find recurrent semantic categories (such as the occurrence of 'people or organizations' with *comply with*). We may find recurrent syntactic categories, or colligations: these (and other) features may also co-occur. The concordance in Figure 2 shows a recurrent colligation in a 200,000 word corpus of academic texts in social sciences (*MicroConcord Corpus B*: Murison-Bowie 1993c), namely that *worth* is frequently followed by a gerund. The most frequent collocate to realize this colligation is *noting*, but a number of other gerunds following *worth* (*seeing*, *looking* and possibly *singling out*) are quite close to *noting* semantically. *Discussing*, *enquiring* and *reporting* seem to form another semantic group. Re-sorting the concordance by the words preceding *worth* highlights other colligations, such as the impersonal *it is worth*, which occurs in eight lines (and in the forms *it is not/only/ therefore worth* in a further three).

Looking for recurrences generally involves looking for other lines which are in some way similar in form or meaning to see if they can be fitted into the same or a similar category. Wider and more abstract generalizations can then be attempted concerning typical patterns. In this case, for instance, there seems to be a tendency for *worth* to occur in the wider colligation *it is worth* V-*ing*. This pattern also appears to have a typical pragmatic function, that of underlining the importance of the following proposition to the reader.

Analyzing similar instances may also show that particular features tend to recur in particular positions or particular types of texts. In a corpus of articles from *The Independent* newspaper (*MicroConcord Corpus A*: Murison-Bowie 1993b), a search revealed that in 19 out of its 24 occurrences, *talks to* occurs in headlines, 18 of these being headlines to interviews (Figure 3).[4] Further analysis showed that while *talks to* has the interviewer and the interviewee as its arguments, either of these may be its subject: thus we find both *Andy Gill talks to Hardy Fox* and *Chris Isaak talks to Andy Gill*, where Andy Gill is the interviewer in both cases. However the interviewee's name is usually accompanied by an indication of her/his profession (*novelist David Lodge*; *Wilfred Thesiger, explorer*; *wandering American singer and song-writer, Loudon Wainwright III*; etc.),

5. The learner as researcher

```
 1   There is one apposite text which may be worth a closer look. <pb n=247> <qt> If something has been
 2   e point of view, this area was probably worth between one and one and a half million employed men
 3   or other reasons. As a result it is not worth discussing them fully here. One example may suffice:
 4   le for the prolonging of the war, it is worth enquiring why the 'Hitler myth" did not collapse more
 5   by mortgaging it for as much as it was worth: innumerable latent entails were produced to deprive
 6   he trustee was insolvent, they would be worth little. <p> So far discussion has been limited to dis
 7   ts the law at Neratius' time. <p> It is worth looking more closely at the expressions he cites. The
 8   , and there was 'hardly any credibility worth mentioning" left for his last broadcast speech on 30
 9   hin each category. To start with, it is worth noting that the list is <pb n=164> not exhaustive, in
10   servatism with the new right. Yet it is worth noting that one of the most influential works in the
11   ults on the police, and it is therefore worth noting that this offence is committed even though D w
12   ely. The first is more difficult. It is worth noting too that it can arise in different types of tr
13   > is not listed. Two other oddities are worth noting: first, the list does not confine itself to wo
14   n" raises again the issue of the social worth of sport, recreation and dangerous exhibitions. <p>
15   so infinitesimal, that the case is not worth reporting, and therefore, for <i> practical </i> purp
16   it is none the less unhistorical. It is worth seeing whether a historical development can be detect
17   r of the examples cited. Of those it is worth singling out D. 32.95 and D. 33.2.34.1, in which the
18   t the future of the inner cities. It is worth stressing that in <i> each </i> year since 1980 there
19   a (no doubt inflated) valuation of its worth to the legatee. Yet often it cannot have been the cas
20   the concluding remark that 'it is only worth while waging war if the enemy can be destroyed with t
```

Figure 2. *worth* in *MicroConcord Corpus B* (social science texts)

1   MINSTRELS / As the roamers do: Jim White **talks to** wandering American singer-songwriter Loudon
2   THEATRE / Unemployed virtues: Meredith Oakes **talks to** Christopher Hampton and Heribert Sasse about
3   INTERVIEW / The Kane mutiny: Stephen Pope **talks to** the Kane brothers about the new, more intima
4   th with the past: Wilfred Thesiger, explorer, **talks to** Richard North about his lifelong search for
5   ero of cool: Old-fashioned rocker Chris Isaak **talks to** Andy Gill </hl> <bl> By ANDY GILL </bl> CHRI
6   THEATRE / Lights on, nobody home: Andy Gill **talks to** Hardy Fox about the history of American cult
7   arge: Songwriter and performer Anthony Newley **talks to** Mark Steyn about the return of Stop The Worl
8   ersation pieces: Choreographer Siobhan Davies **talks to** Judith Mackrell about the qualities she look
9   ile popular taste with avant-garde design. He **talks to** Roger Berthoud </hl> <bl> By ROGER BERTHOUD
10 <hl> E Germans sceptical as Krenz **talks to** Church </hl> <bl> By STEVE CRAWSHAW and PATR
11 ined to return to Cleveland: Nicholas Timmins **talks to** the doctor facing an uncertain future after
12 ots face Claesen class barrier _ Don Lindsay **talks to** Nico Claesen about the difference between th
13 INTERVIEW / A tissue of truths: Zoe Heller **talks to** Kazuo Ishiguro whose novel, The Remains of t
14 old: At some point in the future, Giles Smith **talks to** Matt Goss about adult rock </hl> <bl> By GIL
15 A rumba life: World Music _ Nicola Mitchell **talks to** Zairean soukous singer, Kanda Bongo Man </hl
16 to scrutinise Civil Service: Peter Hennessy **talks to** Sir Angus Fraser, head of the efficiency uni
17 is leading a 697m pound break-up bid for DRG, **talks to** Frank Kane </hl> <bl> By FRANK KANE </bl>
18 / Industrious relations: Novelist David Lodge **talks to** Mark Lawson about the television version of
19 playing in London after a three-year absence, **talks to** Giles Smith </hl> <bl> By GILES SMITH </bl>

Figure 3. *talks to* in headlines in *MicroConcord Corpus A*

while the interviewer's name is never accompanied by an "our reporter" or the like. The headline then usually goes on to state the topic of the conversation - in 9 out of 13 cases introduced by *about*. From these characteristics we can identify a typical pattern for interview headlines in *The Independent*, consisting of a sequence such as *Wilfred Thesiger, explorer, talks to Richard North about his lifelong search for diversity* (4). It can also be noticed that this pattern does not constitute the entire headline, but usually follows a short eye-catching phrase or summary sentence, such as *As the roamers do* (1), *Unemployed virtues* (2), or, in the case of Thesiger, *Boy's Own adventurer keeps faith with the past* (4).

To arrive at these generalizations, we first compared concordance lines to see whether they shared common features, and the analytic process then moved from the identification of one recurrent feature (the occurrence of *talks to* in headlines), to progressively add others (the colligation 'person-talks to-person', the specification of the interviewee's profession, the extension of the headline with *about*, its introduction by a catch phrase). The process required looking for formal and functional similarities and differences in order to group instances and formulate generalizations which those instances exemplified, progressively extending the scope of these generalizations in the search for (proto)typical patterns. Learners brought up on input filtered by the teacher and textbook are unlikely to be familiar with this process, and need to be helped to develop their skills in identifying recurrences of various kinds in the data, and in making generalizations from them.

3. Introducing learners to corpus analysis

3.1 Identifying recurrences

The analyses in the last section have aimed to show how limited generalizations about language use can be made by observing recurrences in corpus data. Concordance samples are examined to find occurrences sharing similar collocational, colligational, semantic, pragmatic or textual features, and these are then grouped into categories which are as far as possible related to each other. I have suggested that recognizing such recurrences is not an immediate operation and that learners need to be introduced to it gradually.

For these initial steps, a restricted amount of data seems more appropriate than a large corpus (Aston 1997a, Gavioli 1997; for a partially opposing view as far as advanced learners are concerned, see Bernardini, this volume, chapter 9: 4.3). For instance, if we construct small homogeneous corpora consisting of short texts of the same type - job advertisements, news flashes, weather forecasts, short business letters - these can provide manageable quantities of data, but at the same time a substantial number of recurrent features, since the sample texts will have many similarities. Such corpora can be easily put together from printed or electronic sources (see Zanettin, this volume, chapter 7: 2). For the activities to be described here, devised as part of a unit dealing with personal descriptions, two corpora which would hopefully attract the interest of a teenage class were used: one of lonely hearts ads, and one of letters to a newspaper agony aunt.

The lonely hearts ads corpus was tiny, consisting of 41 short texts totalling a mere 2,000 words. The most frequent lexical word in the corpus was *seeks* (most concordancing software will provide lists of all the words in a given text or corpus in order of frequency: e.g. Chandler 1989; Scott 1996; Barlow 1996b). Similarly to *talks to* in interview headlines, *seeks* appears to play a key role in the structure of lonely hearts ads, linking a description of the seeker to one of the person sought. Learners were first asked to look for recurrent features in the concordance of *seek** shown in Figure 4 (the asterisk indicates that a suffix may follow *seek*). Besides the fact that the most common form is *seeks*, they noted two recurrent colligational patterns: it usually occurs as the first word of a clause, following a full-stop, a dash or a comma, and in all but one case it is followed by a noun phrase rather than an infinitive. (The concordance lines are sorted alphabetically, first according to the form of the search word, then according to the first word to its left.)

Another recurrent feature which can be noted in this concordance is that seekers often use a series of adjectives to describe themselves and the person sought. Learners were given a list of the six most frequent adjectives in the corpus, and asked to generate concordances for any three of them. They were then asked to see whether these adjectives occurred as part of a series, and which words they frequently co-occurred with (see Figure 5).

All these adjectives except *good* tend to come in series, and all have recurrent collocates. *Handsome* is preceded by *tall* or followed by *successful*; *tall* is followed by *handsome* or *slim*; *attractive* is preceded by *intelligent* or *classy*; *pretty* is preceded by *very* or *extremely*. *Good* is instead found in two main patterns, *good looking* and *good sense of humour*. Though these concordances (shown in Appendix A) provide too few examples to allow confident generalizations, they suggest that there may be routine ways of organizing series of adjectives, and that there may be a difference between adjectives that come in series and ones that do not.

5. The learner as researcher

```
1   s, freckles, and laugh loudly in movie theaters. I      seek a man willing to try new things - sky divi
2   me, extremely funny, sincere, romantic, creative -   seeking bright, funny, outgoing, sane, very pre
3   truly caring, fun-loving and exceptionally modest.    Seeking a warm, loving relationship with a pret
4   h traditional family values and secure profession,   seeking quality time of fun, home, heart and hu
5   nt is definitely a "man of distinction", seriously   seeking a new and prosperous, compatible marria
6                                    <p> Female 29,       seeks lovable, non smoking man 25-35, for fun /
7   body-builder - Martial arts, funny, unique(!) 29,     seeks handsome, generous soul mate. Note / phot
8          <p> Beautiful, dangerously sincere MD - 39,    seeks future with attractive, accomplished Jewi
9   mantic dinners, music, country drives and animals.    Seeks best friend, 22-32, Jewish, pretty, matur
10  l executive - 42, brown hair, blue eyes, athletic,    seeks smart, very pretty, curvaceous woman for
11  tural/charity events, dynamic people, fine dining.   Seeks selective Manhattan/CT gentleman who appr
12  Youthful, in-shape 39-year-old, jewish, divorced,     seeks to meet a relationship-centered, principl
13  ful - Lovely NJ Widow; war, secure, down-to-earth,    seeks counterpart in quality jewish man, 50-60,
14  orced lady, young 45, many interests, smart dress,    seeks tall slim professional gent, must have go
15  white female, 5'8", ready for marriage and family,   seeks tall, handsome, highly successful, NYC-ba
16  29, not bad looking, genuine, romantic and honest,    seeks female friend 20-32, for friendship and r
17                        <p> Romantic Intellectual -     seeks passion and friendship. Athletic, very in
18  es, dinner by candlelight, plus various interests.    Seeks very pretty, slender, warm and affectiona
19                     <p> Handsome MD, 44 - Renaissance man, seeks slender female, 25-35, for friendship, co
20  merican woman, tall, slim, blonde, living in Rome,  seeking generous and honorable gentleman for mutu
21  h, 36, bright, fun, warm, sensitive and giving ...   seeks similarly special woman. Note / photo. 97
22                                       <p> Soprano     seeks tenor - For harmonic convergence or duets
23  ody, 30s, passionate spirit, unusually successful.    Seeks the joys of friendship and romance with a
24  of humor, medium build, caring and understanding.    Seeks female friend, for friendship, age and co
```

Figure 4. *seek** in the Lonely Hearts Ads corpus

WORKSHEET

handsome   good   attractive   pretty   tall   successful

1. In pairs, choose three of these adjectives and have a look at their concordances.
   - Which words do they most frequently occur with?
   - Do they occur as part of a series of adjectives?

2. Discuss your findings with other pairs, then with the rest of the class.

Figure 5. Looking at adjective sequences: learner activity

While it focuses on relatively simple collocational and colligational features, this activity also has a wider aim, that of showing that there is considerable repetition in language use, and that observing recurrent features can contribute to an understanding of how particular kinds of texts are typically constructed. Not all these features, particularly those relating to sequencing (such as the organization of adjective series), may immediately strike learners' attention or be intuitively obvious. (In another activity where learners were asked to write a short news flash reporting an event they had witnessed, almost all began with the word *yesterday*, only to find that in a corpus of news flashes, *yesterday* occurred, if at all, later on in the text.)

Although quite advanced learners of English, these learners made unexpected discoveries from examining a corpus of short, simple texts which could easily be compared. They rapidly became more sophisticated in their observations, as they realized that there was a wide range of recurrent features which could suggest generalizations about the typical content and structure of lonely hearts ads. For instance, they noticed that in 30 out of 41 texts the seeker is introduced by a noun giving their sex (*male, guy, female, lady,* etc.) or profession (*businessman, self-made millionaire,* etc.). This noun is preceded by adjectives (generally two) referring to physical appearance (*attractive*), psychological or intellectual qualities (*sincere, intelligent*), or civil status (*divorced*). Gay seekers are generally introduced with *gay* as the first word in the ad. Further expansions of the description introduce the seeker's interests (generally two) with verbs like *enjoys* and *likes* (*enjoys rollerblading, movies*; *likes music, nights out*). As for the sought, expansions often include a deontic *must* (*must have good sense of humour*) or a relative clause with *who* as subject (*who is intelligent and attractive*). Descriptions are also often expanded with phrases introduced by *with* (*with good sense of humour*; *with a strong moral sense*). In 33 of the texts the sort of relationship desired is stated, usually introduced by *for* (*for friendship and romance*; *for commitment*).

3.2 Testing generalizations through corpus comparison

In the lonely hearts ads corpus, learners noted that two semantically similar words, *pretty* and *attractive*, were used in different ways. While *pretty* was often intensified by *very* or *extremely*, *attractive* was not. *Pretty* was followed by other adjectives referring to physical or emotional characteristics (*slim, slender, curvaceous, passionate, mellow, expressive*); *attractive* was found with adjectives referring to social or intellectual features (*intelligent, successful, classy, ivy-educated*, etc.). And while *pretty* invariably referred to females, *attractive* was used of both sexes. At this point, it seemed interesting to compare the use of *pretty* and *attractive* with that of another semantically similar adjective, *beautiful*. However, *beautiful* did not occur often enough to reveal any clear patterns in its use - not even that it refers to females, as one might perhaps expect (Figure 6).

Even when the data from a single corpus is sufficient to indicate differences in the use of semantically similar words, it is always dangerous to generalize beyond the type(s) of texts represented in that corpus. Stubbs (1993, 1994) suggests that one of the ways in which more confident generalizations can be made is by contrasting data from different corpora or sub-corpora. For this purpose the next activity introduced a second corpus, consisting of letters to a newspaper agony aunt and the latter's answers. Totalling 230,000 words, this corpus was much larger, and contained texts of a very different type from the lonely hearts ads. But since the letters generally concerned relationships, they too contained many descriptions of the writers and those close to them, which might be expected to share some features with the descriptions in the lonely hearts ads.[5]

Comparing data from different corpora is likely to highlight some recurrences found in only one kind of these, and others which instead recur in both. Comparing concordances of the adjectives *pretty*, *attractive* and *beautiful* in the lonely hearts ads and the letters (see Appendices A and B), learners found that *pretty* and *attractive* always refer to people's physical appearance in both corpora, *pretty* referring to women and *attractive* to either sex. *Beautiful*, on the other hand, also refers to music and home in

```
1  somewhat tall - 5'7" to 5'11", who is strikingly beautiful and is also in exceptional physical shape -
2                                              <p> Beautiful Asian body-builder - Martial arts, funny, u
3                                              <p> Beautiful, dangerously sincere MD - 39, seeks future
```

Figure 6. *beautiful* in the Lonely Hearts Ads corpus

the letters. A further difference noted was that in the letters, neither *pretty* nor *attractive* generally occurs in a series of adjectives. In contrast *beautiful* tends to occur in a coordinate structure with another positive adjective (*mature and beautiful*; *beautiful and well-behaved*; *beautiful and wonderful*; *sweet and beautiful*).

As well as comparing data from two different kinds of texts, it may also be interesting to compare data from small, homogeneous corpora with data from larger, heterogeneous ones. This may further reveal the extent to which particular features are limited to specific text-types or are instead more generalized. While in the letters corpus, *beautiful* recurs in a coordinate structure, in one of its three occurrences in the lonely hearts ads we find a similar instance, *strikingly beautiful and also in exceptional physical shape*. Looking at a larger and more varied corpus, this time of different kinds of newspaper texts (*MicroConcord Corpus A*: Murison-Bowie 1993b), learners found that *beautiful* came in a coordinate structure in approximately a third of its occurrences, suggesting that this pattern is in fact quite a general one. Gradually introducing them to larger and more heterogeneous corpora can help learners see how far such generalizations can be widened, and at the same time help them learn to handle larger quantities of more varied corpus material (see also Bernardini, this volume, chapter 9).

4. Using the concordancer to produce texts

4.1 Producing routine language

Concordances focus the attention on patterns that are repetitive and seem in some way typical. Thereby, they make it evident that syntactic rules are much less productive in practice than a traditional approach to the study of grammar might suggest (Sinclair 1991a). While grammars suggest that the number of word combinations is potentially infinite, concordances suggest that this number is in practice much more limited. In the letters and lonely hearts ads corpora, for instance, the adjective *pretty* always referred to girls, and where it functioned attributively (*I'm a pretty girl*) rather than predicatively (*I'm pretty*), it always modified either *girl* or *face*. While this may be a consequence of the nature of the corpora, and the number of occurrences is very limited, it suggests that there may be some general constraints on the use of *pretty*.

The written component of the British National Corpus (Burnard 1995; cfr. Aston, this volume, chapter 1: 6) contains over 90 million words from a wide variety of types of text. A search for occurrences of *a pretty* found 1161 occurrences. Analysis of a hundred of these, randomly selected, revealed that though considerably more varied than in the letters corpus, there are still clear recurrent features of a semantic nature. Leaving aside fixed idioms such as *a pretty penny* and *a pretty pass*, four main semantic categories of words follow *a pretty*: a 'girl/woman' category (*lady, maid, face*, etc.: about 30%); a 'place' category (*village, garden*, etc.: 20%); a 'picture/sight' category (15%), and a 'dress/furniture' category: 10%).[6] Even when carried out using large representative corpora, concordance analysis suggests that word combinations are far more repetitive than might be expected.

As noted in section 1 above, the fact that language is repetitive is in line with Bolinger's (1976) theory of language production, according to which speakers tend to reproduce multi-word chunks of language that they have memorized as such, rather than generating them through the application of grammatical rules. This idea may seem inefficient to language learners: memorizing huge numbers of multi-word chunks seems far more work than learning a more limited lexicon and a relatively small number of combinatory rules. It may also seem to reduce the scope for individual choice, reducing language production to a matter of repetition. The fact that language is repetitive, however, does not mean that choice is completely excluded, merely that "once a register choice is made [...] then all the slot-by-slot choices are massively reduced in scope or even, in some cases, pre-empted" (Sinclair 1991a: 110).

Considering language use in this way in fact suggests that learning should concentrate not only on recurrent behaviours, but also on the ways in which typical patterns leave space for choice. The next activity (Figure 6) requires learners to identify recurrent chunks in the lonely hearts ads corpus, and then to use these to produce a text of the same type. We have already seen that these texts show a typical structure. The activity invites learners to identify possible chunks for each slot in this structure, and to then use these to build up new texts of their own.

The idea of asking learners to produce texts by combining chunks copied from other texts may seem questionable, encouraging them to imitate and cramping their freedom to say what they want. However any corpus will contain a variety of texts, with a variety of chunks that learners can choose from to build up a text of their own. Trying to reproduce a pattern forces them to compare their own ideas of what such texts should be like with what they are in fact like, raising a wide range of issues as to what sounds native-like in the L2 - a key consideration in formal writing and in translation (see Zanettin, this volume, chapter 7: 4).

WORKSHEET

1. In groups of two or three, use the corpus of Lonely hearts ads to identify 4 or 5 patterns which are typically used to do each of the following:
   - introduce the seeker
   - add descriptions of the seeker
   - introduce the sought
   - add descriptions of the sought

   You can generate concordances to get suggestions.

2. Use the patterns you have identified to produce at least two new lonely hearts ads. Complete any missing parts of the text as necessary.

Figure 7. Identifying and using recurrent chunks: learner activity

4.2 Producing unusual language

As well as accounting for the predictability of language, reflecting its typical use, observing recurrences can also help cast light on atypical, unconventional behaviour. It is rare for all the lines in a concordance to follow exactly the same pattern. Often, categorizing citations will leave over a small group which are 'different' from the others in some respect. For instance, in an analysis of a corpus of 18 million words from the Bank of English, Louw (1993) found that the word *utterly* is typically used in negatively-connoted contexts. There were four cases, however, where it occurred in positively-connoted ones. Studying these four instances more closely, Louw noted that each time irony appeared to be intended (cfr. Partington, this volume, chapter 3: 4).

Many 'creative' uses of language seem to involve deliberate deviation from typical patterns. Partington (1996) illustrates how newspaper headlines often obtain striking effects by deviating very slightly from typical collocations. Among the examples he cites are *First class male* (alluding to 'first-class mail'), *Murder of the cathedral* (alluding to T.S. Eliot's *Murder in the cathedral*), and *A fridge too far* (alluding to the saying 'a bridge too far'). As well as highlighting conventional uses of language, concordances can also highlight deviations from these, where some special effect may be intended. In the letters corpus, for example, concordances of *attractive* and *pretty* show that these adjectives do not typically occur in series (see 3.2

WORKSHEET

In groups, look at the concordance below and discuss the openings which seem most original or creative to you. Then write a "creative" ad of your own.

```
1   <p> An enchanting Scandinavian lady ... in her early 40s, 1.70, a charming beauty with blonde hai
2   <p> Are you a caring policeman, who wants lots of fun, love and attention? Then call me, I'm peti
3   <p> Are you Miss Special, the lady I gazed at, in the supermarket petrol station at Leek? Red spo
4   <p> Attractive divorced lady, young 45, many interests, smart dress, seeks tall slim professional
5   <p> Beautiful Asian body-builder - Martial arts, funny, unique(!) 29, seeks handsome, generous so
6   <p> Beautiful, dangerously sincere MD - 39, seeks future with attractive, accomplished Jewish man
7   <p> Catch of the year - If you believe all the good guys are taken - you just found one! Sensible
8   <p> Classic wasp- auburn beauty - Fit 5'9", size 6, stylish, stylish, vulnerable, inner beauty, t
9   <p> Classy, attractive, successful - Lovely NJ widow; war, secure, down-to-earth, seeks counterpa
10  <p> Desperately needed, lots of TLC, for male, mid-50s, i have suffered two tragic years, now I n
11  <p> Divorced Irish businessman, 49, 5ft 6in medium build. wants female, any age under 48, somebod
12  <p> Divorced, young looking, 43 male, good job, own house / car, likes music, nights out / in, fo
13  <p> Doing this kills me - But so does bachelorhood. Single Jewish male, 35, (nonpracticing). Cent
14  <p> Exceptional find - very handsome, successful, athletic, Jewish, 36, bright, fun, warm, sensit
15  <p> Extremely cute cardiologist - Jewish male of 30, with a great sense of humor and long-term pe
16  <p> Female 29, seeks lovable, non smoking man 25-35, for fun / friendship, and possible relations
17  <p> Fun loving, decent male, 29, not bad looking, genuine, romantic and honest, seeks female frie
18  <p> Gay woman, 42, wishes to meet feminine lady, 40-50. If I knew you and you knew me, what a won
19  <p> Gay male, 40s, wants to meet same, professional, reliable, discreet, single, for warm, lovabl
20  <p> Gay Male - Youthful, in-shape 39-year-old, Jewish, divorced, seeks to meet a relationship-cen
21  <p> Gentleman, 45, own home, requires lady, any age, for permanent relationship or marriage. Lanc
22  <p> Genuine professional male, but with a much younger outlook, would like to meet an attractive
23  <p> Good looking male, 28, would love to meet good looking, non smoking female under 33 who is al
24  <p> Good looking, professional black male, 28, non smoker, good sense of humor and long-term pers
```

5. The learner as researcher

```
25  <p> Handsome MD, 44 - Renaissance man, seeks slender female, 25-35, for friendship, companionship
26  <p> Handsome, successful, executive - 42, brown hair, blue eyes, athletic, seeks smart, very pret
27  <p> Herpes and handsome - Widowed businessman, young, 49 (6', 180 lbs.), enjoys movies, dinner by
28  <p> Intelligent, attractive, outgoing European lady, 40, USA citizen, loves to travel. Interested
29  <p> Is receiving and giving - uncompromising love in your heart? ... Versace, Armani and Bennis
30  <p> Italian industrialist - the owner of a global enterprise, 56, 6'0", with subsidiaries in Euro
31  <p> Pretty American woman, tall, slim, blonde, living in Rome, seeks generous and honorable gentl
32  <p> Ready to settle down - 40 years young, Manhattan Wall Street guy who does okay. Ivy League gr
33  <p> Real man, conservative values - Police lieutenant, tall, handsome, educated, smart, honest, t
34  <p> Romantic Intellectual -seeks passion and friendship. Athletic, very intelligent, attractive p
35  <p> She is 45, 5'4", Jewish, attractive - Blond, slim, incurably romantic, emotionally and financ
36  <p> Soprano seeks tenor - For harmonic convergence or duets on show tunes. I have deep brown eyes
37  <p> Special beginning - Extremely pretty, bright and passionate, L1 Jewish girl (36, 5'4", 115, g
38  <p> Straight male, dark, handsome, fit, 27, new to North West would like to meet a woman who is n
39  <p> Successful investor looking for mate - I'm looking for a woman to marry. If you introduce me
40  <p> Surgical Clark Kent - Hopes to be your superman! A joyous, enthusiastic MD / inventor with a
41  <p> Very pretty passionate professional - Single white female, 5'8", ready for marriage and famil
```

Figure 8. Identifying and using creative language: learner activity

above and Appendix B). There is however one case which contains such a series: *nice, smart, funny and pretty*. If we look at the letter this comes from, we find that its writer is a girl who is complaining that she doesn't have a boyfriend. She mentions a series of things that 16-year-old girls generally do, such as holding hands, dancing, being kissed, and being asked out, and she complains that none of these have ever happened to her (notice the repetition of *never* in the first two sentences). The series of positive adjectives occurs in the very last sentence, underlining the strangeness of this situation:

> Dear *xxx*:
> I'm 16 years old, thin with long blond hair and blue eyes, yet I have never had a boyfriend, held hands or danced or been kissed by a guy. I've never even been asked out by someone who is unattractive or unintelligent! My good friends don't understand because they all have boyfriends. I don't know what's wrong with me. I'm nice, smart, funny and pretty.
> *Confused and missing*

The deviance of this occurrence with respect to the typical patterns shown in the concordances suggests that here a particular effect is being aimed at, arguably one of deliberate emphasis. The unconventional formulation of the writer's attributes asserts her typicality, but at the same time seems to confirm that she is in some ways strange.

As well as helping learners become aware of deviation and its possible meanings, analyzing such occurrences may also help them produce effective deviations of their own. They can be asked to use corpora to produce 'creative' as well as conventional texts. For instance, while generally repetitive in their organization, lonely hearts ads sometimes open in unconventional ways - presumably with the aim of attracting the reader's attention. Learners can be asked to look for openings which seem original in this respect, and can subsequently be asked to write unconventional ads of their own. (The concordance on the worksheet in Figure 8 was generated by a search for the tag <p>, which in this corpus indicates the beginning of an ad, and was sorted according to the word following it.)

In this activity, learners are asked to focus on those occurrences which capture attention because they deviate from the typical opening pattern. There in fact seem to be recurrent ways of producing such deviations. While most of the ads open with a series of adjectives providing a literal description of the seeker (*very pretty, passionate professional*: line 41), there are also some clearly metaphorical formulations, such as *Soprano seeks tenor* (36) and *Surgical Clark Kent - Hopes to be your superman* (40).

There are also occasional polar questions, such as *Are you a caring policeman?* (2), *Are you Miss Special?* (3), or *Is receiving and giving uncompromising love in your heart?* (29), as well as summary phrases such as *Catch of the year* (7), *Exceptional find* (14), *Doing this kills me* (13). The discussion may be extended to consider ways in which authors attract readers' attention by 'marked' uses in other genres, such as jokes and newspaper headlines, and this discussion may give learners further ideas for producing 'creative' ads of their own.

Corpus-based concordancing, then, can highlight typical ways of assembling words and chunks as far as both routine and more creative uses of language are concerned. The activities proposed aim to help learners observe such features as they show up through concordance analysis, and to derive generalizations from them. They also invite learners to use concordances as a basis for their own language production. As well as introducing a research perspective into their language learning, such activities aim to lead learners to view language use as a negotiation between conformity and originality, inviting them to consider both the consequences of following convention and those of deviating from it.

5. Conclusion

Proposing corpora and the concordancer as instruments for autonomous research involves more than simply teaching learners a new technology. In the first place, they need to acquire appropriate methods of analysis. They need to appreciate that corpora and concordances provide samples rather than examples, and that analysis should aim at identifying recurrences and inferring patterns which appear in some way typical of certain contexts. Such analysis may be problematic for many learners: since raw concordance data are not filtered pedagogically, categorizing them may not confirm any particular initial hypothesis, and patterns of many types (collocational, colligational, semantic, pragmatic and textual) may emerge, with very different degrees of generalizability. Besides giving learners guided opportunities to practice concordance analysis, the activities presented aim at introducing them to the idea that there are typical ways of organizing language within particular genres, and that what makes them typical is largely reflected in repetitive use.

While this approach assumes that language production involves assembling prefabricated chunks rather than combining single words and morphemes, this does not however exclude choice and originality. When analyzing concordances, learners' interest may be stimulated not only by discovering typical structures and what chunks typically fit particular slots in these, but also by discovering what options those conventions leave open. Working with corpora should enable them to consider both what is conventional and what is unconventional, and what each implies.

It should be stressed that the activities outlined have the primary aim of teaching a methodology of corpus analysis, and guiding learners to appreciate its potential as a learning tool. The findings reported have no claim to being adequate as linguistic descriptions: they are simply conclusions which learners performing these activities found relevant. Any good grammar will say much more about the constraints on the use of adjectives than these learners were able to discover from the corpus of lonely hearts ads.

In order to progress from such partial findings to more general and reliable facts about the language, I have suggested that it may be useful for learners to compare the results of analyses of small homogeneous corpora with ones of larger and more heterogeneous ones. This does not however mean that findings from analyses of small corpora may not be of value to them - for instance, one student reported that studying the corpus of lonely hearts ads had helped her appreciate that the title of the film *Desperately seeking Susan* was an allusion to this genre.

Even if restricted in their descriptive potential, corpora such as those employed here nonetheless seem to offer several pedagogic advantages.

- Since the total quantity of text is relatively small, learners can easily become familiar with the entire corpus, relating frequency data to a known set of texts rather than to a statistical abstraction.
- Since the texts are similar and short, particular patterns can easily be related to particular positions and functions in those texts, encouraging learners to go beyond the immediate lexicogrammatical context in their analyses.
- Since the genre is a familiar and relatively standardized one, analyzing such a corpus can demonstrate that familiarity with a standard does not necessarily imply awareness of how this standard is constructed. Analyzing the lonely hearts ads, learners noticed a number of recurrent features which they had not previously thought of, for instance that *must* is used in descriptions of the sought, but not of the seeker, or that there are typical ways of organizing series of adjectives in these texts.
- Since the language of the corpus is 'easy', there is little problem in understanding particular texts and citations, allowing learners to focus their attention on the features these have in common. While a fair number of authentic instances may be required to observe recurrences

and identify typical patterns, these instances do not have to be 'difficult' in order to raise interesting questions. Data from small, single-genre, single-topic corpora seem particularly suitable to clarify the notions of recurrence and typicality, highlighting "the working of various types of speech behaviour as individual and social mechanisms in recurrent situations" (Firth 1937: 14), and facilitating the acquisition of those mechanisms as potentially productive communicative procedures.

The activities described aimed to help learners see how the analysis of corpus data can support intuition and memory in relation to features of language which are traditionally problematic, such as idiomatic and register-specific uses. Concordancing small specialized corpora provides a means to investigate many of these. Much work however remains to be done in identifying those areas in which concordance analysis is most effective as a learning tool, distinguishing between, for instance, its use in reception and production, and between conventional and creative behaviours. Not least, closer study of the appropriateness of particular data in relation to learners' own needs and purposes is essential if corpora are to fulfil their potential as instruments of autonomous learning.

Notes

1. In this paper I do not deal with the handling of specific software, which obviously needs to be taught if learners are to generate concordances for themselves, rather than using teacher-prepared printouts (cfr. Brodine, this volume, chapter 6: 3).

2. In the Letters corpus, <p> indicates the beginning of a new paragraph: in the Lonely Hearts Ads corpus, it indicates the beginning of a new advertisement.

3. Annotated corpora, in which more abstract grammatical and/or semantic information has been manually or automatically added to the words of the plain text, can facilitate this process by making it possible to retrieve occurrences of these more abstract features (see Garside et al. 1997; Partington, this volume, chapter 2: 3.2).

4. This is shown by the presence in the context of the word /INTERVIEW/, and of the tags <hl> and </hl>, indicating the beginning and end of a headline.

5. The adjective *good*, for instance, is very frequent in both corpora (it is the most frequent adjective in the letters, and the second-most in the lonely hearts ads, after *handsome*). The next most frequent adjectives in the letters (*old, better, best, sexual, long, normal*) are however all different from those in the lonely hearts ads (*attractive, pretty, tall, successful*). And while, in the lonely hearts ads, *good* mainly occurs in the phrases *good looking* and *good sense of humour*, its most frequent collocations in the letters are *good for you, in a good mood, a good idea, a good reason, a good relationship, good advice* and *good friend*.

6. Similarly, in an analysis of the collocations contained in the *Collins COBUILD English collocations on CD-ROM*, based on 200 million words from the Bank of English, Stubbs (1998) notes that the word 'seeks' shows a striking tendency, even in this large corpus, to occur in lonely hearts ads.

Appendix A: *handsome, good, attractive, pretty, successful, tall* and *beautiful* in the lonely hearts corpus

```
 1  ctive - a 34-year-old businessman, 5'11" tall.  Handsome,  athletic and trim. Enjoys rollerbladin
 2  conservative values - Police lieutenant, tall,  handsome,  educated, smart, honest, truly caring,
 3  , 35, (nonpracticing). Central NJ, 5'9", slim,  handsome,  extremely funny, sincere, romantic, cr
 4                            <p> Straight male, dark, handsome, fit, 27, new to North West would like
 5  der - Martial arts, funny, unique(!) 29, seeks  handsome,  generous soul mate. Note / photo. 8766
 6  h wit, charm and a zest for life. He is 40-45,  handsome,  healthy, wealthy and wise, with a str
 7  8", ready for marriage and family, seeks tall,  handsome,  highly successful, NYC-based male coun
 8  passionate, even-tempered, well- educated and   handsome.  I practiced law for ten years and am a
 9                                            <p>   Handsome   MD, 44 - Renaissance man, seeks slender
10              <p> Exceptional find - very         handsome,  successful, athletic, Jewish, 36, brig
11                                      <p>         handsome,  successful, executive - 42, brown hair
12  stic MD / inventor with a good sense of humor,  handsome,  tall, strong and gentle, hard body, 30
13                              <p>Herpes and       handsome   - Widowed businessman, young, 49 (6', 1
```

```
 1  I love travel, fine dining, theater,            good  entertainment and exotic cars. Who am
 2  <p> Catch of the year - If you believe all the  good  guys are taken - you just found one! Sensib
 3       <p> Divorced, young looking, 43 male,      good  job, own house / car, likes music, nights o
 4                                         <p>     Good  looking male, 28, would love to meet good l
 5                                         <p>     Good  looking, professional black male, 28, non s
 6  <p> Good looking male, 28, would love to meet   good  looking, non smoking female under 33 who is
 7  king, professional black male, 28, non smoker,  good  sense of humour, medium build, caring and u
 8  , seeks tall slim professional gent, must have  good  sense of humour, smoker, for long-lasting r
 9  n! A joyous, enthusiastic MD / inventor with a  good  sense of humor, handsome, tall, strong and
10  s, looking for a honest young lady 36/37, with  good  sense of humour. Ring voicebox: 0660 20562
```

1 dangerously sincere MD - 39, seeks future with **attractive**, accomplished Jewish man. 8790.
2 <p> She is 45, 5'4", Jewish, **attractive** - Blond, slim, incurably romantic, e
3 <p> **Attractive** divorced lady, young 45, many intere
4 <p> **Intelligent**, **attractive**, outgoing European lady, 40, USA cit
5 ion and friendship. Athletic, very intelligent, **attractive** professional, ivy educated, well-tra
6 man who would like to start a family. Please be **attractive**, sincere, intelligent. Most of all,
7 <p> **Classy**, **attractive**, **successful** - Lovely NJ widow; war,
8 woman who is not those, who is intelligent and **attractive**, who likes life both in and away fr
9 h a much younger outlook, would like to meet an **attractive** younger female for fun times. Ring v

1 <p> **Pretty** American woman, tall, slim, blonde, livin
2 <p> Special beginning - Extremely **pretty**, bright and passionate, L1 Jewish girl (3
3 n hair, blue eyes, athletic, seeks smart, very **pretty**, curvaceous woman for romance, adventure
4 and animals. Seeks best friend, 22-32, Jewish, **pretty**, mature,expressive and fun-loving. Please
5 - seeking bright, funny, outgoing, sane, very **pretty**, mellow, single female for partner on lif
6 <p> Very **pretty** passionate professional - Single white f
7 andlelight, plus various interests. Seeks very **pretty**, slender, warm and affectionate female (3
8 st. Seeking a warm, loving relationship with a **pretty**, slim, commitment-minded woman, 35-45, wh

1 and life's finer things. Be 50 plus, 6' plus, **successful**, affluent, confident, honorable, marr
2 Exceptional find - very handsome, **successful**, athletic, Jewish, 36, bright, fun, w
3 <p> **Handsome**, **successful**, executive - 42, brown hair, blue eye
4 <p> **Successful** investor looking for mate - I'm looki
5 <p> **Classy**, **attractive**, **successful** - Lovely NJ widow; war, secure, down-
6 rriage and family, seeks tall, handsome, highly **successful**, NYC-based male counterpart (40s). 86
7 e, hard body, 30s, passionate spirit, unusually **successful**. Seeks the joys of friendship and rom

5. The learner as researcher

```
1  for? A woman in her 20s to early 30s, somewhat tall - 5'7" to 5'11", who is strikingly beautifu
2  man, conservative values - Police lieutenant, tall, handsome, educated, smart, honest, truly c
3  le, 5'8", ready for marriage and family, seeks tall, handsome, highly successful, NYC-based mal
4  perspective - a 34-year-old businessman, 5'11" tall. handsome, athletic and trim. Enjoys roller
5  , young 45, many interests, smart dress, seeks tall slim professional gent, must have good sens
6             <p> Pretty American woman, tall, slim, blonde, living in Rome, seeks genero
7  inventor with a good sense of humor, handsome, tall, strong and gentle, hard body, 30s, passion

1  mewhat tall - 5'7" to 5'11", who is strikingly **beautiful** and is also in exceptional physical sh
2                     <p> **Beautiful** Asian body-builder - Martial arts, fun
3                     <p> **Beautiful**, dangerously sincere MD - 39, seeks fu
```

Appendix B: Concordances of *attractive*, *pretty* and *beautiful* from the letters corpus

```
 1   go back to her house for a little sex. She is attractive and smart but I hear many guys say th
 2   kid at school I really want to meet. He's very attractive and hasn't got a girlfriend, so far a
 3   p in the same room with her. At 39, she's very attractive and has no trouble picking up guys. I
 4             Dear Beth: I'm a 16-year-old, very attractive and popular girl. I've had a lot of b
 5             Dear Beth: I'm 19. I'm smart, attractive and have a great sense of humor. I am
 6   y disgusted with you. Drugs do not make people attractive, and your going with someone else beh
 7             Dear Beth: My son is a really nice, attractive but not very confident boy. He has re
 8   ng to get me to go to bed with her. I find her attractive, but she's my sister, sort of. Help m
 9   o raise her self-esteem. Assure her she's very attractive, but don't mention dating. Gradually
10                          PAUL     You sound attractive enough, but I suspect that you aren't
11   but don't know how to go about meeting young, attractive gay girls.      ALONE
12   ould be that some guys are intimidated by very attractive girls and don't show their feelings f
13   y mixed background keeps boys from finding her attractive. I am a young racially mixed guy and
14   to friends who get better marks, or seem more attractive, or more popular, etc. If the answer
15   r about yourself, and that makes everyone more attractive. So get busy on an exercise program,
16   boyfriend who's a really respectful friend and attractive, too.
17   duces your self-esteem. That makes people less attractive. Urge her to enjoy the friends she ha
18   the nice things you can think of that make her attractive. When she's ready to listen, explain
19   he dorm. Keep this up. Some girl who finds you attractive will prolong the conversation. Then i
20             Dear Beth:     I'm an attractive young lady. Not a lot of guys seem to
21   y in September. But the other day I met a very attractive young woman and I'm sexually attracte
```

5. The learner as researcher

```
 1  I like her. I wrote in her yearbook about how pretty she is. I asked when I could call her. I
 2  s kids think they should emulate adults. Being pretty and thin and having the right clothes ta
 4  they come to me to solve their problems! I'm a pretty girl with lots of friends, get good grad
 5       Dear Beth: My daughter is 14. She's a very pretty girl, but quite overweight. She won't li
 6  a support group for overweight teens. "Such A Pretty Face: Being Fat In America," by Marcia M
 7  because I was promoted twice. Friends say I'm pretty but none of the guys will go out with me
 8           Dear Beth: My girlfriend is very pretty, which of course I like, but it is a rea
 9  poke at you. But suppose you said, "You are so pretty. Your hair looks lovely and your comple
10  I don't. I'm unhappy. The problem is, I'm too pretty. Worse, I'm kind of shy, and other girls
11  Everyone thinks I've got it made because I am pretty. I don't. I'm unhappy. The problem is,
12  it. This girl knows I like her. She is really pretty. I asked her out once, but she said, "No
13  My daughter is 16. She is very bright and very pretty. Her only problem is that she has big hi
14  t's wrong with me. I'm nice, smart, funny and pretty.         CONFUSED AND MISSING OUT
```

```
 1       Dear Beth: We have an unusually mature and beautiful 11-year-old daughter. I don't allow h
 2  nsequences for the rest of that child's life. "Beautiful and well-behaved" is appropriate for
 3  ear Beth: My daughter is physically mature and beautiful and only 11 years old. I don't allow
 4              Your children might also be beautiful and well behaved if you had never spa
 5           Dear Beth: My college roommate is a beautiful and wonderful young woman. You wou
 6  g put down by the other kids. I'm not the most beautiful girl for 2 1/2 years. She caught me c
 7  f you can't share and enjoy it with others. My beautiful girl in school, but I'm not ugly, eit
 8  r penis: A cello doesn't necessarily make more beautiful home is a lonely place because I have
 9   son and 14-year-old daughter and they are now beautiful music than a violin; it depends on th
10              Dear Beth: There are two beautiful, well-behaved human beings. I agree t
11  wife's nose!" If people you love think you are beautiful women, Pam and Judy, in our town, and
12                                                 beautiful, you learn to think so too!    D.A.
```

6 INTEGRATING CORPUS WORK INTO AN ACADEMIC READING COURSE

Ruey Brodine

1. Introduction

In many courses of English for Academic Purposes, especially in foreign language settings, the top priority is to enable students to read in English for their other courses and in view of their future professional needs. In this chapter I examine ways in which work with corpora and concordances can contribute to a course of this kind by building up knowledge and skills in ways that support reading. As teachers, what we typically do with a resource (whether it is as familiar and low-tech as a blackboard, or as sophisticated as corpora and concordancing software), is to use our store of experience of teaching practices to devise and adapt ways to exploit it, bearing in mind a variety of factors such as the constraints of the setting, the learners' needs and expectations, the course objectives, as well as our own theoretical convictions and preferences. Using such 'teacher's reasoning', and taking examples from two commercially available corpora, *MicroConcord Corpus A* (newspaper texts: Murison-Bowie 1993b) and *Corpus B* (academic texts: Murison-Bowie 1993c), along with a third corpus consisting of the main documents in the course textbook (Haarman et al. 1988), I investigate ways in which concordance work can provide learners with

- a source of information about the language (including an awareness of typical lexicogrammatical patterns and other regularities);
- an opportunity to apply procedures which serve reading (such as using context to reduce ambiguity);
- an aid to memorizing this information and to internalizing these procedures.

The chapter is structured as follows. I first outline my theoretical perspective on reading, and relate this to some of the processes involved in using concordances (section 2). I next describe relevant features of the teaching situation I am concerned with (section 3). I examine in detail one particular issue - that of acquiring lexical knowledge - and its relation to ùconcordance work (section 4), as an illustration of the premises underlying a range of classroom activities to support learning in academic reading (section 5).

In order to clarify the central issues, the terms of the discussion are somewhat simplified. In particular:

- I treat reading as if it was separable from other abilities, focussing on a situation where English is learned for and largely *through* reading, instead of the more usual case in which reading is not the major component;
- I focus mainly on cognitive aspects of reading, rather than its role as a socially situated process;
- I focus on those types of knowledge which readers draw on to interpret 'local' rather than 'global' aspects of meaning in texts;
- I focus on features which would appear relevant to academic reading in general, rather than on features of specific fields, such as terminology.

I shall also not deal in any detail with problems of how to introduce concordances into the classroom - an area treated more fully in this volume by Zorzi (chapter 4) and Gavioli (chapter 5) - or how to individualize corpus-based work (Bernardini, chapter 9).

2. Reading as an interactive process

Reading theory and teaching practice have been strongly influenced in recent years by the idea that reading is 'interactive', a notion which has been interpreted from both social and psychological perspectives:

- it involves not "*reaction* to a text but [...] *interaction* between writer and reader mediated through the text" (Widdowson 1979: 174; his emphasis);
- it involves the interaction of different levels of processing and knowledge (Carrell et al. 1988; Grabe 1988).

It is this second sense which is more germane to our concerns here. 'Interactive models' see reading as a process which requires the reader to link many different kinds of knowledge, accessed in ways that are roughly classified as knowledge-driven, or 'top-down', and text-driven, or 'bottom-up':[1]

> Top-down processing is the making of predictions about the text based on prior experience or background knowledge, and then checking the text for

confirmation or refutation of those predictions. Bottom-up processing is decoding individual linguistic units (e.g. phonemes, graphemes, words) and building textual meaning from the smallest unit to the largest, and then modifying pre-existing background knowledge and current predictions on the basis of information encountered in the text.

(Carrell 1988: 101)

Originally developed to account for reading in the mother tongue (see, among others, Rumelhart 1977, Weber 1984), interactive models assume that "skills at all levels are interactively available to process and interpret the text" (Eskey and Grabe 1988: 224). It has taken some time for this view to penetrate the field of L2 reading, where all through the 1980s the psycholinguistic perspective prevailed (cfr. Bernhardt 1991). ESL/EFL instruction now typically includes activities designed to build top-down skills: to activate latent knowledge of the topic or the genre, to predict meaning at various levels and adjust predictions while proceeding in the text, to develop appropriate interpretative schemata, to check hypotheses of meaning and so on. Learners are often not very good at exploiting such skills without guidance, and training often brings rapid signs of improvement. In contrast, bottom-up skills (and the knowledge of lexis and grammar that supports them) develop more slowly, and yet they have often received less emphasis in teaching.

It makes sense to encourage learners to bring *all* relevant skills and knowledge to bear in the difficult task of getting meaning from texts. Eskey and Grabe recommend a double approach in teaching, with time devoted not only to top-down skills but also to

such relatively bottom-up concerns as the rapid and accurate identification of lexical and grammatical forms. Even students who have developed strong top-down skills in their native languages may not be able to transfer these high-level skills to a second language context until they have developed a stronger bottom-up foundation of basic identification skills.

(Eskey and Grabe 1988: 227)

At a university level, where learners' command of the L2 inevitably lags far behind their knowledge of the world, their cognitive abilities, and their reading proficiency in their own language, concordances offer one means of providing this stronger foundation. Paradigmatic areas where identification skills are often lacking involve features which facilitate production for learners, but conversely are troublesome for reception. For instance, the morphological simplicity of English and the correspondingly large numbers of polysemous items (e.g. *book* as a noun meaning 'volume'

6. Introducing corpus work into an academic reading course

and as a verb meaning 'reserve'; *-ing* forms: cfr. 5.2.1 below) can lead to difficulties in identifying word class, recognizing co-reference, interpreting syntactic relations and segmenting sentences (e.g. recognizing the boundaries of groups). To reduce ambiguity in these areas, learners need to learn to exploit clues in the immediate context.[2]

Reading concordances requires basic identification skills and the exploitation of the immediate context to arrive at local meanings, just as reading texts does. However, it does not require the same attention to global meanings. I hope to show how this selective focus can promote reflection on features of texts that are relevant to bottom-up processing, developing knowledge and skills in this area. The underlying assumption is that learners may need to deal with the complexity of reading by focussing in turn on different aspects of the process and of the text itself. If learners deal with a limited number of problems at a time, focussing alternately - for instance - on top-down and bottom-up aspects, this may help them develop and become aware of metalinguistic and metacognitive strategies that can facilitate the reading process. For instance, initial contacts with a complex text may include skimming to facilitate global predictions, and/or scanning to locate specific information for limited decoding. Subsequent activities may focus on features such as cohesive reference, connectors and implicit logical links, rhetorical conventions and the identification of clues to the text structure or to writer attitude. Work with concordances can contribute to construct such a shifting focus, which may help learners realize that for comprehension of a difficult text, several re-readings are usually better than a single slow, painstaking deciphering chore, and that comprehension is not the same thing as mental translation into the mother tongue.

3. The setting and the students

In many courses of English for Academic Purposes, the primary concern is that students should acquire the ability to read academic texts, and resources are deployed in such a way as to stress reception rather than production. The intermediate-level course I refer to here is taught in a Political Science faculty in Italy, where students' fields of specialization vary - economics, history, public administration, sociology, and communication studies - a broad range which makes precise assessment of their language needs difficult. The design of the course has involved various radical choices, with an emphasis on written academic varieties relating to the social sciences, and a very limited oral component (lessons are conducted partly in Italian if the class cannot handle them in English).

The chosen textbook, *Reading Skills for the Social Sciences* (Haarman et al. 1988, hereafter *RSSS*), is one of the few reading textbooks designed to be used as a principal coursebook and not simply as supplementary material. The (debatable) decision to forego the learning potential of oral interaction and of students' desire to speak the language has determined a clear focus on meaning rather than form in order to foster motivation and interest.

In evaluating the potential of concordance work in this context, the following additional factors appear relevant:

- Few technological aids are available. There are no classroom computers or data-display facilities, and no laboratories in which students can use computers on a self-access basis. Consequently concordances can only be presented as printed handouts or OHP transparencies.
- Students have the same mother tongue. As the teachers are native speakers of British and American English who also speak Italian, this facilitates a contrastive perspective with the students' L1.
- While students come from a wide variety of backgrounds, it is generally the case that:
  - They are unsophisticated about language and language learning in general. They often believe that reading is translation or that what they need to improve their reading ability is a better mastery of explicit grammar. Greater awareness of the *range* of the knowledge drawn on in reading, at local and wider levels, may help them make fuller strategic use of it.
  - Their knowledge of English can be very limited. In such cases their lack of lexis and grammar makes academic reading laborious, highlighting the need for supplementary activities. While the work they do on assigned texts aims at fairly thorough, non-reductive comprehension, the linguistic difficulties encountered may well prevent them from learning as much from their reading as their more competent classmates.
  - Few are interested in achieving native-like ability in production. Thus most are not primarily concerned with avoiding errors or inappropriacies in speaking and writing.
  - With the exception of grammar, most do not consider explicit linguistic descriptions important. They have little interest in learning *about* the language, except where this clearly helps them to read more effectively.
  - Their lack of basic grammatical concepts and of metalanguage,

even relating to their first language, makes it difficult for them to elicit the explanations they need. They can gain from a recognition that formulating suitable questions about language and texts - whether addressed to themselves, their teachers or to their various resources - need not hinge on elaborate metalanguage.

4. Concordances and reading: acquiring and interpreting lexis

If the major course objective is improving the students' ability to read academic texts, what sort of input is called for, and how - besides through the actual reading of texts - is it best provided? On the basis of the outline of the reading process provided in section 2 above, I underlined the importance of bottom-up as well as top-down skills, along with the knowledge on which they are based, and suggested that concordance work might provide a means of focussing on these. I also suggested that the use of a variety of activities dealing with different aspects of the reading process might help develop metacognitive and metalinguistic abilities which can facilitate the interactive process. I now turn to examine some ways in which concordance work might develop the kinds of knowledge and skills needed by learners such as those just described, taking as an example the area of lexis.

4.1 Reading and lexical knowledge

Although all theoretical models of reading acknowledge the importance of lexical knowledge, interactive models consider it a prerequisite to fluent reading skills (Eskey and Grabe 1988: 226). According to one estimate, learners who read well in their first language need to know about 3,000 word-families in the foreign language in order to be able to transfer their reading skills effectively (Laufer 1992). Nagy and Herman (1987) argue that writers of academic and professional texts assume that their readers have a vocabulary of over 40,000. Two less daunting estimates are that the 2,000 most frequent words account for 80% of the words in a typical ninth-grade level text (Coady et al. 1993: 219), and that a knowledge of the 500 most frequent words - and their typical contexts of occurrence - permits comprehension of 75% of language in use (Sinclair 1996c).

Sinclair's qualification suggests that numbers do not tell the whole story. Broadly speaking, lexical knowledge has two facets: how many words are known, and what is known about those words. Compared with written dictionaries, the mental lexicon "contains far, far more information about each entry" (Aitchison 1994: 13), and learners too need more lexical knowledge than they can find in dictionaries, and more, for that matter, than they can be explicitly taught. Goodfellow, for instance, argues that computer-aided vocabulary-building materials based on mnemonic techniques are too simplistic to be effective because

> the ways words function to represent meaning, e.g. by denotation, by collocation, as sense relations, by extension, as metaphor, are too complex. Word meanings are not autonomous static data - they depend on interaction within a context.
>
> (Goodfellow 1994: 53)

But how many of the ways in which words represent meaning are relevant for reading? Meara (1993) points out that while you might pick up the idea that *burgle* "has something to do with stealing things from somewhere", to *use* it correctly you need to know the answers to questions like these:

> Can you *burgle* a person, or somebody's wallet? Can you *burgle* an idea? If you take something from a shop without paying for it, have you *burgled*? What exactly is the difference between *burgle*, and other words you might know with a similar meaning like *shoplift*, *loot*, *pinch*, *mug*, *embezzle*, *hold up* and so on.
>
> (Meara 1993: 15)

From the viewpoint of production, knowing a lexical item involves knowing "the range of words with which a lexical item can occur", and "the syntactic patterns into which each word can slot" (Aitchison 1994: 14). And yet for the reader there may well be many cases in which it is enough to know that *burgle* "has something to do with stealing things from somewhere", or that an adjective's connotations are positive (*sound*, *tasty*, *nimble*, *snug*, *deft*, *lush*) or negative (*faulty*, *awkward*, *loathsome*, *harsh*, *ill*, *shoddy*). And in any case, partial or approximate knowledge is better than none (Aston 1995b). Remembering the class of a word or its general semantic area can be one step towards a hypothesis of meaning, and hence a step towards a more adequate knowledge of how a word is actually used.

The view that partial knowledge, rather than simply being a shortcoming, is the terrain in which more complete and complex knowledge may take root, has important implications. The ability to capitalize on partial knowledge is one which native speakers and expert non-natives regularly make use of, and which learners need. It is an ability, however, which needs to be built up, by working on lexical items in context. It is this possibility which perhaps most clearly distinguishes relatively decontextualized vocabulary-building and work starting from texts. But if an ability to capitalize on partial knowledge may help the learner, the inherent vagueness of lexical meaning represents an additional difficulty:

> There are a small number of words such as *square* or *bachelor* which appear to have a fixed meaning; that is, they are words for which we can specify a set of necessary and sufficient conditions. The majority of words, however, do not behave in this way. They suffer from one or more of the following problems: first, it may be difficult to specify a hard core of meaning at all. Second, it may be impossible to tell where 'true meaning' ends and encyclopedic knowledge begins. Third, the words may have 'fuzzy boundaries', in that there may be no clear point at which the meaning of one word ends and another begins. Fourth, a single word may apply to a 'family' of items which all overlap in meaning but do not share any one common characteristic.
> (Aitchison 1994: 48-49)

One of the principal ways in which language users, learners and native speakers alike, compensate, in reception, for the natural fuzziness of words in use, the high proportion of polysemous items, and the shortcomings of their own lexicon is by exploiting information in the immediate context.

4.2 Chunks, chunking, and concordances

Much of the concordance work presented elsewhere in this volume is aimed at improving learners' production by making it more native-like (cfr. Gavioli, chapter 5: 4; Zanettin, chapter 7: 4; Bertaccini and Aston, chapter 8: 3). Not all such work is relevant to the requirements of those learners who primarily need to read effectively. For instance, a concern with production might counsel comparing the environments of semantically-related lexical items - e.g. *big/large/great* - to help the learner know when to select each. A concern with reading might instead counsel comparing environments of a polysemous item or homograph - e.g. *sound* as a noun, verb or adjective - to help the learner find the necessary clues in the immediate context to assign the right meaning.

The process of using the immediate context to find clues to meaning can be considered from two perspectives. When words are viewed across a range of occurrences, their typical collocations and colligations, their status as components of fixed and semi-fixed expressions, idioms, and other pre-assembled chunks (cfr. Bolinger 1975; Gavioli, this volume, chapter 5: 2.1) constitute things to know *about* them. As elements in particular texts, however, words need to be seen in terms of knowing *how to* deal with them, of the procedures to use when they are encountered. A term which

1   stood as referring to this law. And so it is possible in these few words to dism
2   Over the top, I hear you say, and so it is _ splendidly over the top and a mom
3   in order to see if, over a month or so, it is going up, down or staying the same
4   has already allowed the child to do so. It is saying too little in that to ask f
5   as fought <i> seventeen duels </i> (so it is said). </qt> Tailhade, who was then
6   how cytoplasm can form muscle. Even so, it is a very impressive example of the r

Figure 1. The word sequence *so it is*

is relevant to both these perspectives is *chunk*, in its twin senses as a noun and a verb. On the one hand, we are concerned with knowing which words go together as chunks (remaining conveniently vague as to the exact nature of their relationship - cognitive, textual, etc.). On the other hand, we are concerned with chunking as a mental process of "grouping items in a text into meaningful patterns" (Coady 1993: 12). Both types of knowledge are indispensable to effective reading, and in practice must interact. Thus to make sense of the words "so it is" in the concordance lines in Figure 1, the reader must be able to chunk them appropriately. S/he may be assisted by the familiarity of particular chunks ('it is possible', 'a month or so', 'to do so', 'even so'), as well as by the writer's chunking device, punctuation.[3]

The use of such concordances can consequently be seen as having three main functions:

- *providing lexical information* (e.g. which chunks recur frequently). Such concordances are a convenient tool for examining the local environment of lexical items with the aim of making and testing hypotheses regarding their recurrent uses, and hence of learning *about* them.
- *developing procedures to interpret lexis* (e.g. the ability to chunk text quickly, effectively and appropriately). While in the usual reading process, attention needs to be principally engaged by global meanings and can be guided 'top-down' by the overall context, concordances focus attention on local meaning, thereby engaging bottom-up procedures that utilize clues in the immediate context to reduce lexical ambiguity, guess the meaning of unknown items, and identify the boundaries of chunks. They hence provide opportunities for learning *how to* deal with lexis.
- *helping to memorize this information and to internalize these procedures*. Insofar as the various lines provide a series of partially analogous local contexts, they provide a degree of focussed repetition which may facilitate the memorization of information and the consolidation of interpretative procedures.

4.2.1 *Providing lexical information*
Among the kinds of knowledge relevant to the bottom-up processing of local meanings is a familiarity with frequently used lexicogrammatical patterns. Here I shall touch on this function of concordance work only briefly: Partington (this volume, chapter 3) illustrates the wide range of information concerning such patterns which concordances can provide - information which is not always readily available in dictionaries or other

reference works. Familiarity with such patternings makes for more effective reading, since recognizing a chunk is quicker and easier than recognizing each component word of the chunk. Recognizing the first part of a pattern makes the rest more predictable: portions of text such as *no sooner said than ...* or *visible to the naked ...* leave little doubt as to the next word. Likewise, patternings in the immediate context may make it easier to distinguish between words which look similar (*though*, *through* and *tough*), but whose collocations and colligations differ.

"Semantic prosodies" (Sinclair 1987b; Partington, this volume, chapter 3: 4) are a particularly clear illustration of how familiarity with recurrent patterns can help predict meaning: the favourable or unfavourable connotation of an element acquired 'by contagion' from its typical collocates entails that the presence of that element can be used to predict the presence of meanings associated with those collocates. Competent language users often draw on this knowledge without being fully conscious of it (e.g. things that *set in* tend to be unpleasant, although intuitively the phrasal verb itself probably seems neutral: Sinclair 1991a). Learners often have difficulty determining subtly signalled attitudes in texts, and may find a contrastive perspective an aid in seeing that differences in connotation can be as important as differences in denotation in creating 'false friends' (Partington 1995).

4.2.2 *Developing procedures to interpret lexis*

The role of the linguistic environment in attributing meaning to an element of a text is especially clear in two areas that I have already mentioned as posing problems for learners: guessing the meaning of unknown items and interpreting polysemous ones. Because learners will inevitably encounter unknown low-frequency words, learning to exploit the context effectively in guessing has come to be regarded as one of the main reading strategies that should be taught (Dubin and Olshtain 1993: 181). What is less often stressed is that because most words are polysemous or fuzzy in meaning, readers are continually required to reduce their ambiguity on the basis of the context of use, and learners need strategies for doing this as well.

Selecting or guessing an item's meaning typically entails restricting the range of possibilities. Disambiguating a polysemous item involves selecting the correct meaning from a limited set, exploiting a context which - if competently written - has been constructed in such a way as to minimise ambiguity (and hence processing difficulty) for the target audience. Guessing the meaning of an unknown item, too, involves a search for clues in the context, but the solution may lie in a far wider array of possibilities. Moreover, readers who have less knowledge of the language,

```
1   business'? Plausible as this may sound, the proposition is flawed; the
2   s if we were committing one. The sound of my father's voice had the unex
3   e bone which in lizards conducts sound from the eardrum to the inner ear
4   slate information in the form of sound waves in the air into patterns
5   er. The fact that this rule is a sound, valid or sensible rule is a r
6   ged in consensually by adults of sound mind, and there was a brief dis
```

Figure 2. Interpreting lexis: *sound*

culture and subject matter than the intended reader may have difficulty locating sufficient clues to identify the meaning of unknown or polysemous items. And a wrong guess can be worse than no guess at all: mistaken hypotheses of meaning, if they go uncorrected, can create more serious problems of misinterpretation than the unknown word which the reader chooses to ignore as of marginal importance. This makes effective hypothesis-checking strategies especially critical when a reader has less knowledge than is presumed of the target audience.

Competent readers, on the other hand, carry out most of the necessary operations in reducing ambiguity without much conscious thought, distinguishing quite easily between key elements and redundant ones requiring only cursory attention. Even the limited context in the concordance lines in Figure 2 provides enough information to decide promptly whether *sound* is a verb, a head noun or a modifier. The local context is also adequate to identify the right sense in the three cases that *sound* is used as a modifier: namely, 'noise' (line 4), 'good judgment' (5), and 'good condition' (6) (to use the guide words in the respective entries in the *Cambridge International Dictionary of English*: CIDE 1995). The competent reader is assisted by such familiar chunks as *sound waves* (4: a hypothesis confirmed by *in the air*), *sound of* [someone's] *voice* (2), *of sound mind* (6), *sound* + [noun entailing judgement, e.g. argument, advice, rule] (5: confirmed by the semantically related adjectives *valid* and *sensible*), and [adjective] *as* [something] *may sound* (1). In all these examples the reader can select the correct meaning of *sound* without misreadings or undue effort.[4]

How are learners to learn to recognize and exploit contextual clues? Activities in which learners group concordance citations according to different meanings of an item can cultivate procedures for making distinctions like the ones noted in the *sound* concordance, and build up the knowledge that they rely on. Nation and Coady (1988: 104-105) outline a five-step strategy for guessing from context which includes identification of the part of speech of the unknown word, examination of its immediate and its wider context, formulation of a hypothesis as to meaning, and checking of that hypothesis. Among the clues which can lead to hypotheses of meaning, Nattinger (1988: 63) identifies grammatical structure, topic, and discourse features such as parallelism, anaphora, and redundancy (including relations such as synonymy, antonymy, cause and effect, association between an object and its purpose or use, description and example). All of these seem likely to be available in the limited contexts provided by concordance data: Huckin and Bloch (1993: 175) found that in 70% of cases where learners successfully exploited context in guessing, the principal type of clue they used was some word located in the same sentence. Thus the concordance of *sound* (Figure 2) revealed such helpful discourse features as the series of near-synonyms *sound, valid or sensible* (line 5), the contrastive structure *Plausible as this may sound, the proposition is flawed* (1), and the object-function association in *bone which [...] conducts sound from the ear-drum to the inner ear* (3). Even topic can often be inferred from a concordance line, as in the case of *sound waves* (4: cfr. note 4). And to note just one of the ways in which grammatical structure cues interpretation, in *the sound of my father's voice* (2), *sound* fills a slot for a noun. Examples of other relations mentioned by Nattinger will be seen in 5.3.1 below.

Nation and Coady (1988) provide a further reminder that interpretative procedures, linguistic knowledge, background knowledge and global comprehension work together, synergically. Successful guessing requires

> firstly that the learners are able to follow the ideas in the text they are reading, that is, that they have sufficient command of vocabulary, grammar and reading skills in order to achieve basic comprehension of the text, and secondly that the learners bring some relevant background knowledge to the text.
>
> (Nation and Coady 1988: 104-105)

Competent exploitation of context means combining elements which, taken singly, would not be enough to understand a word, but which together solve the problem adequately. And being able to classify a word - say *robes* or *rags* - syntactically (e.g. as a plural noun), and to categorize it semantically at the levels of denotation (e.g. as clothing) and connotation (positive or negative) is sometimes adequate to reach a precise enough meaning for some reading purposes, and to support hypothesis-checking.

Concordances in which the search word has been blanked out (Stevens 1991, Murison-Bowie 1993a, Johns 1997) can provide linguistic problem-solving activities which give the learner an opportunity to practice observing contexts and reinforce other skills that aid disambiguation and guessing. In them the learner needs to exploit whatever clues the verbal environment offers to formulate hypotheses as to the meaning of the missing item, just as when guessing an unrecognized word. They make the item's wider context unavailable, but they provide more than one example of local patterning to examine critically, first to trigger the guess and then to test the hypothesis. How many lines does the reader need to guess the word that has been omitted in the concordance in Figure 3?

To identify the word, the competent reader will presumably pick up

152   Ruey Brodine

```
1   sonal finances, according to an _____ poll, writes Leonard Doyle. His comm
2   hern Ireland, in the considered _____ of the august assessors from the RIB
3   years ago. <p> Biggs is of the _____ that Mason would be unlikely to surv
4   nly way I could show that in my _____ they were absolutely wrong was to st
5   the game, Henderson has a high _____ of himself, and thrives on psycholog
6   has served to polarise popular _____ on modern architecture. Richard Roge
7   avis, has been seeking a second _____ on the knee injury that forced him o
8   world is not based on a public _____ poll but purely on my own feelings .
9   n them feel moved to express an _____, either positive or negative. We cont
10  reat opportunity to turn public _____ against Salman Rushdie, an Islamic s
11  said that, contrary to popular _____, traumas caused by such a disaster we
```

Figure 3. Guessing the missing word

```
1   are few patterns as varied and _____ as those made by the feathers of
2   e and active lives, Rachel was _____ but Liah was the fertile one. Gre
3   hio </i> , Trimalchio having a _____ clock in his dining room. Neverth
4   Harold Owen makes clear in his _____ evocation of those golden weeks:
5   e things and expressed them in _____ language. <p> Clement combined hi
6   ust do not feel up to it? Your _____ scheme is ruined. You let things
7   did not seem to appreciate the _____ simplicity of his achievement, an
8   nce on plasmids can be seen as _____ supporting evidence for the conje
```

Figure 4. A more difficult word to guess

collocations to the right and left of the missing word: *an* ____ *poll; in the considered* ____ *of* [someone]; [to be] *of the* ____ *that; in my* ____ *; has a high* ____ *of himself,* etc. Learners will probably have to look harder to find familiar chunks or patterns, but they should be able to locate clues such as the article *an* (indicating that the missing word starts with a vowel sound: lines 1, 9), the two cases of *popular* immediately to the left (6, 11), the recurrences of *poll* (1, 8) and *on* + [noun group] (6, 7) immediately to the right. They might notice that in the two cases preceded by *public,* the missing word is a modifier (8) and the head (10). This search for clues to support interpretation is a more conscious version of the flexible sort of processing that effective readers carry out fairly automatically as they read.

However the next concordance (Figure 4) shows that not all contexts provide the basis for a confident hypothesis as to the word that has been omitted. The contexts suggest an adjective with positive meaning, but it is difficult - especially when the lines are considered singly - to come up with the missing word, *beautiful.* Whether 'positive adjective' is a close enough guess in an actual reading assignment will depend on the text itself and on the reader's purposes. In the concordance in Figure 5, it is again difficult to identify the missing item, but not to narrow down the range of possible meanings. The missing word is clearly an intensifier, and for comprehension, that is probably close enough. Identifying which one - *utterly* - is irrelevant to reception. While the degree to which the context supports guessing may vary considerably, so may the degree of precision required in any given reading situation.

Concordance-based activities combine reading and the acquisition of the knowledge which effective readers possess. The learner practices observing local contexts and picking out relevant elements, and encounters both familiar patterns and chunks and new ones. Such activities thus link chunking and recognizing recurrent chunks. They also sharpen the learner's awareness that a word can have multiple meanings, that local contexts play a vital part in distinguishing between them, and that hypotheses of meaning need to be checked.

4.2.3 Memorizing information and internalizing procedures
Learners not only have the problem of discovering facts about the language: they must also remember them. As well as engaging particular bottom-up procedures on a one-off basis, they must also consolidate them as skills. It seems likely that memorization can be aided by concordance work in various ways. Take, for instance, the principled guessing of meaning of unknown words (like guessing blanked-out items in a series of citations). While it can be argued that

```
1 _____ is a great responsibility to be _____ honest about the experience of war bec
2 _____ ir Master by failing to see how _____ new his message was. He therefore set
3 _____ police, which would have been _____ unacceptable in the climate of early n
```

Figure 5. Guessing the category of the missing word

> the very redundancy of information in a given context which enables a reader to successfully guess an unknown word also predicts that same reader is less likely to learn the word because he or she was able to comprehend the text without knowing the word
>
> (Coady 1993: 18)

this effect may be offset when the guessing process involves greater effort. Citing Craik and Lockhart's (1972) research, Nattinger stresses that

> There is a tight relationship between 'cognitive depth' and retention. What this means is that the more we actively work out a solution to a problem (the more commitment we make to the task of learning something, that is), then the more likely we are of storing this information permanently.
>
> (Nattinger 1988: 65)

Further variables which may contribute to memorization are saliency (cfr. Brown 1993) and frequency (Eskey and Grabe 1988: 228). While saliency in a text depends on the centrality of the item to global meaning, a concordance highlights the item's relationship to the local context, providing multiple instances in a form which gives salience to recurrent patternings. Concordances also increase the number of occurrences of the item which learners encounter, as well as exposing them to related expressions that they might not otherwise meet in their normal reading. From all of these perspectives concordance work seems likely to aid not only the discovery and effective use, but also the retention of lexical knowledge. Similarly, the fact that reading concordance lines will tend to repeatedly engage particular procedures seems likely to consolidate them as effective skills.

5. Using concordances to exploit and extend reading activities

Following this mainly theoretical discussion of the possible functions of concordance work on the level of lexis, I now return to the specific practical teaching situation described in section 3 above, extending these functional distinctions to other linguistic levels. A product of 'teacher's reasoning', the concordance-based activities to be described here aim to provide relevant information about the language, to build up procedures for observing and interpreting text, and to facilitate retention of this knowledge and consolidation of these skills, for these students in this setting. Although particular examples may highlight one or another of these functions, they are in practice inseparable: while looking to concordance lines for information, users employ procedures to observe and interpret them, thereby increasing the likelihood that both the information and the procedures will be available for future use. These examples should not therefore be interpreted as vocabulary-building exercises in a narrow sense, nor as operations in language description, but rather as activities designed to help learners build up and flexibly draw on different resources while reading.

Concordancing software blindly finds and displays all the occurrences of a particular string in a corpus: indeed, it may supply too many, or provide an unpredictable mixture, including ones which are irrelevant to the problem at hand. Examining the question of what data to give learners, Zorzi (this volume, chapter 4: 3.1) distinguishes between unedited, unsorted concordances (where users may have to select occurrences that suit their research question and disregard others), and ones which are filtered by the teacher through (a) preliminary editing to adjust the amount of context or to eliminate difficult, irrelevant or repetitive cases, and/or (b) sorting to group instances which share particular patterns. Gavioli (this volume, chapter 5: 2.3), who draws a distinction between "samples" (raw data) and "examples" (specially selected illustrative cases), stresses that filtering concordances may have its costs, deleting data which might be found significant, reducing information on frequency, and encouraging particular interpretations at the expense of others which may be equally valid. Most of the concordances reproduced here have been edited, both in order to provide examples which fit the pedagogic objectives and give an appropriate amount of context, and in order to avoid taking up undue space on overhead projector slides, student handouts, and the pages of this volume. Some have additionally been sorted in order to highlight patterns preceding or following the search word.

The activities outlined in 5.1 and 5.2 below start from reading passages taken from the students' textbook (Haarman et al. 1988: *RSSS*). The first example (5.1.1) shows how a specific problem of semi-specialized lexis, the use of *price* in economics texts, can be associated with a more general problem for readers, that of determining the boundaries and structure of a complex noun group. The next example (5.1.2) looks at the apparently unproblematic item *known as* (used in the passage to introduce a technical term), to show how concordances can provide 'parallel passages' in which to investigate such functions as definition, and to develop procedures for resolving problems of cohesive reference. The final section (5.1.3) offers some ideas for additional work on lexis.

The activities based on the second passage examine a specific grammatical feature in the passage (present participial post-nominal modifiers: 5.2.1), going on to the more general problem of distinguishing between the many functions of *-ing* forms (5.2.2).

The activities in 5.3 instead start from an extract from the *MicroConcord corpus B* of academic texts (Murison-Bowie 1993c), to investigate the use of the general noun *problem* in 'problem-solution' structures of discourse organization (Hoey 1983, 1994), and to develop procedures for identifying 'problems' and 'solutions' in texts.

5.1 Starting from lexis

The extract below is the first part of a 400-word passage used as a gap-filling exercise in a unit in *RSSS* dealing with reading economics textbooks. The gaps are selected to call attention to specific features of academic texts, such as the use of 'matching relations' in lexis (e.g. *prices/wages* or *rise/fall*: Hoey 1983) and syntactic parallelism (e.g. *organizing output/keeping markets responsive to people's tastes*). In the textbook, the words to be used in filling the gaps (underlined in the passage below) are listed above the passage, along with their word class.

> *Prices and Inflation*
> The third major macro-economic objective is to ensure *price stability with free markets*. Price stability means that prices neither <u>rise</u> nor fall too rapidly; that the rate of inflation (measured as the rate of change of prices from one period to the next) be close to zero. The desire to maintain 'free markets' is based on the political judgment in the United States that prices and <u>wages</u> be set in decentralized private markets or bargaining rather than by government fiat. The desire for this form of organization is based on the economic judgment that free-market-determined prices are an efficient way of organizing <u>output</u> and keeping markets responsive to people's tastes.
> The most common way to measure the <u>overall</u> price level is the *consumer price index*, popularly known as the *CPI*.
> (Haarman et al. 1988: 27: italics in the original)

5.1.1 *Noun groups with* price
Price is clearly a key word in this text, both in terms of frequency (it occurs once every 43 words in the full passage) and centrality to the global meaning. It belongs to one of the most problematic categories of lexis for ESP and EAP students, namely, a general word which is used in a special way in the genre (Mparutsa et al. 1991), appearing as a component of two complex noun groups (*price stability*, *consumer price index*) that are treated as technical terms and are explained in the passage.

```
1   tries, or during times of wartime price controls in market economies. A frozen p
2   l price level is the <i> consumer price index </i>, popularly known as the <i> CP
3   t avoid hyperinflation, where the price level rises a thousand or a million perc
4   common way to measure the overall price level is the <i> consumer price index </i
5   pical urban consumer. The overall price level is often denoted by the letter <i>
6   rate of growth or decline of the price level, say, from one year to the next. <
7   ent in 1947. <p> The objective of price stability with free markets is more subt
8   stability with free markets </i>. Price stability means that prices neither rise
9   onomic objective is to ensure <i> price stability with free markets </i>. Price s
10  ols in market economies. A frozen price structure would prevent the <i> invisibl
```

Figure 6. *price* in the original text

```
1   ical process is probably too steep a price to continue paying for that privilege
2   into everyone's living room, but the price the American public has had to pay in
3   for example, evading tax may be the price for business survival; competition fr
```

Figure 7. *price* in the main documents in *RSSS*

Students on the course often have difficulty in decoding complex noun groups. This is particularly so when the group contains nouns as modifiers, and/or when there is no clear indication (such as a determiner) of where the group begins. In the absence of clear syntactic marking, a great deal of expert knowledge can be required: analyzing the sentence from a science textbook *Lung cancer death rates are clearly associated with increased smoking*, Halliday (1988: 176) points out the potential ambiguity of *lung cancer death rates*: is it how quickly lungs die from cancer, how many people die from cancer of the lung, or how quickly people die if they have it?

Given the frequency of *price* in the full text, a first concordance can be generated of only these examples (Figure 6). Sorted by the first word to the right of *price*, it shows that *price* here is invariably a modifier, though not always the first word in the noun group. It thus confronts the reader with the problem of looking to the left and right to identify the boundaries of the group. While these noun groups are shorter than many found in academic texts, they still display a variety of relationships between components: e.g. *wartime price controls* (controls during wartime on prices: line 1), *consumer price index* (index of prices paid by consumers: 2), and *overall price level* (overall level of prices: 4, 5).

A larger corpus can provide further practice in identifying and interpreting noun groups that include *price*. A concordance from the business section of *MicroConcord Corpus A* (totalling approximately 200,000 words: Murison-Bowie 1993b) includes *offer price, issue price, cash price, market price, sale price, share price, purchase price, takeover price*, as well as *price cuts, price drop, price control, price tag*. Provided learners are made aware that the business pages of a newspaper may not be strictly comparable with academic prose, this seems an acceptable way to expand the problem beyond the original text.

By contrast, a concordance of *price* compiled from the main documents in *RSSS* yields a very different picture (Figure 7). It occurs only 3 times in 14,000 words, always in a metaphorical sense, and never as a modifier in a noun group. Although the inexpert reader might not easily notice without guidance, this tiny sampling is enough to suggest that when *price* collocates with *pay*, the meaning is often metaphorical - a suggestion which can be followed up by examining a concordance of forms of *pay* in the context of *price* in a different corpus.

5.1.2 Known as: *providing terminology*
The concordances of *price* provided starting points for lexical and

grammatical reflections. Other expressions can occasion work focussing on discourse-related features. A concordance of *known as* in RSSS reveals its frequent use in academic texts as a marker of definitions and reformulations, in such patterns as *also known as, become/come to be known as, better/commonly known as*. The concordance below has been edited to include only a sampling of these uses, providing a series of short parallel passages with cohesive reference involving the expressions underlined:

1. People in Britain spend about £20bn a year using plastic cards. The processing of <u>these transactions</u> on behalf of shops - **known as** 'merchant acquisition' in banking jargon - is worth no less than £400m annually.
2. Marx and Engels argue that we must understand ideas as products of people engaged in this natural process and see the production of ideas as an aspect of the general enterprise of making a living from nature. <u>This</u> is the position **known as** materialism; it is opposed to idealism which, in a broad sense, sees the basis of human existence as abstract spiritual concepts whose origin cannot be explained by natural circumstances.
3. The occasion-setting procedure involves explicit discrimination training; in <u>the procedure</u> **known as** feature-positive training, for instance, the subject experiences reinforced trials in the presence of the occasion setter and nonreinforced trials in its absence.
4. And, of course, talk of cost must never overlook <u>what</u> are **known as** opportunity costs: time, effort, and money spent on one thing necessarily means a lost opportunity to spend them on something else, which may be of just as much value.

This concordance illustrates some of the problems that may have to be solved in order to ascertain what is *known as* what. In line 1, readers must be able to interpret the anaphoric noun group *these transactions* as the credit card spending referred to in the previous sentence. Line 2 illustrates a familiar pattern of academic discourse in which a term (*materialism*) is not only defined but also contrasted with a related term (*idealism*). In lines 3 and 4, the relevant information for interpreting the reference items follows rather than precedes it, in patterns that, though frequent, may not be quite the sort of cataphoric reference exemplified in textbooks. The problem in line 3 is one of putting together several relevant pieces of information: the scenario of *feature-positive training* and the fact that this is an instance of *explicit discrimination training*. In line 4, *opportunity costs* is interpretable on the basis of the explanation which follows, namely, that *time, effort, and money spent on one thing necessarily means a lost opportunity to spend them on something else*.

Why should concordances be used to create decontextualized examples of reference problems in discourse when learners can encounter all kinds of contextualized instances in their assigned reading materials? One reason is that juxtaposing instances in brief, judiciously selected parallel passages makes it easier to see both regularities and a range of variability. Within this environment of similarity and difference, learners can note how different types of knowledge and different procedures are involved in reading - being brought into play not discretely, but interacting with each other.

A next step might be to examine further examples so as to correct excessively reductive generalizations. Students can be shown that *known as* is not the only way terminology can be introduced (e.g. by examining a concordance of *called*), and that it also has other functions, such as that of specifying nicknames (line 1 below), reasons for fame (2), reputation (3), identity (4):

1   [...] the received view of Haydn as a benign old man in a white wig, universally **known as** "Papa" and naughtily given to inserting loud bangs in quiet passages to wake his audiences up?
2   Perhaps best **known as** the scene of Jack the Ripper's murders, it was developed as an early eighteenth-century city suburb [...]
3   His successor, although by no means **known as** a reformer, has so far shown that he is prepared to introduce an element of glasnost.
4   What business is it of the State if someone now wishes to be **known as** a woman, where previously she was considered a man?

By initially narrowing the focus of this activity to cases where *known as* introduces terminology, I am not saying that other means of performing this function and other uses of *known as* are unrelated, or not useful for learners to know. Rather, I am once again using 'teacher's reasoning' to eliminate examples that might distract students from what I have chosen as the initial focus. Subsequently, the range of investigation can be expanded as appropriate.

5.1.3 *Further lexical tasks*
Even after completing and correcting the "Prices and inflation" gap-filling exercise in *RSSS*, less proficient students still find the lexis of this densely technical text problematic. And yet it is very difficult to find appropriate supplementary materials for these students: materials on the market which are easy enough for them are usually based on oral language, and therefore unsuitable for their needs. Concordances offer a means of providing further work relating to some of these problems.

- Distinguishing, on the basis of context, between homographs belonging to different word classes, e.g. *price, rise, fall, rate, change, desire, form, tastes, level, close*. While relatively easy, this does not mean that such a task is unproductive. Effective readers make such discriminations rapidly and virtually automatically, and learners need to see that some meanings are quickly accessible.
- Distinguishing between different senses of polysemous words, e.g. the various uses of the verb *set*. Learners might be asked to find L1 equivalents in each case, using a dictionary as necessary. Although they may need to be dissuaded from considering mental translation a comprehension strategy for full texts, translating chunks involving different senses can foster awareness of the distinctive patterns associated with different uses in each language.
- Distinguishing the contexts of easily-confused expressions, such as false friends. To help Italian learners remember that *major* (unlike *maggiore*, which means 'greater/larger') is not comparative, they can be given a blanked-out concordance in which they must select the lines in which the blanked-out word is *major* and those in which it is *larger* or *greater*.

5.2 Starting from grammar

Students often have trouble grasping syntax. Lacking the metalanguage to make their linguistic reasoning explicit or to elicit appropriate grammatical information, they may assume the solution is learning explicit grammar rules. Concordances can show them that learning a syntactic rule or regularity is not dependent on having the metalanguage to express it.

5.2.1 -ing *forms*

A case in point is the present participial post-nominal modifier, as exemplified by the italicized expressions in the following passage from *RSSS*:

> The wide range of activities in the shadow economy can be divided into two broad categories. There are monetary transactions concealed to avoid tax - people *doing* odd jobs for cash payment, a businessman *failing* to declare part of his turnover, and so forth - which, following popular usage, we have called the 'black economy.' Then there is a wide range of productive activities which do not involve monetary payment - housework, DIY, voluntary work - which we have simply called the 'wider shadow economy.'
> (Stephen Smith, "The other economy", *New Society*, 17 October 1986)

Such post-nominal uses, which receive scant treatment in learner grammars (Biber, Conrad and Reppen 1994), are often problematic for these students, in whose native Italian present participles are rarely used in this manner.

A search for *ing in the 14,000-word *RSSS* corpus yields 18 occurrences of this use. In the (edited) concordance below the post-modified nominal group is italicized:

1   kinds of business most involved in the black economy are likely to be *smaller businesses **selling** labour-intensive services to private households and individuals* - building, decorating, cab driving

2   But the kind of tableau much favored by U.S. media consultants - *the candidate apparently **chatting** with ordinary voters in the marketplace* - turns up in German sports too. In fact, Penniman and

3   The students were asked to read a fictitious passage which described *a New Zealand airliner **crashing** en route to the South Pole*. There were 264 passengers on board, representing 21 nationalities.

4   centuries. 1924 is not a good place at which to stop, because *the most dramatic changes **resulting** from the Bolshevik takeover* - the social and economic transformation of Russia undertaken by Stalin

5   book on experimental psychology or studied the subject, and they completed *a questionnaire **consisting** of 21 questions*, each of which embodied a principle related to the working of the memory.

Providing a grammatical explanation that accounts adequately for these cases would intimidate many a teacher, let alone learners.[5] Rather than learning an explicit rule, it may be more useful for readers simply to be aware that this form occurs frequently in English, with a range of different meanings as to tense. They also need to encounter it often enough to be able to recognize it, identifying the head noun - with or without premodifiers - and the participial clause with all its complements. Asking learners to identify these elements obliges them to contend with the boundaries of syntactic groups within the sentence.

5.2.2 Grammatical polysemy
The 18 post-nominal participial uses are only a small proportion of the 319 occurrences of *-ing* forms in *RSSS*. A much more frequent problem for these readers may be distinguishing between different functions of the *-ing* form, as can be seen from the concordance of *-ing* in Figure 8. This is taken from an early unit of *RSSS* (34 occurrences in 870 words: a very frequent form indeed). Rather than applying categories and labels from standard metalanguage, learners can be asked to devise groupings of their own, and to discuss the criteria adopted. In this manner, there are no single

```
1   ed a poster which read 'earn $5 by answering 21 questions about behaviour'' in a
2   eading (an optimum level of stress being necessary for successful learning), or
3   and a theoretical explanation. <t> Eating people is wrong </t> Attitudes to the R
4   sis o their own common sense. This finding that most hard-won psychological kno
5   ess being necessary for successful learning), or that teaching the children to r
6   ived remedial teaching improved in reading accuracy. No group improved in readin
7   worked against any improvement in reading (an optimum level of stress being nec
8   at this was an effect of increased reading practice. <p> The authors suggest tha
9   ing accuracy. No group improved in reading speed - and this even <I> decreased <
10  ne of two control groups had daily reading tests (as did the three experimental
11  d the attention they gave to their reading. <p> So while relaxation may be of ge
12  ress seems to be less helpful than reducing its cause - failure.
13  tice. <p> The authors suggest that reducing stress may have worked against any i
14  axation may be of general benefit, reducing the symptoms of stress seems to be l
15  here were 264 passengers on board, representing 21 nationalities. When the rescu
16  dramatically immediately after the shooting down of the Korean civilian airliner
17  kely to eat human flesh before the shooting down of the airliner, but jumped to
18  aining; and the third had remedial teaching based on phonics and comprehension.
19  group which had received remedial teaching improved in reading accuracy. No gro
20  their learning can be improved by teaching relaxation. <p> This study involved
21  elped more by them to read than by teaching them to relax, according to Christop
22  ; the second was given relaxation training; and the third had remedial teaching
```

Figure 8. Distinguishing the function of *-ing* forms in a unit of *RSSS*

correct answers, only more or less convincing arguments as to how instances may reasonably be grouped (Zorzi, this volume, chapter 4: 2).

This kind of activity is best done sorting instances on-screen, but it can still be done using printouts cut up into separate lines for learners to arrange into groups. Learners should not have trouble seeing similarities between *after the shooting down of the Korean civilian airliner* (16) and *before the shooting down of the airliner* (17), with a high proportion of identical or related words. Can they also link the cases where the *-ing* form is the object of a preposition, or perhaps group together the ones where it is preceded by *by*? Can they see the pattern linking *improved in reading accuracy* (6) and *improved in reading speed* (3), and distinguish it from *any improvement in reading* (7)?

An activity of this kind is highly flexible. Classification and discussion need not continue until all cases are fully accounted for. If desired, the concordance can be edited to reduce the range of functions represented, limiting it to those which students are most familiar with or which the teacher wants to focus on. And the teacher can use her discretion as to just how much metalanguage to introduce - for instance terminology that will help students to use their dictionaries more effectively.

5.3   Starting from discourse: the 'problem-solution' pattern

The activities discussed so far all start from reading materials in the textbook, using corpora as sources of parallel examples. However, corpora can themselves be a source of reading materials for learners: for instance, the following extract was selected from a concordance of the word *problem* from *MicroConcord Corpus B* (Murison-Bowie 1993c). It was chosen to illustrate a particularly common rhetorical pattern in academic texts, that of 'problem-solution' (Hoey 1983, 1994), in order to investigate the linguistic features associated with it and to develop procedures for their interpretation.

> Unfortunately, slow music and fast music altered how they performed the tests so music is now forbidden during testing sessions. *Another problem* is that the tests show practice effects; that is, for the first day or so of testing, subjects' performances improve greatly (and so mask any daily rhythms) as they are getting used to the tests and are developing their personal ways of tackling them. To counteract *this problem*, subjects are given sufficient practice tests before the experiment to ensure that this effect has worn off.

Like concordance citations, this incomplete extract provides only local contextual clues to assist interpretation. Readers may feel handicapped by the lack of an explicit topic and of information provided earlier in the text (such as the referent for *they* in the first sentence), but various types of knowledge interact to trigger and confirm hypotheses which can compensate for the missing information. There are enough local clues to suggest that the topic is the reliability of experimental research procedures, that *they* refers to the subjects whose performances were being measured, and so on. That the passage discusses problems is clear from the referential noun groups *another problem* and *this problem*, and the 'problem-solution' pattern is also signalled in other ways. Thus in the first sentence, with the cue *unfortunately*, alteration in the way subjects performed the tests can be identified as a problem, and music as the cause of that problem; *so*, signalling consequence, indicates that forbidding music during testing sessions is to be interpreted as the solution. For the problem referred to in the final sentence, we again have adequate clues to realize that the great improvement of subjects' performances is - positively-connotated lexical choices notwithstanding - another problem, something that masks information which is significant.

5.3.1 *Posing 'the problem'*

Extending the investigation of *problem* to *MicroConcord Corpus B* yields a lengthy concordance, sorted in Figure 9 according to the first and second words to the left. Even after being edited to about 15% of its original size to reduce repetitions, obscure cases, and the range of issues raised, it offers a great deal of further information as to the way problems are written about.

A variety of patterns involving the word *problem* can be observed here. In some cases there is simply a variant of "*x* is a/the problem", "the problem is *x*", or "there is a problem". Other cases can instead be classified according to the semantics and grammar of particular collocates. Verbs, for instance, may express:

- the occurrence of problems: e.g. they *exist*, *emerge*, *arise*, etc.;
- their source: situations may *give rise to* or *lead to* them;
- typical things that are done to them, at various stages of problem-solving: problems are *posed* and *raised*, upon which they may be *approached*, *addressed*, *tackled* and *dealt with*, in the course of which they may be *examined*, *studied*, *analysed* and *discussed*, and - if *ways out* are found - they are ultimately *solved*, *resolved*, *settled*, *corrected*, *eliminated*, or at least *alleviated*: otherwise, they *remain* or are *left unanswered*;
- preclusion: problems can also be *avoided* or at least *denied*.

6. Introducing corpus work into an academic reading course

```
 1  t abolish the effect. What remains a    problem  is to explain why exposure to the c
 2  ind. <p> Self-cutting is sometimes a    problem  in impatient psychiatric units, esp
 3  Thus, a reasonable goal related to a    problem  of boredom in an adolescent because
 4  8.4. <p> This result raises another     problem. In the absence of the second wave,
 5  method of attacking and studying any    problem  in architectural design which may b
 6  <p> In each of these cases the basic    problem  is the same: a will has been made,
 7  s control these changes is a central    problem. <p> The changes are not due to alt
 8  79 onwards. It also posed a delicate    problem  for the Home Secretary himself, sin
 9  insouciant attitude to the economic     problem, arguing at one stage that there sh
10  ce-Hall (1980) model faces a further    problem  in attempting to deal with contextu
11  ine its retrievability. <p> A futher    problem  arises from the fact that the exper
12  developing world, the global-warming    problem  will never be solved. Consider Chin
13  main source of the greenhouse-effect   problem. <hd> 15.7 Conclusion </hd>.
14  ical language, there is an important   problem  here: namely, how is it that Conser
15  of course, is tackle the inner-city    problem  nor indeed is it designed to do s
16  views. But neutral or not, the main    problem  is to find any reason for supportin
17  act was necessary. Liz felt the main   problem  was finding a way to talk to her pa
18  heir toxicity. Resistance is a major   problem, particularly in countries where th
19  . But at this juncture another major   problem  emerges, in that it is very difficu
20  ison. There seems to be virtually no   problem  of sexually transmitted infection a
21  evelopment gave rise to a perplexing   problem. For Zarathustra had spoken of the
22  orities. Unemployment is a political   problem, as is a worsening balance of trade
23  t concerned with an urgent practical   problem  which has to be settled one way or
24  h. That there is a real and pressing   problem  was made clear by that case. What w
25  were simply left aside. <p> The real   problem  here, then, is the use of the word
26  e from emotional bias, when the real   problem, that of marriage, is considered. S
27  zed 'rustic' masses posed no serious   problem  except the pastoral one of how to i
28  is no denying that this is a severe    problem. But it must be addressed. Let me r
29  m has been defined as a major social   problem. It has attracted not only widespre
30  sisted that he wished to tackle some   problem  in his home yet arranged to go out
31  anything provided you set about the    problem  in the right way. It is not necessa
32  contemplating it. First of all, the    problem  exists of determining whether in fa
33  it was believed, would alleviate the   problem. <pb n=29> <p> The Finlay Committee
```

```
34  If the therapist had approached the problem in this way she may well have avoid
35  government censorship to correct    the problem. Senator René Bérenger was to bring
36  rate this approach by discussing    the problem of how animals find their way about
37  governed by A), thus eliminating    the problem identified with the between-subject
38  writer who has recently examined    the problem has considered that in nature it mu
39  arge." A comprehensive review of    the problem of attempted suicide and its manage
40  nd ideas. <p> Another way out of    the problem of fraud could be to require from
41  orly developed made him aware of    the problem of setting up too rigid a sequence
42  ed with an infuriating denial of    the problem, 'Just look at our figures. We have
43  ed in terms of the dimensions of    the problem being dealt with. <p> What, then,
44  onstituted a breach of duty. <p>    The problem is best analysed in the following s
45  n the experimental protocol. <p>    The problem is to decide what such an influence
46  ual conviction". For their part,    the problem faced by the proponents of epigenes
47  heir condition, continue to pose    the problem of euthanasia. The appropriate resp
48  formation. <p> Patterning poses    the problem of how the cells know what to do, h
49  can turn blue, or white, or red.    The problem is to generate a pattern that looks
50  care of that, but there remained    the problem of infection in the population at l
51  was Palm Sunday. <p> To resolve    the problem of Easter and other points of disp
52  i> Écuyère </i> ''and so resolve    the problem he had first posed in the 'Missing
53  soner's Dilemma type situations.    The problem does not arise merely through lack
54  e. How is a land animal to solve    the problem of acquiring oxygen without losing
55  ine, and the best way of solving    the problem is to apply some local anaesthetic
56  es too late adequately to tackle    the problem. It is unlikely that the continuous
57  al children and this can lead to    the problem of bedwetting. <p> What all this wo
58  tructure. This leaves unanswered    the problem of how and why the ancestral struct
59  the War Office for dealing with    the problem of sexually transmitted diseases, t
60  esigns shown in Table 5.1 avoid this problem. <p> The first of these designs was
61  s turn comes. The resolution of this problem is interesting and is worth discuss
62  deteriorating, but perennial, urban problem rapidly became the most acute aspec
63  warfare agents once again an urgent problem. In Britain, and later in the Unite
64  to be slow. If you have had a weight problem for a long time, do not expect a mi
```

Figure 9. *problem* in *MicroConcord Corpus B* (edited)

Noun groups with *problem* as the headword may include adjectives expressing:

- evaluation of the importance or gravity of the problem, by means of a qualifying adjective: it can be *central, delicate, major, perplexing, pressing, real, serious, severe, urgent*, and the like;
- specification of the general type or area of the problem, by means of a classifying adjective: *social, urban, economic*, and the like.

Assertions of the lack of problems may be hedged: *seems to be virtually no problem of ...* (20); *posed no serious problem except ...* (27).

From a procedural perspective, these categories can be linked to an investigation aimed at helping learners predict where they are likely to find certain sorts of information in the context of *problem*, beginning with the very rough distinction of what tends to come to the left or right of it. Some regularities - e.g. that attributive adjectives precede the noun, while relative clauses and participial post-nominal modifiers follow it - are determined by English word order. And word order, as an indicator of syntactic relations, is an area in which awareness of typical patterns can be as useful as explicit rules.

The data in the concordance suggest a variety of other generalizations. For instance, forms of *be* and other linking verbs can occur on either side of *problem*, since the latter can be a subject (e.g. 6, 16) or complement (7, 18). Existential intransitive verbs with *problem* as subject, such as *arise* (11), *emerge* (19), and *exist* (32), typically come to the right. The position of other verbs depends mainly on whether they are active (left) or passive (right), with the systematic exception of full or reduced relative clauses: *problem which has to be settled* (23), *the problem being dealt with* (43), *the problem he had first posed* (52). Obvious as these observations may appear, the operations involved in identifying and interpreting the various semantic and grammatical roles associated with *problem* can be anything but obvious for learners, especially in complex text.

Questions aimed at a fuller understanding of the 'problem-solution' pattern can lead to further interesting concordance work. In a text, a problem is what the writer calls a problem and wants the reader, too, to see as a problem. What is it in such cases that allows the competent reader to identify an element in the immediate context as a problem? Examination of the concordance lines reveals that although there is no single answer to this question, in a surprising number of cases it is possible to guess quite confidently that certain elements are in fact part of a specification of the problem. Even if brief contexts like the following leave some doubt as to its nature, we can confidently predict that the problem is in each case explained by the text to the right of *problem*:

6   the basic **problem** is the same: a will has been made,
25 The real **problem** here, then, is the use of the word
41 made him aware of the **problem** of setting up too rigid a sequence

The reader clearly draws on a broad range of types of knowledge to achieve even partial understanding in such cases: it may be the negatively connoted language to signal that there is a problem (*too rigid*: 41), or the use of routine lexicogrammatical patterns (*the basic/real problem is ...*: 6, 25). Learners can be asked to examine the full concordance to look for regularities of this type. For instance, we find that the nature of the problem may be indicated by:

- a noun modifier preceding *problem*: *global-warming problem* (12), *greenhouse-effect problem* (13), *inner-city problem* (15), *weight problem* (64).
- *the problem of* + [noun group]: *boredom* (3), *attempted suicide* (39), *fraud* (40), *euthanasia* (47), *bedwetting* (57), *sexually transmitted infection/diseases* (20, 59);
- *the problem of* + [noun clause]: *setting up too rigid a sequence* (41), [explaining/understanding] *how the cells know what to do* (48) (i.e. how to do something); *acquiring oxygen without losing ...* (54) (i.e. how not to do something).
- *the problem is* + [gerund or *to* + infinitive], where the non-finite clause expresses something difficult to do: *What remains a problem is to explain why exposure to ...* (1); *Liz felt the main problem was finding a way to talk to her ...* (17), *The problem is to generate a pattern that ...* (49).
- apposition, with *namely* and/or a colon, indicating that the problem is what follows: *the basic problem is the same: ...* (6); *there is an important problem here: namely, how is it that ...* (14).

When looking for such regularities, the reader also needs to be able to weed out cases that only apparently follow the pattern. While *the problem is to ...* is a commonly used way of specifying a problem, it must not be confused with constructions like *the best way of solving the problem is to apply some local anaesthetic* (55), where what follows is not a specification

6. Introducing corpus work into an academic reading course 171

of the problem, but its solution. Such analyses require students to focus on meaning, and not simply work mechanically.

6. Conclusions

6.1 Summing up the activities

This chapter began with a discussion of the sort of work which might be specifically appropriate to the needs of readers in an EAP setting. Recapitulating, those needs include:

- Knowledge of a wide range of lexis and lexicogrammatical patterns belonging to registers and genres that will be read, and the ability to recall them when needed. This knowledge will vary from the vague and incomplete to an increasingly rich mixture of more precise meanings, with a sense of what is typical and frequent, awareness of typical collocations, colligations, semantic prosodies, etc.
- Procedures for getting meaning from text, e.g. recognizing and capitalizing on relevant contextual clues to 'chunk' the input and reduce ambiguity, making plausible hypotheses as to the meanings of polysemous or unknown elements, and to the roles and relationships of different words and chunks.

The proposals for concordance work outlined as possible responses to those needs can be summarized as follows:

- Activities aimed at developing lexicogrammatical knowledge and bottom-up processing skills, with attention to
  - knowledge that helps readers resolve lexical and syntactic ambiguity (polysemous elements such as *-ing* forms; segmentation of complex noun groups);
  - typical collocations and recurrent chunks (*problem*, *price*);
  - markers of roles and relationships of textual elements (*known as*, cohesive reference).

  Analogous activities might focus on other accepted points in reading instruction, such as word formation and linkers.
- Activities aimed at increasing awareness of the range of types of knowledge drawn on in reading and the strategic use of context.
- Activities aimed at encouraging reflection on ways of classifying instances and ways of asking relevant questions about them, as well as of relating these to information in dictionaries.

In all of these areas, these proposals aim to complement and extend existing tasks and materials in an integrated and flexible fashion.

6.2 Concordances and teachers' choices

Teachers' first steps in using concordances are likely to be cautious, probably involving activities on paper rather than online. The work I describe is cautious enough to be used in this way, allowing the teacher to control the situation as she investigates the potential strengths and limits of the tool. Edited printouts of concordances can provide transitional material for learner and teacher, groundwork for subsequent activities in which learners follow up features more independently, and in which teachers experiment with less controlled applications. Learners and teachers alike need to get a sense of the rationale behind concordance use and to learn by steps what can be looked for in a concordance or a corpus, developing suitable procedures for doing so, in ways that Zorzi (this volume, chapter 4) and Gavioli (chapter 5) discuss in detail. And common sense suggests that the less language the learners know, the less sophisticated they are as linguists, and the less experience they and their teachers have had with concordances, the more carefully their first contacts need to be planned. As in every other area of teaching, we are continually called on to decide what is most relevant, interesting and productive to make the learning setting more efficient and less frustrating for the learner.

Two aspects of concordance work that have not been addressed here are how to differentiate between what is likely to be easy or difficult for learners, and how to meet the differing priorities of learners with different levels of competence. These are both crucial matters: when learners can't read the concordances, they can't carry out the procedures; what is relevant to one learner's needs may be an old story or a baffling subtlety to another. Some strategies to help learners whose basic knowledge of English is limited - the ones who most need extra work beyond what their textbook provides - can however be derived from familiar ways of helping low-level readers deal with authentic materials (yet another reminder that solutions to problems arising from new technology are often already available in established teaching practices: cfr. Aston, this volume, chapter 1: 3.1).

- *Select simple materials.* The obvious way is to select the concordance lines themselves, limiting the number of lines and eliminating irrelevant difficulties (cfr. Zorzi, this volume, chapter 4: 3.1.2). Increasing the context size may also help support comprehension. Another way is to select an easy corpus (cfr. Gavioli, this volume, chapter 5: 5), though this may mean settling for different registers or

genres from the ones learners will eventually have to deal with. Yet another way is to use concordances based on texts which students have already read (Seidlhofer 2000). Concordances based on the textbook, introduced halfway through their course, gives them the chance both to revise previously-encountered cases and to anticipate ones they will encounter in the future.
- *Provide guidance.* Lead full-class discussion, provide help on demand, have students pool their knowledge in pairs or small groups, and the like. Sort concordances to facilitate observation of particular patterns.
- *Simplify the task.* Choose an activity that requires less precise comprehension, tolerating more approximate knowledge. Some categorization activities (semantic fields, connotations, word classes) may work even when comprehension is only partial. Avoid asking learners to look for information in concordances which is not relevant to their present learning needs: some types of knowledge seem less germane to learners' earliest approaches to academic reading, including much of the 'core' grammar and lexis of everyday life at the heart of general courses, many explicit grammar rules, and other knowledge which is more relevant to production than reception (knowledge of what to avoid, constraints of register, etc.).

Most of the activities described in this chapter are based on edited concordances. However, it is worth noting that even though filtered by the teacher, they can still allow for fairly open-ended activities. If learners attempt to discover what a number of concordance lines have in common, or how they could be grouped, they can often arrive at observations of their own that had not occurred to the teacher. And where edited data leaves issues hanging, there is nothing to prevent the use of unfiltered data and/or other corpora to test hypotheses further (cfr. Gavioli, this volume, chapter 5: 3.2). Of course, concordances that have been edited and sorted to the point that they lead only to well-defined questions and unproblematic answers will do little to encourage learners to adopt a "research perspective" of the kind that Gavioli proposes (cfr. Johns 1991a). Such concordances can become very like display questions to which the teacher already knows the answer, and being designed to suit the group, they may not meet individual learning needs. Ultimately, the right mixture of guidance and freedom depends on the teacher's preferences and the students' response, with some sort of negotiation to find an acceptable match between the two. Not everyone - teachers *or* students - will find relatively unguided concordance work equally stimulating and worthwhile.

There is also the question of cultural background. Might such work, for instance, seem less valuable to some learners whose traditions tend to discount data-based approaches? Concordance work seems potentially able to enhance many of the characteristics of the 'good language learner' (see R. Ellis 1994: 546-550 for a review): attention to the formal properties of the target language, attention to meaning, the ability to switch flexibly to and fro in attending to meaning and form, active involvement in the language learning process, and perhaps also awareness of the learning process, with the capacity to use "metalingual strategies, [i.e.] higher order executive skills that may entail planning for, monitoring, or evaluating the success of a learning activity" (O'Malley and Chamot 1990: 44). But adapting innovations appropriately is a task that requires tact, perceptiveness and sensitivity to a host of variables in the setting. It is because the teacher plays such a central role in the success or failure of such adaptations that I have tried to weave a thread of personal choices through this chapter - choices which might not be everybody's.

I hope that some of what I have said will sound familiar, and sound like common sense. One of my intentions has been to show how we teachers put together our knowledge and insights to solve problems, and incorporate new ideas and new technology into our teaching practices. We are in some ways in a privileged position, since we can cull the literature for ideas that fit our current notions of teaching and learning, and apply them without having to take sides in current debates. Thus, to experiment with concordances we need not take a precise stand on what sort of models of reading and learning to espouse.

There are however some teaching experiences from which we cannot turn back, because they allow us to see things we hadn't seen before, or hadn't seen so clearly: they permanently alter our vision of classroom reality. It may well be that concordance work is such an experience. Whether or not they stimulate our interest in language descriptions, corpora give us a view of the language that is simply not accessible through our own intuitions or through someone else's description. They offer learners the same opportunity, though their experiences will not be identical to ours. The opportunities for discovery, and the energy which springs from discovery, can continue as long as we maintain our research perspective, our curiosity towards the data and our involvement in what we teach.

Notes

1. In an influential discussion of the role of mental models in reading, Sanford and Garrod (1981) make a similar distinction between "concept-driven" and "data-driven" cognitive processes. The data-driven mode (sometimes also called input-constrained processing) makes use of information which is available locally, typically in the current sentence. Concept-driven processing, instead, draws on the reader's background schemata:

   First, schemata provide the basis for 'filling the gaps' in a text: no message is ever completely explicit, and schemata permit a coherent interpretation through inferential elaboration. Second, schemata constrain a reader's interpretation of an ambiguous message [...]. Third, it is by establishing a correspondence between things known, as represented by schemata, and the givens in a message that readers monitor their comprehension and know whether they have understood the text.
   (Steffensen and Joag-Dev 1984: 54)

2. Although it is convenient to treat 'receptive' and 'productive' as a dichotomy here, the distinction is simplistic, and fails to take into account - for instance - features of words such as spelling, pronunciation (Stoller and Grabe 1993) and even phonological processing (Bernhardt 1991) that were once considered relevant only to production, but have been shown to influence word recognition.

3. Concordances from the *MicroConcord* corpora (Murison-Bowie 1993b, 1993c) include the following tags:

\<hd\> \</hd\>	beginning, end of heading
\<i\> \</i\>	beginning, end of italics
\<p\>	new paragraph
\<qt\> \</qt\>	beginning, end of quotation
\<t\> \</t\>	beginning, end of title

4. Despite my declared aim to focus on 'bottom-up' processing, it is virtually impossible to rule out recourse to background knowledge in making interpretations and drawing conclusions about meanings even with just one line of text. In the concordance of *sound* (Figure 2), understanding of lines 3 and 4 seems - in practice if not in theory - inseparable from their identification as belonging to a scientific or technical register, with a series of predictions on the basis of this background knowledge. When the wider context is not available, or not considered, bottom-up information thus may trigger 'top-down' interpretations, yet another confirmation that many kinds and levels of knowledge interact in reading.

5. And, to judge from the evidence, even some grammarians. To state that "a present participle clause can be used directly after a noun to indicate that something is doing something" (Cobuild 1990: 134) hardly accounts for "a questionnaire consisting of 21 questions" in line 5 of this concordance. Greenbaum and Quirk (1990), who deal with the form more fully, explain that in "The man *writing the obituaries* is my friend", the italicized modifier could, depending on the context, be equivalent to any of the following: *who + writes/is writing/was writing/will write/will be writing*. They also note that "not all *-ing* forms correspond to progressive forms in relative clauses. Stative verbs, which cannot have the progressive in the finite verb phrase, can appear in participial form" (1990: 372).

However, even locating the relevant information in a reference grammar may require too much metalinguistic knowledge and indeed perseverance for some learners. The appropriate information in Greenbaum and Quirk is the eighth out of nine undifferentiated section references to *-ing* in the index.

7 SWIMMING IN WORDS: CORPORA, TRANSLATION, AND LANGUAGE LEARNING

Federico Zanettin

1. Introduction

Translation can be a means of helping learners to improve their reading and writing skills, as well as of increasing their cross-cultural and cross-linguistic awareness. Translation consists of interpreting a discourse in the language of the source text, and then re-interpreting it by creating another discourse in the language of the target text. By recasting discourse A as discourse B, the translator manipulates language to a meaningful end, transforming a text originally created to fulfil a particular communicative function in a particular context into another whose function and context are somewhat different. Seen from this perspective, translating between languages is in principle no different from translating from one language variety or register to another: all involve a shift in perspective and in recipient design (for further discussion see Newmark 1988, 1991; Snell-Hornby 1988; Hatim and Mason 1990; Bassnett and Lefevere 1990; Gentzler 1993; Chesterman 1997; Nord 1997).

In reading a text in the L1 and trying to formulate a suitable 'equivalent' in the L2, or viceversa, learners have to strive to find the most appropriate words for the new audience. This is not simply a matter of terminological accuracy, but involves comparing higher-level cultural codes and their conceptual and rhetorical structures. Corpora containing texts in two languages which are similar in subject and purpose not only allow for contrastive analysis of individual expressions. They also provide a mapping of the structures and strategies employed by the two language communities for "building discourse in different linguistic and socio-cultural settings" (Marmaridou 1990: 564). This paper illustrates the use in a translation task of such 'comparable corpora' - two collections of texts, one in L1 another in L2, selected on the basis of such similarities and stored on computer.

I am distinguishing here between 'comparable' and 'parallel' corpora, two terms which overlap in much of the literature. The term 'parallel corpus' is generally used to designate a collection of texts in language A and of their translations into language B (see for example Leech and Fligelstone 1992; Baker 1995; Marinai et al. 1991). The best known such collection is probably the proceedings of the Canadian Parliament (Hansard), which are published in both French and English (the original text may be in either language).[1] Corpora of this kind are generally *aligned* on a sentence-by-sentence or phrase-by-phrase basis, either through reference to a bilingual dictionary (Picchi 1991), through statistical elaboration (Langé and Bonnet 1994), or a combination of the two (Johansson et al. 1996), so that instances of any textual string can be retrieved along with its translational equivalents in the parallel text. Such corpora have been extensively used as a basis for the creation of bi- or multilingual terminology databases and thesauri, and for developing machine translation software.[2] The term 'parallel corpora' has also been used, however, to refer to collections of texts which are not translations of each other, but are simply selected on the basis of analogous sampling criteria. These may either be taken from different varieties of the same language, such as the Brown and LOB corpora, respectively of American and British English, and the various components of the ICE corpus, taken from a range of geographical varieties (Leech and Fallon 1992; Greenbaum 1992; cfr. Partington, this volume, chapter 2: 3.1), or else from similar varieties of different languages, for instance laws in French and Danish (Dryberg and Tournay 1990), service encounters in English and Italian (Gavioli and Mansfield 1990), public signs from various English- and German-speaking countries (Snell-Hornby 1984). It is this latter type that I refer to as 'comparable' corpora.[3]

In this chapter I discuss the basic operations necessary to create and use small comparable corpora as translation aids, and suggest ways in which the procedures involved may contribute to language learning. The data reported derives from an experiment where Italian undergraduates were asked to produce an English translation of an Italian newspaper article. The objective was to write a text which would sound as if it had been taken from a British newspaper, with the aid of a corpus of comparable English and Italian newspaper texts and concordancing software. While in this case the translation was from the students' native language (Italian) into a foreign language (English), the methodology would seem equally appropriate to translation into the mother tongue.

The original Italian text and one student's translation of it are shown in Figure 1. In what follows, I illustrate the main steps which led up to the translation. I hope to show how by comparing features in the two corpora which are similar formally but may differ functionally (false friends, loan words, near synonyms, metaphorical expressions, etc.), and by comparing segments of text which are functionally similar but may differ in their formal realizations (propositional and rhetorical structures, contextualizing

7. *Swimming in words: corpora, translation, and language learning* 179

IN VASCA

Sorvegliato speciale è Matt Biondi, che cerca di vincere l'oro per la terza volta consecutiva ai Giochi, sul gradino più alto del podio ben cinque volte nell'edizione '88. Si esibisce nei 50 e 100 stile libero, oltre che nella 4x100 stile libero. Re del mezzofondo è l'australiano Kieren Perkins, primatista mondiale dei 400, 800 e 1.500 stile libero.

SWIMMING

Matt Biondi, the defending champion, will be trying to win gold in his third successive Olympic Games. After gaining no less than five gold medals in 1988, this time he is back to contest the 50 and 100m freestyle, and 4x100m freestyle. Kieren Perkins of Australia, the world record holder for the 400m, 800m, and 1,500m freestyle, is top performer over the longer distances.

Figure 1. The source text and its corpus-aided translation

information, logical connectors, terminology, etc.), this student was not only able to enhance the specific translation, but was also provided with a wide range of learning opportunities. It should be stressed that while the final product was written individually, much of the research using the corpus was carried out in groups.

2. Making comparable corpora

Some of the most readily available sources of computerized text are newspapers, many of which are now published on the Internet, or commercialized on CD-ROM at an affordable price. A CD-ROM usually contains up to a year of issues (8 to 10 million words of text) from which selections can be downloaded to the user's hard disk. While not all CD-ROMs and online newspaper services use the same search and retrieval software, there is a tendency to standardization and some basic operations are common to most of them. Any user (teacher or learner) who is computer/network-literate should be capable of creating collections of text from these sources.

The criteria for selecting the texts to be included in comparable corpora depend on the uses to which these are to be put. If, for example, we want to investigate the use of high-frequency words which supposedly serve similar functions in the two languages, then probably any collection of roughly similar materials will do. If, on the other hand, the purpose is to investigate how two different cultures treat a particular topic within a particular domain and/or genre, then the selection must target for that topic, domain and genre. For the activity discussed here, the aim was to create two corpora regarding one event (the 1992 Olympic Games), from one domain/genre (the sports sections of newspapers), drawing on CD-ROMs of *The Daily Telegraph*, *The Independent* and the Italian *Il Sole-24 Ore* for 1992.

To retrieve articles from a newspaper CD-ROM, it is generally enough to specify keywords (a keyword being a string of characters, which may include wildcard characters such as * or ?). A first search was run using the keywords *olympic** and *olimp** in the English and Italian data respectively. This however found quite a few articles which had little to do with the '92 Games: *olympic* and *olympics* also appeared in book reviews, and the adjective *olimpico* (which also means 'calm') turned up in a wide variety of contexts. Since the search systems on most newspaper CD-ROMs allow queries to be restricted by author, date, and section of the newspaper, as well as to particular parts of articles (headlines or body), the search was rerun specifying the sports section and a date span (June 1st to September 1st, the period in which the Games took place). This yielded 150 articles from *The Independent* (about 95,000 words), 307 from *The Telegraph* (160,000 words), and 77 from *Il Sole-24 Ore* (65,000 words), all of which were saved as ASCII files. Overall, the English corpus thus consisted of about 250,000 words, while the Italian was roughly a quarter of this size. These figures seemed sufficiently small to allow students to browse through the corpora and become familiar with the texts (100,000 words are the equivalent of 250 pages or so). Too much data can confuse the learner, increasing the number of citations to be dealt with and hindering understanding of the relationship between citations and their contexts (Gavioli, this volume, chapter 5: 3.1).

3. Swimming and navigating

The process of querying a corpus with a concordancer may be described as 'navigation' - to use a metaphor employed by Internet 'surfers' - since each citation displayed in a concordance can lead to the discovery of unexpected features and prompt further searches (Bernardini, this volume, chapter 9: 3). It is up to the user to decide what to look for next in each case, and learners have to develop strategies for navigating through the corpus they are dealing with. Rather than trying to report on particular 'routes' which

3.1 Proper names

were followed, I shall focus here on the kinds of strategies which were adopted for the purposes of this translation task.[4]

As a concordance is a list of different contexts for the same word or pattern, an obvious starting point is to examine words which are likely to be present in both corpora, such as proper names. A concordance of *Biondi* in the English corpus produced 35 occurrences (see appendix A), many of which were followed by a phrase giving information about the Olympic champion. These citations were examined for possible translations of the first sentence of the source text, which states who Matt Biondi is, and what he is trying to do. They included:

> **Biondi** expects to be back to his best
> **Biondi** is the big man of swimming,
> Matt **Biondi**: Swimmer. Won five golds, a silver
> Matt **Biondi**, the defending Olympic champion,
> Matt **Biondi**, the defending champion
> Matt **Biondi**, the first man to win seven swimming golds
> **Biondi**, who gained five golds in 1988,
> Matt **Biondi**, winner of five gold medals
> **Biondi**, with five golds last time
> Matt **Biondi** will try to slip into his 'Superman' guise

In the source text, Biondi is introduced as *sorvegliato speciale*. This is a phrase that belongs to the language of law, being used to refer to a person under police surveillance. Here it is used metaphorically to convey the idea of Biondi, champion of the '88 Olympics, being under attack and defending his supremacy. Thus among the descriptions in the English corpus, *defending champion* seemed a feasible translation.

The other proper name in the source text is that of Kieren Perkins, often referred to in the English corpus as *Australia's Kieren Perkins* or *Kieren Perkins of Australia*. This surprised our student, who had hypothesized using *the Australian Kieren Perkins* in his translation. By generating sample concordances to compare the use of adjectives of nationality, country names as possessives, and *of* followed by the country name, he found that the *of* form was quite the most frequent way of referring to contestants' origin in the English corpus, and duly selected this as a translation.

3.2 Key words and their equivalents

Work with concordancing software favours an approach which starts from a relatively low level of text constituency, where what the learner wants to know is "how do you say this in English?" - the equivalent of a particular word (Baker 1992; Brodine, this volume, chapter 6: 4). The first sentence of the source text contains two other propositions about Biondi: *cerca di vincere l'oro per la terza volta consecutiva ai Giochi* (lit. "trying to win the gold for the third consecutive time at the Games"), and *sul gradino più alto del podio ben cinque volte nell'edizione '88* (lit. "on the highest step of the podium no less than five times in the '88 edition"). For each of these propositions, students generated concordances of key lexical words and their hypothesized equivalents: *oro* ('gold'), *podio* ('podium'), and *consecutiva* ('consecutive').

A concordance of *gold** (Figure 2) produced nearly 850 lines. Sorting these by the words to the left/right and skimming through them, a number of patterns were noticed, for instance that one can *win/gain/earn/get the/a gold (medal)*, or *win golds*. By also generating a concordance of *or** in the Italian corpus (109 lines: Figure 3), these expressions could be analyzed contrastively. In Italian you can *vincere/conquistare/prendere la/una medaglia d'oro* (lit. "win/conquer/take the/a medal of gold"), *vincere/conquistare/prendere un oro* (lit. "win/conquer/take a gold"), or *vincere/conquistare/prendere ori/medaglie d'oro* (lit. "win/conquer/take golds/medals of gold"). However, while in English you can *win gold*, Italian requires a definite article (*vincere l'oro*).

3.3 Cognates

Students rapidly discovered that the other two key words in the first sentence of the source text, *podio* and *consecutiva*, had cognates in the English corpus, *podium* and *consecutive*. The question was: if there is a cognate form in English, is it a true or a false friend (Holmes and Guerra Ramos 1993; Partington 1995)? As can be seen from the concordances in Figures 4 and 5, *podium* does in fact correspond to *podio* in this context.

It was noticed, however, that there was a difference in the relative frequency with which these terms occurred. There were 27 occurrences of *podio* in the Italian corpus as opposed to only 22 of *podium* in the English one, even though the latter was four times as large. Inspecting the citations revealed that the expression found in the source text, *il gradino più alto del podio* (lit. "the highest step of the podium"), was used repeatedly in the Italian corpus to mean 'winning the gold medal' (6 occurrences: cfr. lines

7. Swimming in words: corpora, translation, and language learning

```
1   996 is a long way ahead. I badly wanted to win gold but I accept I probably won't now.' Fox gam
2   he 800 is wide open,' he said. 'Anyone can win gold.' Robb's Liverpool Harriers team-mate Steve
3   yo. In that run she destroyed the field to win gold with one of the greatest track performances
4   Yet, next day, they sailed brilliantly to win gold. Windsurfers Barrie Edgington, 25, and Penn
5   ssumed god-like status in Turkey after winning gold in the 60kg in Seoul in 1988, had been said
6   ld medal to their tally, Romas Ubartas winning gold in the discus for Lithuania. When Atlanta c
7   ore she reduced strong men to tears by winning gold in Munich aged 33. Brasher (3,000m steeplec
8   silver and bronze, and Ann Brightwell, who won gold and silver. So you can imagine how I felt w
9   ics his older and, for a long time, better won gold; when he was collecting bronze medals in th
10  mming as anywhere else - East German women won gold and silver in all events at the 1986 world
11  n both the 200m and 400m medley while Hong won gold in the 100m butterfly. BRITISH SWIMMING TEA
12  anistan. When Mike McIntyre and Bryn Vaile won gold medals in South Korea four years ago, saili
13  onal attention. Pattison, a naval officer, won gold in the Flying Dutchman class in 1968 and 19
```

Figure 2. *gold* with *win*/won* immediately to the left, sorted by word to left of *gold*: every third citation

```
1   mo_ dice il ct Velasco_ non solo non si vince l'oro, ma non si arriva alla finale>. Nella pall
2   ritorno di Pablo Morales, un ragazzo che vince l'oro nei 100 farfalla a 28 anni (per il nuoto,
3   o speciale e' Matt Biondi, che cerca di vincere l'oro per la terza volta consecutiva ai Giochi,
4   era coperto di ridicolo. Due bulgari vincitori dell'oro erano risultati positivi agli steroidi
5   , mi sono detto, io prendo un sabbatico e vinco l'oro". Spitz, forse il piu' grande nuotatore di
6   ro vecchietto", Maurizio Damilano, che ha vinto l'oro nella 20 chilometri di marcia addirittura
```

Figure 3. *or** with *vinc** within two words to the left, sorted by the second word to the left: all citations

```
1   on yesterday Michael Carruth was standing on a podium in the boxing arena here, listening to t
2   . You can't finish anywhere better than on the podium of an Olympic Games.' Ever since his con
3   enough to win. But I was proud to stand on the podium after a race like that. 'It's a great wa
4   ust one game away from a definite place on the podium after crushing Australia 98-65 in the fi
5   s ago only two Americans stood on the winner's podium to salute the anthem. True that duo, Mat
6   o threw 86.60m. Despite his climbing on to the podium along with Zelezny and Raty, there was n
7   registered as Skah stepped jauntily out to the podium matched that which accompanied his feroc
```

Figure 4. *podium**, sorted by the word to the left: every third citation

```
1   dell etiope Abebe), conosceva la sua ascesa al podio (terzo posto) dopo un quarto d'ora quando
2   avano con spettacolare autorita' la scalata al podio piu' alto del torneo a squadre costringend
3   cross), Massullo e Bomprezzi sono lontani dal podio. Nella vela un avvio in sordina dopo la bo
4   00. Oggi favoriti per il gradino piu' alto del podio Scarpa e Josefa Idem; outsider Rossi-Dreio
5   (la gara era mista) sul gradino piu' alto del podio, la cinesina Zhang Shang. La seconda, con
6   Le fiorettiste azzurre che hanno sottratto il podio piu' alto alle tedesche. Da sinistra: Giov
7   mente, 21,6 e 10,8 milioni. Il terzo posto sul podio equivale, quindi, a una vittoria in una ga
8   ro, per esempio, se Michael Jordan salira' sul podio alla cerimonia di premiazione del torneo
9   opo 32 anni di esilio, il Sud Africa torna sul podio: i tennisti Ferreira e Norval si sono infa
```

Figure 5. *podio**, sorted by the word to the left: every third citation

7. Swimming in words: corpora, translation, and language learning

```
1        Spain, making their first Olympic appearance, gained the women's gold medal for hockey after
2   sion can complete their convincing progress by gaining gold medals, but at least they are hand
3   sh: Bill Colwill on how Spain and Germany made gains in the gold market in the hockey tourname
4      eoul when lifting three times his body weight, gaining the gold medal for Turkey and then goin
5        ut they could be in a week's time. Biondi, who gained five golds in 1988, will again be the ma
6        oached it all wrong.' Not so Tamas Darnyi, who gained Hungary's second swimming gold medal of
```

Figure 6. *gain** with *gold?* within five words to the left, sorted by the word to the left of *gain**: all citations

4-5 in Figure 5), a figurative use which did not occur in the English corpus. Consequently, our student decided not to use *podium* to translate this expression, resorting instead to the more literal but attested *gaining five gold medals*.

The other cognate to be hypothesized as a translation in the first sentence of the source text, *consecutive*, also posed the question of whether it was a false friend. One student, who suspected that *successive* might be more appropriate, compared the two Italian and the two English words *consecutivo/successivo* and *consecutive/successive*. The concordances showed that the English terms were almost always preceded by a number, and seemed to be synonyms (Figure 7), while the Italian ones differed (Figure 8). *Consecutivo* (the citation form is the masculine singular) seems more or less equivalent to the English *successive/consecutive*, while *successivo* means something like 'following', appearing two out of four times in the phrase *gli anni successivi* (lit. "the following years") - which led this student to also investigate the behaviour in the English corpus of *following* and *next*.

3.4 Discourse structure

Corpora consisting of similar texts not only allow comparison of the uses of individual words, but also of features of discourse structure and their realization (Aston 1997a). To translate the source text headline *In vasca* (lit. "In the swimming pool"), the strategy adopted was to focus on its function as a headline indicating that the following article is about swimming. In the search for expressions in the English corpus which might fulfil this function, a concordance of *swim** quickly revealed that an equivalent might be *Swimming*, 14 out of 102 instances of this word being found in headlines.[5]

3.5 Stylistic appropriacy

Even where students were relatively confident in proposing a translation, the corpus evidence would often surprise them. As well as terminological accuracy and functional appropriacy, many of their searches related to style: is a certain phrase 'native-like', and would it be used in a British newspaper? For instance, in the second sentence of the source text, the phrase *50 e 100 stile libero* intuitively had a direct equivalent in *50 and 100 freestyle*. With the corpora at their disposal, some students tried looking for numbers by searching for words matching the pattern **0* in the Italian and the English data. As this resulted in hundreds of citations, the search was narrowed by adding other characters, and using the patterns *?00* and **00m*.

7. Swimming in words: corpora, translation, and language learning 187

```
1   felt Christie could beat him after a run of 10 consecutive defeats at the distance aroused an u
2   hown us ways to lose we never knew existed. At successive Olympics, World Championships and Com
3   ualify for the final of the same event in four successive Olympics? 13 Who came second behind S
4   hampion for the first time in 1986 and then in consecutive years, 1990 and 1991, but has had to
5   ir failed to post a final total for the second consecutive year. Twelve months after breaking h
6   t he will need to be if he is to win his third consecutive Olympic gold medal. He and his partn
7   Italy, who are themselves seeking their third consecutive Olympic gold in the coxed pairs toda
8   pairs rowing. Following Steve Redgrave's third successive rowing gold on Saturday, Johnny, 23,
9   ity is the floor exercise where she does three consecutive back-flips, in which her hands never
10  the Antwerp Games in 1920, has collected three successive gold medals. Redgrave bridged 72 year
```

Figure 7. *consecutive/successive*: every fifth citation

```
1   ta in due salti. Carl Lewis, per la terza volta consecutiva campione d'Olimpia, l'ha vinta al p
2   avano ancora sull'ultimo ostacolo. Per 122 gare consecutive e dieci anni, fra il 197 e il 1982,
3   telli d'Italia puntano la prua al mito, tre ori consecutivi alle Olimpiadi insieme al timoniere
4   re solo i due che, in termini di monetizzazione successiva della medaglia d'oro, sono piu' lont
5   con le opportune modifiche apportate negli anni successivi, riusci' a rendere competitivo. <I b
```

Figure 8. *consecutiv*/successiv**: every third citation

This revealed that in the English corpus, race distances were expressed specifying the unit of length, as in *100 metres freestyle* or *100m freestyle*, while in Italian they also appeared without the unit, as in *100 stile libero*. The only exception in English was in coordinate constructions (*50 and 100 metres freestyle*).

3.6   Chance discoveries

Some discoveries were purely casual. While examining the data related to numbers, our student happened to notice the following citation:

> Games, is back to contest the 100 metres, but Carl Lewis, the man who

of which he proceeded to view an enlarged context:

> Ben Johnson, banned for two years for drug abuse after the Seoul Games, is back to contest the 100 metres, but Carl Lewis, the man who inherited his gold medal, will not be there, or in the 200m, following his failure in the trials. In the 110m hurdles the world champion, Greg Foster, and world record holder, Roger Kingdom, also failed to come through the trials, as did Antonio Pettigrew, the world 400m champion, and Dan O'Brien, the world decathlon champion and subject of a massive pre-Olympic publicity campaign.

This was not an article about swimming, but it nonetheless contained what seemed particularly appropriate solutions to the problems of translating *si esibisce* (literally "exhibits him/herself") and *primatista mondiale* ("world record holder") in the source text, neither of which terms refer exclusively to swimming. Translating *si esibisce* had proved particularly problematic, with searches being run in the Italian corpus for forms of synonymous verbs such as *gareggiare* and *disputare*, and in the English corpus for cognates and functionally equivalent words to these, such as *dispute* and *perform*. However, a search for *perform** showed that out of 219 occurences, only 21 were verb forms, the rest mainly being the noun *performance* (17 of these in the compound *performance-enhancing drugs/ substances*). Here are some typical examples of *performance*:

> His magnificent **performance** at Tokyo attracted a warm tribute ...
> Another masterly **performance** by Steve Redgrave and Matthew Pin ...
> McKean's **performance** was reminiscent of other runs he ...
> ... Carruth's gold medal-winning **performance** from the ringside.
> Moorhouse's **performance** tomorrow, and that of his team ...

Rather than attempting to rearrange the text to include this nominal form, our student opted to use the phrase *is back to contest*, which in the text on the last page refers to the runner Ben Johnson, but could equally be applied to the swimmer Matt Biondi.

Casual discoveries of this kind were worth checking systematically, however. The paragraph about Johnson also included the expression *world record holder*, which appeared to be equivalent to *primatista mondiale*. Examining concordances for both these expressions confirmed that they were used in similar contexts, but also showed that *world record holder* was usually used with the definite article, unlike its Italian equivalent (Figure 9).

3.7 Follow-up

To sum up, these comparable corpora allowed students to contrast the source and target languages at various levels, from single words and phrases to discourse functions and organizations. By looking for patterns and regularities in the English and Italian texts and comparing the uses of words and expressions which they felt had some kind of relationship either within or across languages, they were able to find evidence to formulate and to support (or to reject) specific translation hypotheses. As a final step, after completing the translation, they were invited to check how far the patterns they had observed in the English data might be generalizable to other contexts, by comparing concordances from the Olympics corpus with ones from a more general newspaper corpus (*MicroConcord Corpus A*: Murison-Bowie 1993b).

4.   Learning to create meaning

Like any other process of discourse construction, translation involves creating meaning, the difference being that translation is "*guided* creation of meaning" (Halliday 1992: 15). Using comparable corpora in this process increases the guidance available, enabling the text to be built up from ready-made chunks of language which have been used in similar contexts on similar occasions, selecting those which seem most appropriate to convey the desired meaning.

This does not mean, however, that translating simply becomes a 'cut and paste' activity. The various pieces found in the corpus will rarely fit together exactly, but must be adjusted and linked in order to create a text which is more than just a patchwork of pieces stolen from elsewhere. For instance, in the first sentence of our student's translation in Figure 1 above

```
1   ans grouped around Said Aouita, the 1,500m world record holder prevented by injury from competi
2   14, and is now a double world champion and world record holder. There is also a men's 200m free
3   eoul', Melvin Stewart, the 200m butterfly world record holder, said. Mike Barrowman, who holds
4   drive him to the Olympic title. The former world record holder said a combination of the heat a
5   over', observed Leroy Burrell, the former world record holder who ran the second leg in the re
6   the end of the year because the 400 metres world record holder had competed while banned for st
7   lona, despite the fact that the 400 metres world record holder had failed a drugs test. Confusi
8   o win the 100m backstroke. Jeff Rouse, the world record holder from Petersburg, set the early p
9   t this could be his year but he wanted the world record holder in the race to prove he could be
10  in thrower. European champion, three times world record holder By MIKE ROWBOTTOM TALKING AT G
```

Figure 9. *world record holder*, sorted by the first word to the left: alternate citations

(*Matt Biondi, the defending champion, will be trying to win gold in his third successive Olympic Games*), only the nominal group *Matt Biondi, the defending champion* was pasted from the English corpus without modification. The rest of the sentence combined bits and pieces from three different concordance lines, none of them exactly matching the wording finally adopted:

> ... a third consecutive gold medal ...
> ... won his third consecutive gold medal ...
> ... to win gold in three successive Olympic Games ...

The learner not only has to select relevant chunks of language according to their perceived meaning, but also to fit them together according to the desired overall outcome. Instead of dealing with individual lexical items and their grammatical combination, as is typically the case in translation activities, the learner works with multi-word units, their adjustment and integration. This process arguably parallels that engaged in by fluent writers, who must operate with multi-word units in order to "perform at a level acceptable to native users" (Cowie 1992: 10; see also Aston 1995b), and may help the learner to develop skills of accommodation and monitoring in the light of the purposes and style of the discourse. For instance, while in the source text the information that Biondi had won five golds in the 1988 Olympics is found in the first sentence, in his translation our student moved this information to the second in order to avoid using the word 'gold' twice in the same sentence.

Such operations involve the creation of a coherent and cohesive text above the sentence level - a fundamental feature of all writing, not just of translation. For instance, the source text provides two pieces of news, respectively concerning the top performers over the short and middle distances, Matt Biondi and Kieren Perkins. The latter is said to be *re del mezzofondo* (lit. "king of the middle distance"). But while *mezzofondo* can function as a head noun in Italian ("middle-distance race"), a concordance of *mid** in the English corpus found *middle-distance* (16 occurrences) only as a qualifier (e.g. *middle-distance runner*). Our student solved this problem by using an adverbial phrase (*over the longer distances*) which makes the comparison with the earlier statement about Biondi explicit: besides being a phrase present in the English corpus, it functions as a cohesive link. The non-attestedness of *middle distance* as a head noun in the English corpus obliged the student to focus on the coherence of the target text as a whole, rather than just assembling a series of sentences from equivalent words and phrases.

5. Learning about the language and the culture

This brief example of a translation activity illustrates a variety of potential learning benefits which may accrue from the use of comparable corpora. We have seen, for instance, that it may enhance awareness of the relationships between words which are possible translation equivalents in the two languages. Hypotheses as to equivalences may be drawn from intuition, or from monolingual and bilingual dictionaries. But whereas dictionaries contain "pre-digested information" (Fontanelle 1994: 50), comparable corpora of the kind presented here simply provide collections of raw data: words are not defined, but are given meaning by their contexts. By supplying meaningful instances of real language in use (whose wider context is always available at a keystroke), concordances offer greater safety of numbers and greater certainty of contextual appropriacy than dictionaries do. This argument concerns grammar as well as lexis. Article use, for instance, seems particularly difficult for learners to master from pedagogic grammars, whereas the corpora provided clear evidence as to the use of articles with such phrases as *win gold* and *world record holder* and their Italian equivalents. They similarly highlighted regularities in the grammar of proper names, showing the preferred constructions used to refer to a country of origin (cfr. 3.1 above). Last but not least, the corpora also constituted a source of extralinguistic (world) knowledge, providing information about people, places and institutions.

The specific information drawn from these small comparable corpora must not of course be treated as generalized 'facts' about the language as a whole. The corpora do not claim to be representative of the universe of written discourse, and their features should not even be interpreted as necessarily typical of sports journalism. They are reliable to the extent that particular features are attested with a certain frequency, in contexts which are credibly analogous. While some findings, such as the preference for nominal constructions with *performance* over verbal ones with *perform*, could be of more general import, such hypotheses must always be checked against other data before being generalized, and the learner needs to be wary of the influence which the specific composition of the corpus exerts on the meaning and function of items of all kinds (see Zorzi, this volume, chapter 4: 3; Gavioli, chapter 5: 3.2).

It is particularly important to be careful about what may be domain-specific uses. For instance, the word *golds* occurs over 50 times in the English Olympics corpus. Yet *gold* is usually classed as an uncountable noun in EFL textbooks (see e.g. Fowler et al. 1983: 71), and there are no examples of *golds* at all in the much larger and more varied *MicroConcord*

A newspaper corpus (Murison-Bowie 1993b). This suggests that the plural *golds* may only have the specific sense of 'gold medals' in reference to sporting events like the Olympics. In contrast, both *gold* and *golden* occur in the Olympics corpus as adjectives, *golden* being sometimes used where in Italian we find *d'oro* (as in *ragazza d'oro*: "golden girl"). The latter example suggests that whereas *gold* indicates the metal, *golden* indicates the metaphorical quality - a hypothesis which is this time confirmed by a search in the *MicroConcord A* corpus. While not immediately useful for the translation, where it was clear from the start that the English for *medaglia d'oro* was *gold medal*, this finding illustrates how analyses of comparable corpora can throw up discoveries which may be noted and investigated as spin-offs for potential use elsewhere.

Perhaps the most striking type of result to emerge in using comparable corpora is the disconfirmation of initial hypotheses. For instance, a search in the English corpus for an appropriate translation of *re* in *re del mezzofondo* (lit. "king of the middle distance") revealed that *king* was almost exclusively used to refer to the king of Spain, Juan Carlos. The sole metaphorical instance referred to an activity rather than an individual:

> Basketball is the king in Lithuania and they were hoping to use the sport to strike a blow against the Commonwealth of Independent States - which they still regard as a symbol of the old Soviet regime.

Another possible translation of *re* was *big man*, a phrase which had been found referring to Matt Biondi in the corpus (see 3.1 above). This hypothesis was rejected for the reason that it appeared not only metaphorical but also literal (*Biondi is the big man of swimming, standing 6ft 7in tall and the winner of six Olympic gold medals*). A further candidate was the adjective *top*, which had also been noticed during a previous search. A search for *top* found one occurrence of *top performer*, and two of *top dog*. Both the latter, however, were in quoted statements, suggesting that this expression might be more typical of spoken registers, and *top performer* was the form eventually chosen. But this example may make clear that as much, if not more, may be learned from investigating hypotheses that are subsequently rejected as from investigating ones which are finally adopted in the target text.

6. Conclusions

Using comparable corpora and concordancing software as aids in translation activities can help learners gain insights into the languages and the cultures involved and develop their reading and writing skills. Of its nature, translation is an activity in which meaning is negotiated through the written medium, where the translator interacts both as a reader with the producer of the source text and as a writer with the recipient of the target text. While these interactions are *in primis* individual activities, they do not exclude the possibility of group work and oral discussion, as learners exchange and debate their ideas and discoveries (Duff 1989; Aston, this volume, chapter 1: 3.1). Comparable corpora can provide a natural springboard for such activities, as learners discuss search strategies and evaluate their findings. Besides the clear reward of a more natural-sounding product - Appendix B gives examples of other translations of the same source text carried out without the aid of the corpus - I have tried to show that much else can be learnt through the use of corpora as translation aids.

Notes

1. Other aligned parallel corpora include those being developed from EC official journals and telecommunication texts (McEnery and Wilson 1994), from the multilingual technical manuals of computer companies like IBM or Microsoft, as well as from more heterogeneous sources (Johansson et al. 1996). Parallel concordancing software suitable for classroom use includes *MultiConcord* (Woolls 1997) and *ParaConc* (Barlow 1995).

2. While machine translation (MT) issues are not within the scope of this paper, it may be useful to briefly point out some areas of overlap, as much of the work carried out with parallel and comparable corpora has been for MT applications. Wills (1993) distinguishes between four different procedures which go under the heading of MT: (a) word-for-word substitution, (b) machine-aided human translation (MAHT), (c) human-aided machine translation (HAMT), and (d) fully automatic machine translation (FAMT). Word-for-word substitution is simply "a form of the interlinear version known from the Middle Ages" (Wills 1993: 405) and is generally of little use; MAHT consists essentially in a word processor equipped with the capability of interfacing with dictionaries and terminological data banks, which "may contain [...] a device to specify certain words in certain contextual environments" (ibid.); HAMT, which requires human intervention in either the editing and/or the post-editing phase, is the area where most commercial software has been developed, ranging from professional tools such as *IBM Translation Manager/2*, *Trados Translator's Workbench* and *Globalink* to less sophisticated programs such as *Microtac Language Assistants*. HAMT is also the main field of application for 'parallel corpora' of the Hansard type, which has been used as a testbed for

IBM's *Translation Manager/2* (Somers 1993; Langé and Bonnet 1994); FAMT, which requires a fully implemented formalization of implicit knowledge, has only proved effective in very narrowly defined, formulaic linguistic domains, such as the METEO software for translating meteorological bulletins (Lewis 1992). Many of the techniques and procedures of MAHT and HAMT use parallel or comparable corpora in ways that are relevant to machine-aided language learning and to the training of translators (cfr. Zanettin 1998).

3. Laffling (1992) calls this category "globally parallel corpora", while Baker (1995) refers to those involving different languages as "multilingual corpora", giving as an example the Council of Europe Multilingual Lexicography Project, which has collected analogous texts in seven European languages. Baker (1993, 1995, 1996) also proposes a different use of the term 'comparable corpora' from that adopted here, when she advocates the setting up of what she terms, "for lack of a better term", "comparable corpora", consisting of a corpus of texts originally written in language *A* and another corpus of texts translated into language *A* from different source language(s), covering "a similar domain, variety of language and time span" (Baker 1995: 234). The analysis of such corpora, she argues, may cast light on the translation process. For further discussion of these terminological issues see also Zanettin (1994, 1998); Peters and Picchi (1998); Bowker (2000).

4. The text to be translated in this experiment was taken from one of the articles in the Italian corpus. While in this case the corpus had been defined prior to the task, it is equally feasible to construct a corpus for the purpose of a particular translation or translations, provided care is taken in the choice of selection criteria (Pearson 2000). In designing a corpus to translate the Matt Biondi article, for example, one might be tempted to select all the articles containing the keywords *swim*/swam* from a newspaper CD-ROM. Such a procedure would however retrieve many articles having little to do with swimming as a sport, and ignore those dealing with other sports in the overall context of the 1992 Olympics.

5. This finding was confirmed by a search run on *MicroConcord Corpus A* (Murison-Bowie 1993b), which contains one million words from different sections of *The Independent* for 1989. Here, *Swimming* appeared as a headline in 3 citations out of 9.

Appendix A: *Biondi* in the English corpus

```
1   laced him in the centre lane. On his right was Biondi, 26, with Jager, 27, on his left. The Am
2   r finalists showed no respect for reputations. Biondi, 26, made a brave attempt to add to his
3   mpting to force his way into the record books. Biondi, a giant of a man in both stature - he i
4   rd of 21.91 sec. Foster was sixth in 22.52 and Biondi, a five-time winner in Seoul, missed out
5   when he emerged from the dive just behind Matt Biondi and Alexander Popov it did not augur wel
6   ll the way for Spain it was disappointment for Biondi and Evans in the 100m and 400m freestyle
7   z-Zubero as the United States favourites, Matt Biondi and Janet Evans, failed to retain their
8   which includes the outstanding talent of Matt Biondi and Tom Jager, of the United States. The
9   the pool last night, which, on a day when Matt Biondi and Janet Evans were racing, was a shock
10  dium to salute the anthem. True that duo, Matt Biondi and Janet Evans, heard it often enough t
11  il. At first Borges was given the same time as Biondi but after the officials looked at the vi
12  ht US swimming golds were awarded to the pair,' Biondi collecting five. Yesterday Evans had to
13  e on my side and my shoulders get cramped up.'  Biondi expects to be back to his best by the ti
14  s in the 100m and 400m freestyle respectively.  Biondi is the big man of swimming, standing 6ft
15  he 100 and 50-metre freestyle, and two relays.  Biondi is hoping that a combination of less tra
16  chael Johnson, Sergei Bubka, Mike Powell, Matt  Biondi, Li Jing, Michael Jordan, too. What does
17              DTL 30 JUL 92 / Olympics '92:      Biondi must conquer the threat of Popov - Swimm
18  the 50m freestyle title, writes Colin Gibson.   Biondi (pictured), 27 the day after the Games,
19  ile going for a run in the morning. Perversely  Biondi's recent dip in form - he was third in t
20  , a silver and a bronze in Seoul          MATT  BIONDI returns to the Olympic fray in Barcelona
21  . 'It's more of a factor of working too hard,'  Biondi said. 'Fortunately, we're over the aerob
22  ) and Mark Foster (50m freestyle) might ruffle  Biondi's supremacy. The women's chances are les
23  famous footsteps over the next fortnight? Matt  Biondi: Swimmer. Won five golds, a silver and a
24  ory in the sprint freestyle relay to make Matt  Biondi the first male to win seven swimming gol
25  o main contenders are the American duo of Matt  Biondi, the defending Olympic champion, and Tom
26  ies, who failed to qualify for the final. Matt  Biondi, the defending champion, and Tom Jager,
27  she became too upset to speak and walked out.   Biondi's vulnerability was first hinted at in th
```

```
28    he silver, he was crying in the practice pool. Biondi, who was fifth, said: 'The prospect of wi
29    the moment but they could be in a week's time. Biondi, who gained five golds in 1988, will agai
30              By COLIN GIBSON        MATT BIONDI will try to slip into his 'Superman' guis
31    eestyle to Alexander Popov. The main threat to Biondi will again be Popov and Tom Jager, who fi
32    record holder. Later in the week American Matt Biondi will be attempting to force his way into
33    es so, he will face tough opposition from Matt Biondi, winner of five gold medals, including on
34    f competing this time around - but 26-year-old Biondi, with five golds last time and one in 198
35    but at one point it looked very unlikely that Biondi would return as an individual competitor.
```

Appendix B: Translations without the aid of corpora

The translation of the source text on the left was carried out by a professional translator and native speaker of English without the help of reference instruments, and the one on the right by an Italian learner of English using traditional reference tools.

At the pool all eyes are on Matt Biondi who is trying to win the Gold for the third time running at the Games, having won no less than 5 times in 1988. He swims in the 50 and 100 metres freestyle, and in the 4 by 100 freestyle. King of the middle distances is the Australian Kieren Perkins, world record holder in the 400, 800, and 1500 metres freestyle.	In the pool nearly unbeatable, Matt Biondi, who won 5 gold medals in the 1988 edition, tries to win his third gold medal in a row at the Games. Besides the 4 x 100 freestyle relay he will compete in the 50-m and 100-m freestyle. King of middle-distance races is Australian Kieren Perkins, world-record holder at 400-m, 800-m and 1,500-m freestyle.

8 GOING TO THE CLOCHEMERLE: EXPLORING CULTURAL CONNOTATIONS THROUGH AD HOC CORPORA

Franco Bertaccini and Guy Aston

1. Introduction

Most of the work described in this volume exploits small corpora of one or more kinds of texts which have been created *prior* to the identification of particular linguistic problems by the teacher or learner. As the previous chapters illustrate, such corpora can document a wide variety of features which may be problematic for the learner. However they will not always document features which are comparatively rare. Many lexical items and combinations of lexical items may be absent from even very large corpora, and the information available from conventional reference tools, such as dictionaries, may be inadequate to allow confident decisions to be made.[1] In this paper we illustrate how problems involving rare lexis may be solved by constructing small corpora to deal with them on an *ad hoc* basis, drawing for the purpose on the massive archives of text available on CD-ROMs and through the Internet.

The example we shall discuss is taken from a translation task. Here, there may be a need both to understand expressions in the source language text, and to hypothesize and verify equivalents in the target language (cfr. Zanettin, this volume, chapter 7). However, the procedures we describe would not seem limited to translation. The need to understand lexical meanings is common to all reading, and the translation strategies we shall consider - transfer from the source language, cross-cultural analogy, and paraphrase - are all potentially relevant as communication strategies in L2 writing (Faerch and Kasper 1983; Duff 1989).

Our example comes from a French newspaper article entitled *Les festivals de jazz et de rock: du bon usage de la musique*, published in *Le Monde* in 1992, which we used with Italian undergraduates majoring in translation. This is a quite lengthy discussion (1500 words) of the spread of jazz and rock festivals in Europe. The final paragraph reads as follows:

(1)   [...] par une sorte de courtoisie où le mythe est intéressé et la rentabilité modeste aux postes de commande, le pays organisateur (en l'occurrence la France et ses quatre-vingt-trois festivals) s'offre le luxe d'ignorer en quatre-vingt-trois occasions ses propres musiciens et sa propre créativité. Les

8. Going to the Clochemerle: exploring cultural connotations 199

> musiciens européens n'osent plus s'en plaindre, de peur de passer pour corporatistes. Mais c'est qu'il ne s'agit pas forcément de musique... On serait plutôt dans un phénomène de Disneyland en négatif, soit un phénomène convenablement positif: le mythe de l''autre' Amérique (noire, inventive, délurée, créatrice de culture) circule en aimable caravane, de 'vrais' châteaux anciens en 'vraies' stations balnéaires. Le tout pour faire une vraie bonne action. On retrouve sur le versant rock de cette industrie saisonnière les mêmes configurations. *C'est-à-dire le ballet des stars sur les routes de France que l'on croirait réglé par Bison fûté; les enjeux touristiques, de marketing, clochemerlesques, mal dissimulés; les enjeux esthétiques phagocytés par les précédents.* [...]
>
> (*Le Monde*, 26/5/92: our emphasis)

One of the most difficult pieces to translate proved to be the sentence italicized, and in particular the word *clochemerlesques*. None of our students knew that this was a reference to Gabriel Chevallier's comic novel *Clochemerle* (1934), in which contending factions in a little town in the Beaujolais battle over the installation of a public urinal. Neither *Clochemerle* itself, nor forms derived from it, appear in a major French dictionary such as *Le grand Robert* (1997). And the aspect of its meaning that needs to be understood here, namely its sociocultural connotations, is in any case unlikely to be found in conventional reference tools (see Partington, this volume, chapter 3: 4). While students might have found an account of Chevallier's novel in an encyclopedia, they would almost certainly not have discovered that Clochemerle has come to be a symbol of petty provincialism in French culture. It is this connotative meaning, however, which is essential to an understanding of this sentence, and which a translation needs to convey.

With the help of a variety of CD-ROMs of French and Italian newspapers, and searches on the Internet, our students eventually came up with two alternative translations of *clochemerlesque* into Italian. The first, *guareschiano*, substituted the reference to Clochemerle with one which has analogous connotations in Italian culture, Giovanni Guareschi being the author of the *Don Camillo* stories, which recount the feuds between the parish priest and the communist mayor in a small town by the Po. The second, *strapaesano*, employed a paraphrase, denoting rather than connoting the required meaning: a major Italian dictionary defines *strapaesano* as "emphasizing strikingly characteristic features of local country life" (Treccani 1994, our translation). In what follows we recount the steps by which our students arrived at these two translations - both of which seem quite appropriate - and at the same time expand the question to consider how *clochemerlesque* might be rendered in English.

2. Understanding the source text

Concordances of corpora can often cast light on the connotative meanings of particular lexical items by revealing their tendency to recur in certain semantic and/or pragmatic environments (Sinclair 1991a; Louw 1993; cfr. Partington, this volume, chapter 3: 4). No preconstituted corpus, however, is likely to offer a sufficient number of citations of such rare forms as *clochemerlesque* (or *Clochemerle*) to allow recurrent patterns to be identified. Its unexplained use in the French source text, a piece of divulgative journalism, suggests that it is not a technical term from a particular specialized domain. To find other examples of its use, the only possible strategy would seem to involve searching through very large archives of texts.

The resources available to our students included a CD-ROM of a year's issues of *Le Monde* (over 6 million words) and access to the Internet. The search software provided with the CD-ROM allows the user to retrieve and examine all the articles which contain a particular string of characters; similarly, the various search engines on the Web will list those documents which contain a particular string, which can then be retrieved and examined individually. Both these resources, in other words, allow the user to construct small corpora consisting solely of texts which contain a particular expression or expressions, which can then be analyzed using concordancing software.

Internet search engines rely on the output of web crawlers which automatically scan and index every document they find, recording each word-form (with the exception of common grammatical words) together with the title and address of the document. Given the enormous variety of material and the rather simplistic indexing and search procedures, there is no guarantee that every document found will be relevant to the user's concerns, and in any case the indexes are inevitably somewhat out of date. A search using AltaVista (http://www.altavista.com) for the string *clochemerle** found 20 documents, four of which proved to be no longer available.[2] Of the remainder, three were book lists which included Chevallier's novel, and one was an anthology of French prose containing two extracts from *Clochemerle*, neither of which yielded significant information as to its content. A further six contained references to business establishments called Clochemerle - a wine cellar in the Beaujolais (two documents in French, one in English, one in German), a German restaurant (in German), and an Australian club (in English). This last was the only one to provide an explanation of its title:

8. Going to the Clochemerle: exploring cultural connotations

(2) The name **Clochemerle** stems from Gabriel Chevaliers' book of the same name about that French towns' reaction to the installation of a pissoir! *[sic]*

Another document reproduced the table of contents for a French magazine, which included the title "St-Cergue: Clochemerle en Jura", but the text of the article was not provided.

There were only five documents which used, rather than mentioned, the word *Clochemerle* in such a manner as to suggest its potential connotations. One of these was a transcript from the 1950s BBC radio comedy series, *The Goon Show*:

(3)   *Big Ben striking at various speeds (ten times)*
    GERMAN: Shhh... is that you, Seagoon?
    SEAGOON: No, it was the clock. Where's Tom Yakkamoto?
    GERMAN: He's gone to the **Clochemerle**.
    Handbell ringing
    GREENSLADE: *(French accent)* Everybody out. Closing time.

Given the explanation provided in (2) above, this could be interpreted as a pun (*cloche/clock*), with *Clochemerle* meaning *pissoir*. This extract also suggested that the word might not be totally unknown to an English-speaking public, thereby raising the hypothesis - to be discussed in 3.1 below - that it might not after all be necessary to translate *clochemerlesques* in an English version of the source text.

The remaining four documents were all quite lengthy articles from French newspapers and magazines, which, like the source text, compared particular local situations to those described in Chevallier's novel. The first underlined how local politics had interfered with the artistic direction of a cultural event of international stature, the Avignon festival:

(4)   Aux élections municipales, la Ville a basculé à gauche. Le nouveau maire PS, Guy Ravier, y est allé de sa petite phrase assassine: «Le Festival d'Avignon est trop parisien, coupé du terrain»; un quotidien local prévenait: «Des têtes vont tomber.» Il y avait là, en creux, un symptôme - celui d'une reprise en main de la culture par les collectivités locales - qui ira croissant les années suivantes.
        Alain Crombecque avait mis les points sur les i: «je ne finirai pas mes jours ici, je ne changerai pas mes méthodes de travail, je ne travaillerai pas sous la direction d'une équipe municipale.» Un an plus tard, il est toujours là et son contrat a été renouvelé pour trois ans. Comme l'Etat, la Ville a augmenté sa subvention d'un million de francs.

Victoire? A la Pyrrhus. Car Crombecque a dû se séparer d'une collaboratrice, Nicole Taché, qui avait cristallisé toute l'électricité de cette période; et son administrateur, Elias Ozel, a préféré démissionner face à ce début d'«avignonnisation» du Festival. Car, parallèlement, la Ville a créé le poste de «directeur délégué du Festival» en le confiant à Christiane Bourbonnaud, apparatchik de la culture socialiste locale [...] Elle ne s'arrêtera pas là. [...] Pour la première fois, une chaîne de télévision japonaise vient filmer ce festival de renommée mondiale, qui est aussi un **Clochemerle** de la vie politico-culturelle.

The next article came from *Diagonal*, an independent cinema magazine from Montpellier. This too cited Clochemerle as an example of petty local conflict, again in order to stress that important cultural issues were being ignored:

(5) Les jeux sont faits. Et les forces en présence sont soigneusement identifiées. D'un côté, les mairies de Lattes et de Montpellier, alliés objectifs, qui prônent une vision exclusivement industrielle du cinéma à travers les multiplexes. De l'autre, les petits, les indépendants (Diagonal entre autres), dopés par le fantastique engouement qu'a suscité ce combat et, soudain, pressés par le public, d'être à la hauteur de leurs responsabilités. [...] Mais ne nous trompons pas: ce combat, nous ne le voulons pas comme le énième remake de la guéguerre Diagonal/Mairie de Montpellier. Laissons à Messieurs Frêche et Vaillat le soin d'écrire les Mémoires de **Clochemerle** et attachons nous à identifier précisément les moyens objectifs de lutte contre ces projets. Ne sombrons pas, non plus, dans le manichéisme de l'exclusion. Il ne s'agit pas d'une guerre du cinéma d'auteur contre le cinéma commercial, du cinéma français contre le cinéma américain, des intelligents, des cultivés contre les crétins. Ou de la gauche contre la droite. Et encore moins des consommateurs de pop corn contre les amateurs de confit d'oie ou de faisane cendrée. Ce combat est plus simple et concerne tous les spectateurs, y compris ceux qui peuvent être favorables au multiplexe.

The third document was concerned with the role and status of social economists. Once more, Clochemerle was cited to stress that there are more serious and global matters - those debated in academic conferences, for instance - than the petty local rivalries of institutions:

(6) Surtout si leur technicité reconnue va de pair avec une certaine réserve idéologique, ces quantitativistes du social apparaissent alors, aux yeux des autres économistes (pas nécessairement localement, en raison des rivalités de type **Clochemerle**, mais dans les colloques par exemple) comme de vrais

économistes: mêmes concepts, même discours, même rigueur, même façon de structurer les exposés, même mathématisation [...]

The final document referred in detail to a specific episode in the novel. This had nothing to do with factionism, but Clochemerle was again treated as a stereotypical instance of the trivialization of cultural values:

(7) Un évêque irlandais réactualise la confession en la faisant passer par le 156, le téléphone à 2,15 francs la minute, comme pour le porno. Ce qui met l'absolution au même tarif que le péché. Mais cet évêque n'a rien inventé. A **Clochemerle**, après avoir troussé Honorine, sa servante, le curé Ponosse allait à bicyclette à Valsonnas se confesser au curé Jouve qui en usait pareillement avec sa servante Josépha. [...] Et, un jour d'hiver, c'est par ce télégramme: Miserere urgent que le brave curé Ponosse demanda l'absolution à son ami. Elle arriva par le même chemin avec un rosaire pour pénitence. Ce n'est pas sans inquiétude que le curé de **Clochemerle** continua d'user de cette facilité, mais ses scrupules furent atténués par l'idée que le dogme de la confession remontait à un temps où l'invention du télégraphe n'était pas même concevable. Si on en croit Gabriel Chevalier, cela se passait dans le Beaujolais, pays heureux où la joie de vivre était encore bien partagée.

The largely unexplained manner in which the allusions to Clochemerle are introduced in these examples - three of the four do not even mention Chevallier as the author - suggests that as a stereotype it is well-known to educated French laypeople. At this point, our students were able to infer that the use of *clochemerlesques* in the source text was probably meant to imply the author's condemnation of the fact that local politics play a greater role in the organization of music festivals than do cultural issues.

Turning to the *Le Monde* CD-ROM for further examples confirmed this hypothesis, expanding students' understanding of the connotations of Clochemerle and of the contexts in which it is cited. While yielding a smaller number of texts than the Internet search, the CD-ROM provided more which invoked Clochemerle as a stereotype rather than merely mentioning it as a name. This was immediately clear from the headlines of the articles retrieved:

(8) Polémique entre le châtelain et le maire d'un village gascon

(9) Clochemerle à Sébastopol: La flotte, enjeu de la querelle Moscou-Kiev

(10) Trébeurden, le port de la discorde. Un maire inculpé, des habitants divisés, des ministères en conflit, des promoteurs pressés: une histoire exemplaire dans laquelle s'affrontent économie et écologie

(11) Esprits d'entreprise: Crise à l'aéroport de Nice

(12) Une France frileuse

(13) Polémique à Cambridge: Jacques Derrida, docteur dérangeant

(14) Nessie, le mythe du loch

(15) *Civilisations*. Clochemerle en plein Bled

(16) *Point*. Les relations franco espagnoles: Un tissu associatif renouvelé

(17) Guérilla dans les Pyrénées: Le projet de tunnel routier du Somport et le sort des derniers ours provoquent des incidents répétés

(18) *Cinema*. American Clochemerle: *City of hope* de John Sayles

(19) *Sans visa*. Macuro, l'empreinte de Colomb

(20) Rêve nordiste au Cameroun: Fragilisé et appauvri, le nord du pays espère retrouver sa place sur l'échiquier politique, à l'issue des élections législatives du 1 mars

While not all of these are immediately interpretable, the presence of words such as *polémique*, *querelle*, *discorde*, *guérilla*, *crise*, along with the geographical references, suggests that Clochemerle is again generally associated with local disputes. The presence of unexplained uses in the headlines (15) and (18) once more suggests that the stereotype is a well-known one. Armed with this further evidence, our students now felt able to interpret the source text with confidence: *clochemerlesques* was clearly meant as a criticism of the petty vision of the festival organizers.

Yet further information was gleaned by looking through the texts of the CD-ROM articles. While common expressions are assumed to be understandable for the target reader (see Partington, this volume, chapter 3: 2), relatively rare ones often occur with definitions and explanations, especially in divulgative texts (Pearson 1996; Aston 1997a). Several of the *Le Monde* texts, like that of the Australian club in example (2) above, provided parenthetical reminders about Chevallier's novel. Another point to emerge was that certain words, or better, words from certain semantic fields, repeatedly occurred as collocates of *Clochemerle*. The latter information, as we shall see in 3.3 below, can be a valuable aid to the production of an appropriate translation.

3. Hypothesizing a translation

How should we translate *clochemerlesques*? Our students felt that the ideal way would be by alluding to an analogous stereotype in Italian culture, i.e. one which has similar connotations and is similarly well-known. This strategy of analogy would, if successful, engage the reader of the target text in a similar interpretative process to that of the reader of the source text. Alternatively, an expression which directly denoted these connotative meanings might be used, functioning as a paraphrase. This would convey the meaning implied by the original, but without the need for the reader to work out the implicature, with a corresponding loss of rhetorical effect. Last but not least, we should not forget the most straightforward possibility, that of transfer, or non-translation. It might be possible to simply transfer the allusion to Clochemerle to the target language text, on the assumption that it will be correctly interpretable for readers from the target culture. This would probably be the case with biblical allusions - to the patience of Job, for instance. Corpora created *ad hoc* - both in the source and in the target language - offer ways of investigating all of these three strategies. They may provide evidence to support a hypothesized translation (or indicate the lack of such evidence), and at the same time they may suggest other hypotheses. Our discussion will focus on each strategy in turn, considering both Italian and English as target languages.

3.1 The transfer strategy

Of the texts referring to Clochemerle on the Internet, several were written in English rather than in French. In translating the source text into English, one possible strategy thus appeared to be transfer. Leaving aside morphosyntactic issues (should an adjectival or nominal form be employed: *Clochemerlean*? *Clochemerle-like*? *as in Clochemerle*?), the question is whether *Clochemerle* constitutes a recognizable stereotype for the English reader, and whether it has the same connotations as in French.

The Internet documents provided very limited evidence in this regard. There were fewer English than French texts (though there is far more English material on the Internet as a whole), and only one - taken from a radio script of 40 years ago (example (3) above) - alluded to Clochemerle without adding an explanation. Moreover, this example uses Clochemerle as a euphemism for lavatory, rather than for the connotations of petty rivalry which seem typical in French. Turning to examine English newspaper CD-ROMs (*The Daily Telegraph* and *The Independent* for 1992), a further six references to Clochemerle were found, some of which also suggested that it might be a recognizable stereotype:

(21) PARIS - In the Pullman Saint-Jacques Hotel in southern Paris, Japanese tourists sat cramped together behind a sign declaring their seats a 'smoking zone', writes Julian Nundy.
   None was smoking.
   Smokers in their group wandered freely in the rest of the lobby, where smoking is banned. Although the sign was in both English and French, its message was clearly misunderstood. The mischievous could have called the police to impose fines of up to 1,300 francs (£155) on the transgressors. On day one of the stringent new French law to stop smoking in enclosed public places, there was little of the **Clochemerle-style** resistance some cafe-owners have promised.

(22) TEN YEARS on, there seems less reason than ever to 'rejoice' over the Falklands war. 'Two bald men fighting over a comb' was the verdict of the Argentinian writer Jorge Luis Borges - a rather inadequate joke, to my mind, about a tragedy of such gross proportions. The same can be said of Stuart Urban's overlong, self-regarding play, An Ungentlemanly Act (BBC2).
   It is a plausible conceit to set the Argentinian invasion in a **Clochemerle** governed by the Larkins and defended by Dad's Army. But it does scant service to the 255 British troops who died there, even if they did call the place 'Toytown'. How long before some bright TV spark turns the Gulf war's 'friendly fire' tragedy into a Whitehall farce?

(23) Yet however watchable this yarn proved it lacked a little in subtlety and failed on any profound level to illuminate the guilt that engulfs the Catholic psyche when it comes to sex.
   The same verdict applies to another bodice-ripper, Stealing Heaven, based loosely on the love of Abelard and Heloise. This 1978 British film turned the romance of this medieval story of the secret and ultimately doomed love of a canon of Notre Dame and his young pupil into an Emmanuelle in the Cloisters romp. Bringing a good deal more nuance - not to mention the neglected virtue of modesty - to the subject was Roy Dotrice's performance in the 1970s television serial **Clochemerle**, as a priest who strayed but who suffered agonies of doubt because he succumbed to temptation.

(24) WHEN Stephen Hilditch sent off Gregoire Lascube and Vincent Moscato at Parc des Princes a fortnight ago, it seemed to be the two Frenchmen - one dismissed for stamping, the other for butting - who threatened public order.
   When David Bishop was assailed in the players' tunnel at the Parc by Daniel Dubroca after an earlier France-England game, the World Cup

quarter-final last October, was it not the French coach, bellowing 'cheat' and manhandling the referee, who threatened public order?

Mais non. Eventually Dubroca resigned but as anyone would realize who subscribed to French conspiracy theories, on each occasion it was the referee who was to blame. And the French, well some Frenchmen anyway, are not letting them get away with it.

In one tiny corner of rugby's south-western heartland Hilditch and Bishop have had the full weight of municipal sanction brought down on them. They have been banned, as undesirable and a threat to public order, from Moncrabeau (population 792) and will not be permitted to stand in the annual election of the 'king of the liars', nor the triennial world championship of making faces, for which this Lot-et-Garonne village is renowned even more than its rugby.

Ten of the 15 village councillors voted against Hilditch, a Belfast headmaster, and Bishop, who lives a long way from trouble in a remote part of the South Island of New Zealand. 'These people could create public disorder,' the mayor, Christian Lussagnet, intoned. 'The people of Moncrabeau, who believe in fairness, do not appreciate the performance of these two gentlemen during the two last matches.' France lost them both.

After the Lascube-Moscato affaire, the French rugby federation president Bernard Lapasset invited Hilditch to take the temperature of French rugby by refereeing a few club games. It is safe to assume these will not be in **Clochemerle** ... sorry, Moncrabeau.

(25) BUILT by soldiers to withstand the gales of the Channel, there is no mistaking the line of the new outhouse on the Ecrehous, a chain of rocky islets lying halfway between the north-east coast of Jersey and France. But the islands' first flushing lavatory has not been well received by the sailors who have huts there. A **Clochemerle**-style row has erupted over the convenience, which arrived courtesy of the Jersey Customs and Excise (Impots) Department. Last month, it despatched a Territorial Army unit to the reef to build, alongside the Customs hut, the lavatory, water tank and outlet to the sea.

Development on such an extravagant scale has incurred the wrath of Jersey families with holiday retreats on the Ecrehous, including retired Brigadier Raoul Lempriere-Robin. 'The tank has been sited so it almost ends up on the door of someone's hut,' he said. 'Why can't they make do with an Elsan?'

Hut-dwellers have managed with chemical toilets for generations. The plan for the toilet was approved by an officer of Jersey's Island Development Committee under his delegated powers. But the controversy now involves the island's Attorney-General, Philip Bailhache, who has responsibility for the Ecrehous and who did not endorse the planning application.

(26) The piece de resistance of the museum is a superbly detailed scale model of Burton as it was in 1921 - complete with moving railway trains, fire engine, children playing in school yards, women washing, scenery arriving at the Opera House and all manner of impeccably researched architectural and sociological points.

Sadly the bottle-shaped van was away being restored on the day of my visit, but I patted the 'powerful hindquarters' of the giant shire horses in the stables, admired the 'saddle-tank' engine in the reconstructed railway ale-dock and inspected the ornate iron outside Gents (shades of **Clochemerle**).

While suggestive in morphosyntactic terms (*Clochemerle-style*, *shades of Clochemerle*), the number of these examples is still small, and it is debatable how far recognizability is linked to the British television serialization mentioned in (23), which may have since faded in collective memory. Most worrying, however, is the fact that several of these examples again suggest that the connotations of *Clochemerle* in English are different from those in French (or at any rate less clearly univocal), evoking public conveniences as much as petty factionism. Consequently, it seems that the use of a transfer strategy - for example, *Clochemerle-style* - might fail to convey the meaning of the source text adequately, though a final decision would require more careful assessment of the target text's readership. Examining a corpus of texts which illustrate a hypothesized textual rendition does not supplant, but rather ekes out the writer's intuition in this regard (cfr. Aston, this volume, chapter 1: 4.4).

3.2 Strategies of analogy

There was less uncertainty as far as translation into Italian was concerned, where no evidence whatever was found to support a transfer strategy. Not only had none of our students heard of Clochemerle, but there were also no occurrences of *clochmerl** in Italian texts found either on the Internet (where there is, however, far less Italian than English or indeed French material), or in the 1992 CD-ROM of *Il sole-24 ore* (the Italian equivalent of the *Financial Times*, which, like the latter, has a strong cultural section). After rejecting transfer, the next possible strategy which suggested itself was cross-cultural analogy, referring to a stereotype in the target language culture with similar connotations to those of Clochemerle in French.

Excluding the unlikely case of access to a parallel corpus containing previous translations of the same expression,[3] the problem here is that the translator must somehow be reminded of potential analogies in the target language culture. One way in which memory may be jogged is by looking at other texts that use the expression in question, and which may provide better triggers for memorized schemata than the source text does (Schank 1982). Reading the other French documents containing references to Clochemerle brought a number of Italian analogies to mind, one of which was Guareschi's *Don Camillo* stories, with their running battles between the village priest and the communist Mayor and their respective factions. Our students reported being reminded of this by the references to priests and mayors in texts (4), (5), (7), (8), and (10) above. As far as translation into English is concerned, one analogy which immediately comes to mind is from Swift's *Gulliver's Travels*, with its description of the disputes in Lilliput between Big-endians (who maintain that an egg should be broken into at the big end), and Little-endians (who fiercely maintain the contrary). Intuitively, both these analogies seem close to Clochemerle as comic descriptions of petty politics. However it remains to be confirmed that these stereotypes effectively have these connotations in the target culture, and that they are likely to be recognizable for the target reader.

The archives of CD-ROMs and the Internet were again used to provide evidence in these respects, *ad hoc* corpora being this time constructed in the target languages. The results in the two cases were very different. There were plenty of references to Guareschi and to Don Camillo on the Internet, several of them in Italian, as well as a number in the CD-ROM of *Il sole-24 ore*. These showed that Guareschi's stories had similar connotations to Clochemerle, and were recognizable as a stereotype, as the following example illustrates:

(27)   Deng, e con lui l'intera leadership, incita i cinesi a praticare il contrario di quello che sarebbe ovvio attendersi da chi si ostina a richiamarsi - almeno formalmente - ai principi del marxismo-leninismo. Deng lo fa con lo stesso messianico ardore con cui per anni disse di credere al socialismo reale, e le masse lo seguono con lo stesso acritico furore con cui parteciparono al Grande Balzo in Avanti e alla Rivoluzione Culturale. E' un tardivo omaggio a una vecchia e - all'epoca - vituperata intuizione di Giovannino Guareschi: il "Contr'ordine, compagni" che accompagnava alcune sue vignette.

I cinesi, naturalmente, non sono trinariciuti come i comunisti dileggiati dall'inventore di Don Camillo e dell'onorevole Peppone. E il loro accanimento nel disfare tutto ciò che era stato fatto dal 1947 in poi non è dovuto a un errore di stampa sul *Quotidiano del Popolo*. E' dovuto alla possibilità - per la prima volta nella loro storia - di poter finalmente guadagnare per sé, mangiare, consumare e, alla fine, vivere una vita decente.

In contrast, while an Internet search for the strings *big-endian** and *little-*

endian* found several thousand documents, these words turned out to be used as technical terms denoting computer architectures. When those documents which also contained the strings *computer**, *code**, *routine**, *program**, *byte** or *Unix* were excluded, only one text remained - that of *Gulliver's Travels* itself. A second search for *lilliput** was also carried out, but its connotations related to physical size rather than to political pettiness. Regretfully, therefore, the Swiftian analogy was abandoned as a translation hypothesis, there being no evidence to suggest that use of *big-* or *little-endian*, or allusion to Lilliput, would convey the intended connotations to the target reader.

3.3 Generating further hypotheses: the role of collocates

So far we have shown how corpora created *ad hoc* can be used to evaluate hypothesized translations. But there may come a point when the translator runs out of plausible hypotheses to test. In such cases, *ad hoc* corpora may suggest further ideas. Rather than searching for texts which include the hypothesized translation of the problematic expression, we can search for texts which present similar contexts to that for the expression we wish to translate, and see whether these suggest other hypotheses. We can, for instance, search for texts containing words which we would expect to co-occur with candidate translations. Thus in this chapter, we have repeatedly used the words *petty local politics* to describe Clochemerle. By retrieving and examining English texts which include these words, or others like it, we may well encounter, or be reminded of, further possible translations of *clochemerlesques*.[4]

Such an approach poses two main problems. The first is that of identifying target language expressions which are likely to co-occur with candidate translations. The second is that of deciding which of these expressions are likely to be most effective as a means of finding relevant texts. To use the terms of information retrieval systems, we need to balance recall (finding as many relevant texts as possible) with precision (avoiding irrelevant instances: cfr. Aston, this volume, chapter 1: 2.1).

To identify likely collocates of candidate translations, one possible starting point is to list those expressions which co-occur with *Clochemerle* in the source language. If we take all the French texts containing forms of *Clochemerle*, we can then identify other words which recur in a large proportion of these texts. By positing equivalents for these other words in the target language, we can then go on to look for target language texts which contain these equivalents, hoping that they will include candidate translations of *Clochemerle*.

While the ideal procedure would have been to work with words which frequently appeared in the near vicinity of *Clochemerle* (see note 4), this was not possible in this case. Even after combining the four relevant texts from the Internet with the 14 from *Le Monde* (and the source text itself), we still only had 24 occurrences of *clochemerle** altogether, and there were no lexical words which occurred more than twice within the 10 words to either side of these occurrences. A more productive procedure was to use the consistency option in *Wordsmith Tools* (Scott 1996) to examine the words which were found in many of the texts in this corpus.[5] The following lexical words all occurred in over one-third of the 19 texts: *fois* (13 texts); *aujourd'hui* (12); *faire* (11); *france, temps* (10); *années, compte, français, grande, jour, monde, président, question* (9); *culture, exemple, fin, font, jours, nouveau, partie, pays, petite, reste, vient, ville* (8); *bon, bonne, cause, centre, chose, communauté, coup, général, grand, guerre, lieu, moyens, plein, veut* (7). While many of these words are very general, there are a number which recall the *Clochemerle* stereotype, and which can be grouped semantically: *pays/ville/communauté* and *question/ guerre/partie*, for instance.

Scanning the wordlists for this corpus allowed further terms to be added to these semantic groups: in the second group, for instance, *polémique, querelle, discorde, guérilla, rivalité, conflit*, and *rebelle*. It is not difficult to think of possible English words with similar meanings, and (with the aid of a dictionary or thesaurus if necessary) to come up with a list of equivalents, such as *quarrel, squabble, row, bicker, dispute, rebel, battle*, and *rivalry*. Further terms can be added by analyzing the English texts which contained references to Clochemerle (examples (21)-(26) above).

If we were to look for English texts which contain words from this new list, it would seem reasonable to expect that at least some might contain candidate translations of *Clochemerle*. This leads us to the second problem, that of precision. As many of these words are relatively common, they are likely to occur in huge numbers of documents, relatively few of which are likely to provide candidate translations. This proportion may however be greater for some words than others. For instance, a glance in the dictionary suggests that *bicker* and *squabble* have connotations of pettiness which items such as *battle* and *dispute* lack.

Given the risk of finding unmanageably large numbers of texts, it is useful to first get some idea of the probable precision of searches by testing them against a relatively small body of texts. For instance, in *Micro-Concord Corpus A* (a one-million word selection from the *Independent* newspaper: Murison-Bowie 1993b), we find that the frequencies of these words fall into fairly distinct groups:

group A: *bicker** (2); *squabbl** (3); *quarrel** (6); *rivalr** (13)
group B: *rebel** (121); *disput** (131); *battl** (162); *row** (177)

The concordance in Figure 1 lists all the occurrences of the forms in group A in the *MicroConcord* corpus, while that in Figure 2 lists every twentieth occurrence of the items in group B.[6] Scanning these concordances and examining the texts from which they are taken, it appears that items from group A offer much greater precision in finding relevant texts. For instance, although there are only three instances of *squabbl** in *Micro-Concord Corpus A*, two of these describe situations of a Clochemerlean kind:[7]

(28) Because there is no strategic planning authority for London, the siting of the station is the subject of **squabbling** between rival local authorities. Camden is petitioning against the private King's Cross Bill aimed at obtaining approval for BR to build the new station. So too is Newham Borough Council, which wants the station in Stratford.

(29) The dispute has left the bipartisan efforts to reduce the deficit in, at least temporary, tatters.
   The Republicans claim that the capital gains cut (from 28 per cent to 19.6 per cent for two years) would stimulate investment and create jobs. The Democratic leaders insist that the cut is an unwarranted giveaway to the wealthy which will have no significant effect on the economy and deepen the deficit.
   In reality, the **squabble** is more over slogans and symbols left over from the Reagan years than anything substantial. This begs the question why the Democrats and the White House are staging such a divisive quarrel, at a time when agreement on a deficit-cutting budget for 1990 is already overdue (the nominal deadline passed yesterday).

The fact that other items from our lists are also present in these extracts - *quarrel*, *rival*, *dispute* - confirms the relative precision of *squabbl**.

The hope that *squabbl** might provide a fairly precise key to retrieve appropriate texts from the Internet proved however unfounded. Searching with AltaVista found over 5000 documents, and a glance through the first few titles suggested that few of them would be relevant. More encouragingly, the same search using the CD-ROM of the 1992 *Daily Telegraph* found the more reasonable number of 200 documents. When this

8. Going to the Clochemerle: exploring cultural connotations

```
 1   had tendered his resignation. <p> Once the  bickering  and backbiting, which also led to Terry
 2   corrupt priorities as this one." <p> Rodney  Bickerstaffe, general secretary of the public emp
 3   the White House are staging such a divisive  quarrel, at a time when agreement on a deficit-cu
 4   the General Workers' Union (UGT), which has  quarrelled  with the Socialist Party. <p> Mrs Gonz
 5   rds to an association of disparate and often  quarrelling  individuals, bound only by a common l
 6   as simply a press invention, but some public  quarrelling  immediately after the Bitter Suite se
 7   nd East Berlin have now forgotten their past  quarrels  to confront what both see as their commo
 8   knocked some discipline into a coalition of  quarrelsome, microscopic Communist parties and re
 9   ave of IRA attacks have not been hampered by  rivalries  and that different organisations have b
10   trading system now the victim of the ancient  rivalry  with the Chicago Board of Trade. So far,
11   By LARRY BLACK </bl> <st> <p> BLOODY-MINDED  rivalry  between America's two biggest car makers
12   and the powerful delineation of this central  rivalry  gave the whole performance its backbone.
13   the title. <p> However, Jansher's continuing  rivalry  with Jahangir Khan is likely to be the hi
14   e century-long history of Sheffield football  rivalry  when a goal by a Wednesday player has set
15              <hl> BT cuts prices 8% in  rivalry  with Mercury </hl> <bl> By MARY FAGAN, Te
16   nual contests, the fierce but friendly local  rivalry  is as intense as at any of the better-kno
17   . Leaving aside questions of pique, personal  rivalry  and murmurs of an 'MIT Mafia", the two ca
18   was divided over tactics and personalities.  'Rivalry  within the PDPA is a phenomenon that more
19   TV. <p> So, has ITV conceded in the sporting  rivalry  with BBC which has lasted as long as Davi
20   ing in England, in general evolved round the  rivalry  within counties, writes Kim Norkett.
21   erosity is, it seems, partly due to regional  rivalry. Hamburg's local government had seen the
22   and deepen the deficit. <p> In reality, the  squabble  is more over slogans and symbols left ov
23   sco Earthquake: Officials still find time to  squabble </hl> <bl> By MARC CHAMPION </bl>
24   the siting of the station is the subject of  squabbling  between rival local authorities. Camde
```

Figure 1. *quarrel*\squabbl*\bicker*\rivalr** in *MicroConcord Corpus A*

```
1   nge this week in Zimbabwe's biggest election battle before national polls next year. <p> The ru
2   became the focus of a sustained conservation battle which saved the eighteenth-century building
3   vision which brings the state of play in the battle for the sporting viewer into sharp perspect
4                              <h1> Decision near in US battle over cellular phones </h1> <bl> From LARRY
5   rge of flipping your lid", fighting a losing battle against a body armed with a humiliating ars
6   certainty to business and industry, help the battle against inflation, and secure lower rates o
7   est fly through the Soviet Union, across the battlefields of Afghanistan and past the guns of P
8           THE NUNS in Northamptonshire who are battling to save their 5,000 chickens from slaught
9   and 'osmosis" into the dark auditorium. <p> Battling against what sometimes feels like sensual
10  k". He warned that if anyone was hurt in the dispute the minister would be 'faced with calls fo
11  n postponed because of the domestic airlines dispute in Australia. The dispute has badly hit ef
12  ainst her, Ms Bhutto is embroiled in another dispute with President Ghulam Ishaq Khan over the
13  ng Kong must show its 'sincerity" before the dispute could be resolved. <p> On Sunday China ref
14  alks designed to lead to a resolution of the dispute in the occupied territories. The inner cab
15  bitrarily changing the definition of a trade dispute". <p> Ron Todd, general secretary of the T
16  -Knighton talks would agree to tear up their disputed agreement. It has been suggested that the
17  ence is to bring in foreign legislation." He disputes this, stating that: 'A wholesale introduc
18  d 'face to face" by a senior US officer, two rebel officers said they wanted General Noriega to
19  little authority beyond the capital. <p> The rebel movements are almost exclusively tribal — as
20  the Bush administration did not initiate the rebellion but knew about it at least two days in a
21  ng to arrange a more formal meeting with the rebels in Rome on 4 November. <p> It is not clear,
22  y in Poland to negotiate a settlement in the row over the presence of a Catholic convent on the
23  conference. <p> This is the second year in a row that the Opposition leader has claimed to be t
24  anced itself from claims of a constitutional row over Dr Runcie's remarks about Papal primacy a
25  -Arnold replacing Alex Gissing in the second row. <p> Paul Dodge, once the hard centre amongst
26                                          <h1> Rowing: Britain breath fire in last-gasp victory <
27                                          <h1> Rowing: Redgrave in Serpentine test </h1> <bl> By
28  uces three short scenes in which actors have rows, go to industrial tribunals, issue death thre
29  acting consortium. <p> Yet, despite numerous rows with the contractors, he has failed so far to
```

Figure 2. *row*\dispu*\rebel*\batl** in *MicroConcord Corpus A* (every 20th occurrence)

search was further restricted by adding another search term from our second semantic field, *local*, the number came down to 27.

In most of these 27 texts, *squabbl** was used to describe petty disputes between political factions or family members. While often similar in tone to the French source text, none of them however contained allusions to cultural stereotypes which seemed analogous to *Clochemerle*. At this point, the search for cross-cultural analogies was abandoned in favour of an alternative translation strategy, that of paraphase (see 3.4 below).

Clearly, we do not know whether further searches using other combinations of search terms or other CD-ROMs might have come up with candidate analogies. But at some point, a line must be drawn. Indeed, if we see the purpose of this search solely as coming up with a tolerable translation of *clochemerlesques*, it might be argued that far too much time and effort has been invested already. If, on the other hand, we also see it as an opportunity to find out about the language and the culture, in a process stimulated but not confined by a specific translation problem, and to acquire skills which can be brought to bear on similar problems elsewhere, the investment seems more justifiable. Even when unsuccessful, such searches are not necessarily unproductive in learning terms. As Zanettin (this volume, chapter 7: 5) stresses, much of the learning which takes place using corpora involves disconfirming hypotheses, establishing what does *not* occur. And equally, as Bernardini (this volume, chapter 9) illustrates, much learning from corpora is likely to be incidental rather than in relation to previously-formed hypotheses. Corpus use provides learners with microcosms to explore for themselves, picking up knowledge and experience in a self-directed manner, where they themselves must decide where to go and where to set the limits to their enquiries. In the case of the translation into Italian, it was incidental learning which underlay the second translation proposed by our students, that which provided a paraphrase equivalent for *clochemerlesques*.

3.4 Paraphrase strategies

Investigating the collocates of *Clochemerle** and their English equivalents highlights a fair range of lexis which could describe situations of this kind. For instance, *squabble* seems to share the meaning of petty rivalry conveyed by *clochemerlesques*, similarly implying a lack of global perspective:

(30) The blinkered attitudes of local sports administrators, **squabbling** to retain power, are being placed into perspective by visitors whose generosity of spirit has not been fully reciprocated.

(31) As a species, we are quite capable of drowning while **squabbling** over who gets best deck-chair on the Titanic.

In the absence of an analogous stereotype, the use of *squabble* seems a reasonably effective way of translating *clochemerlesques*, even if the meaning of petty rivalry is more denotative than connotative.

This translation hypothesis was arrived at in three stages: examining the collocates of *clochemerle** in an *ad hoc* source language corpus; positing equivalents for these collocates in the target language; and constructing and examining a target language corpus which contained these equivalents. Even though no ready-made equivalent for the source language expression was found, this last phase also suggested other translation hypotheses based on expressions encountered incidentally in the target language texts. For instance, as well as *squabble*, example (30) contains a further term, *blinkered*, which might have come in useful in a paraphrase. Translating into Italian, one of our students arrived at an effective paraphrase in this way, as a result of browsing through the texts mentioning *Guareschi* and *Don Camillo* (the analogous stereotypes to *Clochemerle* proposed in 3.2 above). One of these texts used the word *strapaese* (which literally means 'extremely provincial': see section 1 above) to describe the rhetoric of politicians in a small town.

A search for *strapaes** in the CD-ROM of *Il sole-24 ore* found 11 texts. In ten of these, it was clearly derogatory, implying undue narrowness.[8] Notably, it appeared in a series of three articles criticizing the organization of the 1992 Columbian celebrations in Genoa - a context strikingly close to that of the organization of jazz festivals criticized in the French source text. It also appeared in descriptions of provincialism in other countries (including France), *rivalità strapaesane* ('provincial rivalries') being contrasted with *confronto internazionale* ('international comparison'). These examples confirmed its similarity of meaning to the source text's *clochemerlesques*, providing, like *squabble*, a potential paraphrase to use in the translation.

4. Conclusions

For the record, our final English paraphrase of the source text's *les enjeux touristiques, de marketing, clochemerlesques, mal dissimulés* was *ill-concealed squabbling over the tourist market*: in Italian, our student's proposal was *la posta in gioco turistica, di marketing, strapaesana, mal dissimulata* (Soglia 1995). Neither of these translations is, perhaps, fully satisfying (we have not discussed their morphosyntactic aspects); neither, however, would seem unacceptable. But as few of our readers are likely to want to translate *clochemerlesques*, and fewer of the learners they may teach, let us close by underlining some of the more general principles which emerge from this study as important for corpus-aided language learning.

No preconstituted corpus of manageable dimensions can be expected to adequately document all of the problems a learner may encounter in understanding or producing a particular text. For this reason, we believe that the technique of creating corpora *ad hoc* to deal with specific problems is potentially useful. This implies that learners should acquire experience in creating *ad hoc* corpora and in evaluating potential means for doing so: the number and variety of CD-ROMs to which they may have access is growing, as is the quantity of texts available on the Internet and the variety and sophistication of the search engines for locating and retrieving them.

The particular kind of problem faced in this chapter, that of understanding and conveying cultural connotations, seems to be one where corpora of this kind can be particularly valuable. Central to native-like performance, but traditionally difficult for learners, lexical connotation is an area where conventional reference tools are notoriously inadequate (Neuner 1996). It is one thing to have read *Clochemerle* and to know that its *pissothière* led to open warfare, and quite another to understand its role as a stereotype of petty politics in French culture. It is only by experiencing allusions to it that this role can be appreciated. Here, the value of corpora containing multiple examples from which to infer connotations and their cultural status is apparent, providing a partial alternative to prolonged direct personal experience of the culture in question - a point developed by Louw (1993, 1997) in relation to the appreciation of literary texts, but which seems equally valid for more mundane text-types.

The procedures illustrated also show how constructing and using *ad hoc* corpora may result in incidental, tangential discoveries. What was learnt by our students went beyond the truth or falsehood of prefabricated hypotheses. Indeed, corpora may hardly be the best option for establishing the latter: who would download dozens of documents from the Internet if they could get the same answer from a dictionary or encyclopedia? But like libraries and bookshops, corpora tend to make for casual encounters with data which throw up other problems and make for other hypotheses than those with which one went to them. These problems and hypotheses can in their turn be investigated and tested, in a process which is potentially endless, as one thing leads to another. The texts containing instances of *squabble*, for instance, not only suggested *blinkered* as an alternative paraphrase term, but also suggested further possible cross-cultural analogies for *Clochemerle*, such as the feud between the Montagus and Capulets in Shakespeare's *Romeo and Juliet*, and the scene of the Mad Hatter's tea party in Carroll's *Alice in Wonderland*. Both these stereotypes were in fact rejected as candidate translations, the evidence suggesting that their primary connotations were of tragedy and inconclusiveness rather than of petty factionism. Nevertheless, they seemed ripe for investigation by learners. What in fact are the connotations of *Romeo and Juliet*? Or just Romeo? Or tea-parties? Are all hatters mad? Who are the better paradigms of madness, hatters or March hares? The incidental discoveries made in the hunt for Clochemerle could in so many places have become focusses for further research. This points to another use of corpora (discussed by Bernardini in the next chapter), one which goes beyond that of solving pre-existing problems, to instead give rein to curiosity, and encouraging the learner to exploit the enormous range of opportunities for reading, analyzing and learning which corpora can provide.

Notes

1. This has been one of the major motivations for the continual expansion of research corpora designed for lexicographic purposes, such as the Bank of English (cfr. Partington, this volume, chapter 2).

2. The number of documents found on the Web depends on when the search is carried out and the search engines used. A search using Excite, for instance, found twice as many documents as AltaVista: most of these however turned out to be mentions of an Australian racehorse called *Clochemerle*. Repeating either search today would undoubtedly find many more documents.

3. On the use of aligned parallel corpora for translation purposes, see Zanettin (this volume, chapter 7: 1).

4. Some support for such an approach comes from corpus-based work in multilingual lexicography. Research by Sinclair (1996a) and colleagues suggests that where a word in one language has more than one equivalent in another, as with *know* in English and *savoir/connaître* in French, it may be possible to select the appropriate equivalent automatically by examining the collocates of *know*, and then seeing whether the French equivalents of these collocates match those of *savoir* or those of *connaître*.

5. Scott (2000) has recently proposed a more sophisticated procedure which could be used for this purpose, based on the analysis of "associates" - i.e.

8. Going to the Clochemerle: exploring cultural connotations 219

words which are significantly more frequent than in a large reference corpus and which also tend to co-occur within the same texts.

6. Tags in the concordances in Figures 1 and 2 have the following meanings:

   <p>   new paragraph
   <hl> </hl>   start and end of headline
   <bl> </bl>   start and end of byline
   <st> </st>   start and end of subhead
   <dt> </dt>   start and end of date

7. This sentence, in which we have deliberately used the adjective *Clochemerlean*, highlights a further factor relevant to the choice of a translation or communication strategy - that is, whether the meaning of the expression is negotiated in the text itself, establishing it as a recognizable schema which can then be alluded to in what follows. We use *Clochemerlean* here, in other words, because we have previously explained its meaning. Since our source text contained no other references to Clochemerle or its author, we have ignored this factor in our discussion.

8. The negative connotations of *strapaese* are not noted in major Italian dictionaries, such as Treccani (1994): cfr. Partington (this volume, chapter 3: 4).

9 'SPOILT FOR CHOICE': A LEARNER EXPLORES GENERAL LANGUAGE CORPORA

Silvia Bernardini

> '[...] Nothing seems really to matter, that's the charm of it. Whether you get away, or whether you don't; whether you arrive at your destination or whether you reach somewhere else, or whether you never get anywhere at all, you're always busy, and you never do anything in particular; and when you've done it there's always something else to do, and you can do it if you like, but you'd much better not. Look here! If you've really nothing else on hand this morning, supposing we drop down the river together, and have a long day of it?'
>
> Kenneth Grahame, *The wind in the willows*

1. Introduction

Whilst in recent years activities involving *small* corpus concordancing in the language classroom have been described and discussed by a growing number of researchers, the pedagogic applications and implications of concordancing *large* general language corpora have received much less attention.[1] This paper looks at some reasons behind this lack of interest, and argues that the time is now ripe for wide-ranging exploration of the pedagogic potential of large corpora. Within a pedagogic framework which views communication as a process of meaning mediation and learning as a process of discovery (Widdowson 1990), I shall describe a learner's 'journey of discovery' in the 100-million word British National Corpus, with the aim of illustrating some key features of large corpus concordancing (LCC) and of evaluating these from a pedagogic perspective.

In the last fifteen years, large general corpora such as the Bank of English (presently featuring whole texts, written and spoken, produced in the UK, USA and Australia in the 1990s, totalling 420 million words - henceforth BoE) and the British National Corpus (featuring samples of a wide range of texts produced in the UK between the 1960s and the early 1990s, totalling 100 million words, 10 million of which are spoken - henceforth BNC), have firmly established themselves as aids in linguistic research. They have also helped extensively in the preparation of learners' dictionaries, grammars and pedagogic materials (see for example Cobuild 1987, 1990, 1995; Willis 1990) - 'helping learners with *real* English', as the Cobuild catch-phrase goes. One might have expected exploration of more direct pedagogic applications to have followed in the wake of such descriptive endeavours, as teachers and applied linguists came to appreciate what large corpora could potentially offer to them and their students. To take three fairly uncontroversial points:

- Large general corpora offer large amounts of genuine, unedited language material, showing all the richness, adaptability and subtlety of language being used for communication in different situations and for varying purposes. Therefore, they very often tell a different story from most language teaching materials, which present *contrived* texts chosen for exemplification purposes, or "language put on display" (Widdowson 1978: 53).
- Large corpora can provide an excellent observatory from which to appreciate the role of lexicalization and memorization in language performance. In recent years, the idea has repeatedly been put forward that native-like control of a language rests more on the memorization of a large inventory of lexicalized expressions - following the "idiom principle" (Sinclair 1991a: 110ff) - than it does on the ability to master morphosyntactic combinatory rules - following the "open-choice principle" (Sinclair 1991a: 109-110; cfr. Gavioli, this volume, chapter 5: 2.1). By highlighting what is typically said and written in similar circumstances, LCC provides an instrument to observe the pervasiveness of idiomaticity in language performance (Bolinger 1976: 3), as well as its (con)textual constraints.
- Large corpora offer a powerful reference tool to check intuitions about a language. Teachers and learners can use them to test their hypotheses and to check the reliability of information provided by dictionaries, grammars and native-speaking informants (Greenbaum 1984: 193). Non-native teachers may thus be in a position to overcome their lack of native intuition and, more importantly, both native and non-native teachers may be able to gather evidence to support their claims, offering students more satisfying explanations than 'it sounds right/wrong'. Learners at intermediate and advanced levels may be stimulated to question the dependability of the generalizations they are fed, thereby developing a certain critical autonomy (Aston 1996: 191).

More than enough, one would have thought, to prompt further investigation and experimentation to find out whether large corpora have a place in the classroom as well as in the offices of grammarians and lexicographers. Yet LCC has not been the subject of significant theorization in language pedagogy, with the literature at most focussing on the concordancing of smaller specialized corpora. Behind this lack of interest in LCC lie a number of practical reasons.

Designed with the aim of providing a reasonably representative cross-section of language performance - i.e. substantial and varied - on which to base linguistic research, large general corpora such as the BNC or the BoE are far more complex than small ones, which are generally assembled in order to represent only a single variety. The BoE has constantly grown in size and range of text-types sampled, being updated and re-balanced yearly. Following a rather different philosophy, the BNC's creators adopted a carefully thought out sampling methodology (Burnard 1995), with the aim of creating a fixed and well-documented tool that would serve as a point of reference against which work on other corpora could be compared. This involved adding a large amount of structural and contextual information about the texts sampled so as to allow contrastive analyses of various kinds, and providing a purpose-designed, user-friendly retrieval application able to draw upon this information (SARA: Aston and Burnard 1998). Clearly, considerable funding and expertise - in both computational and linguistic terms - are necessary to construct such corpora, making their creation an impracticable objective for the majority of researchers in applied linguistics, not to mention single teachers. On the other hand, the increasing availability of texts already in electronic form on the World Wide Web or on CD-ROM, as well as the possibility of capturing material through scanning and typing, make it relatively straightforward to build small, variety-specific, more opportunistically-assembled corpora - requiring generally available facilities, little expertise, and limited expense (Tribble 1997). For instance, the list of small corpora compiled by Ma (1993) and adapted by Flowerdew (1996), shows a prevalence of relatively easy-to-collect texts such as newspaper and journal articles, and a near-total absence of speech of any kind.[2] With large general corpora not easily available, who could discuss their pedagogic use(s), and, more importantly, why should anyone bother?

This situation is now rapidly changing. Although still impossible for single institutions and individuals to construct, large corpora are no longer inaccessible to them, as the builders of large corpora have started to make their products public. The entire BNC, and a 50 million word selection from the BoE, are now accessible over the Internet, and anyone can send simple queries to their demo facilities without even subscribing to the services (see note 1). The structures and expertise required are minimal, as are the costs involved. So not just institutions but many single teachers and students can afford access to large corpora nowadays. But why should they take the trouble?

For almost two years I have been using the BNC regularly as a student, for my own autonomous, open-ended language-learning. In this paper I offer for discussion a distillation of this experience, from the viewpoint of the language learner. At the same time, I have reflected on the theoretical implications of such a procedure in terms of a 'pedagogy of discovery', of the value of its results, and of its applicability and generalizability, and I also offer an account of these reflections, this time from the viewpoint of the teacher and researcher. Both in terms of the learner's need for stimulating and satisfying activities, and of the teacher's/ researcher's requirement for pedagogically sound ones, LCC seems worth the trouble.

2. Learning as discovery

Widdowson (1990) suggests that language pedagogy can be informed either by a *medium* view of meaning or by a *mediation* one. While the former assumes that meaning is intrinsic to language, "a function of the linguistic sign as formal symbol", the latter instead sees it

> not [as] a semantic matter of encoding and decoding messages by reference to linguistic knowledge, but [as] a pragmatic matter of negotiating an indexical relationship between linguistic signs and features of the context.
> (Widdowson 1990: 118)

From a medium viewpoint, learning is mostly concerned with the acquisition of communicative *competence* - in Hymes's (1972) sense of the term - related to the formal features of the language system and their conventional uses. From a mediation viewpoint, on the other hand, learning is primarily concerned with the development of communicative and learning *capacity*, which is necessary to operate on competence, and to consequently increase and progressively restructure it. Whereas learning in a medium-oriented perspective is primarily a cumulative process, operating at the systematic level of formal knowledge, learning in a mediation-oriented perspective is an inherently developmental process, operating at the schematic level of contextual "preparedness for use" (Widdowson 1984: 105).

The pedagogic framework to which I shall relate LCC is a mediation-oriented one, aiming to teach learners how to "communicate as [...]

member[s] of a particular socio-cultural group" (Breen and Candlin 1980: 90) and how to learn ever more effectively and autonomously. As such, it is essentially a pedagogy of discovery, whereby

> language is learned as a contingent consequence of carrying out activities which engage the language with the learners' knowledge and experience of things.
>
> (Widdowson 1990: 120)

Such an approach has a series of pedagogic implications. Here I shall only mention those central to my discussion of LCC, relating to the issues of tasks, autonomy, and authenticity.

2.1 Tasks

Pedagogy becomes mainly concerned with the devising of tasks which require the learner to practice those skills and strategies s/he needs in order to communicate and learn ever more effectively (Brumfit 1984; Prabhu 1987; Skehan 1996a, 1996b, 1998; Willis 1996). Its approach will therefore be process- rather than product-oriented, focussing on "providing learners with contexts for meaningful activities and practice in procedural use of language" (Robinson et al. 1995: 62). Such contexts need to:

- engage the learner's interest through a challenge of some kind (Prabhu 1987: 55-57), favouring intellectual involvement with the task and providing stimuli for communicative interaction;
- create 'reasoning-gaps', which "involve deriving some new information from given information through a process of inference, deduction, practical reasoning, or a perception of relationships or patterns" (Prabhu 1987: 46);
- combine meaning- and form-focussed activity. Different goals of language learning - *accuracy*, *fluency* and *complexity/restructuring* - appear to be in mutual tension, accuracy and restructuring requiring a focus on form, and fluency a focus on meaning (Skehan 1996a, 1996b, 1998). Since the learner's attentional resources are limited, and s/he cannot focus on all aspects at once, tasks should be carefully tuned so as not to sacrifice one aspect in favour of the other(s).

2.2 Autonomy

Viewing learners as actively involved in their overall learning process, a pedagogy of discovery emphasizes the importance of autonomy, motivation and self-confidence. In this sense, its approach will be learner- rather than language-centred, requiring that:

- learners practice learning as self-instruction while still within a formal learning environment: they have a chance to try out strategies and procedures and store successful ones for use in the 'real world', and to appreciate that learning is not only a matter of formal instruction but also of continuing education;
- some measure of self-determination is provided so as to reconcile the individual's need to follow her/his own strategies and procedures - a requirement of successful language instruction, according to Bialystok (1985) and Dickinson (1987) - with the pedagogic need to refine such strategies in order to make them more effective (O'Malley and Chamot 1990). If learners are partly responsible for their learning process, and are allowed to shape it according to their cognitive preferences and developmental competence/capacity, both the stressful feeling of dragging along and the fossilizing one of being faced with unchallenging tasks may be avoided, thereby increasing motivation and, ultimately, chances of success in language learning (Crabbe 1993: 443).

2.3 Authenticity

Viewing meaning not as a built-in feature of the language system, but as a function of the interaction between language, context and text (Halliday and Hasan 1985), a pedagogy of discovery values the authenticity of language used for communication. In this sense, it will be meaning- rather than form-focussed, centering around:

- *authentic tasks*, exploiting the social potential of the classroom and the learners' interests to stimulate "realistically motivated" communication (Breen and Candlin 1980: 98), and to provide opportunities for learners to engage with texts in order to achieve "solutions to problems they feel are worth solving" (Widdowson 1984: 98);
- *authentic texts*, having a set of communicative - rather than merely exemplificatory - purposes, as a consequence of their being "deeply embedded in the processes of persons maintaining themselves in society" (Firth 1952/53: 13). However incomplete, elliptical, context-dependent and potentially unreliable as units of analysis (as claimed by Widdowson 1992: 309), authentic texts at least offer an honest

picture of the language as it is actually used for communication, and one which is sensitive to the role played by lexicalization and memorization in language performance (Bolinger 1976; Pawley and Syder 1983; cfr. Aston, this volume, chapter 1: 2, and section 1 above);

- *authentic discourse*, stimulating learners to engage in the process of mediation which converts text to discourse (comprehension) and discourse to text (production). Activities which require learners to develop strategies for text analysis, and which at the same time draw attention to local aspects such as variation in (semi)-fixed expressions, collocations, colligations, "semantic prosodies" (Louw 1993) etc., and link these to more global aspects such as the organization of information, the presuppositions underlying the text, its overall function(s), register and so on, should also increase critical awareness, and with it the learner's ability to make sense of language input and to communicate successfully. As Carter puts it:

> it is important not simply to look through language to the content of the message but rather to see through language to the ways in which messages are mediated and shaped, very often in the interests of preserving or of reinforcing ideologies.
>
> (Carter 1993: 142)

2.4 Learning as a journey

In section 3 I shall attempt to assess LCC in relation to a set of pedagogic as well as educational objectives ranging from the acquisition of idiomaticity to the development of critical awareness and autonomy. Assuming that learning should take place within an environment rich in intellectual stimuli and language input, with low levels of anxiety and competition and high levels of self-determination and personal involvement, we shall see how LCC can take advantage of the flexibility and potential of corpora designed for linguistic research to stimulate the curiosity of learners in unpredictable ways, resulting in highly motivating 'serendipitous learning'. The metaphor I employ to describe such work, that of *learning as a journey*, builds on Widdowson's (1990) notion of a pedagogy of discovery. It sees learners as explorers, and corpora as realms to be explored. By leaving responsibility for the journey with the learners, this approach favours their active and creative participation. It ensures that learning tasks are always of interest to them, and compatible with their competence/capacity. As a result, I shall suggest that such tasks are also likely to provide a stimulus to engage in discourse, providing material for authentic communicative activities - i.e. "realistically motivated", in Breen and Candlin's (1980: 98) words - such as group discussion and research projects.

Insofar as every journey is unique, LCC cannot be reduced to a set of instructions, nor can the path which a learner will follow be determined in advance. In this sense, LCC cannot be described. We neither know (nor aim to determine) what each individual will use the corpus for, nor what s/he will find in it. To bypass this descriptive deadlock, the next section offers a sample of my own travelling experience. This makes no claim to any kind of comprehensiveness: its purpose is purely clarificatory, to serve as a basis for the ensuing discussion.

3. Diary of a journey

The image of corpus-based learning activities as journeys of discovery may help us appreciate some central aspects of the approach to be described. Faced with a large corpus, learners can be viewed as travellers setting off through unfamiliar territory. While they will probably have a plan and a destination in mind, these will invariably change as unexpected obstacles or opportunities force or tempt them in new directions. The initial stimulus for the activity often becomes a mere pretext: while curiosity, doubts, a teacher's corrections or suggestions are all likely to suggest starting points, the corpus will then see to it that they do not run short of further stimuli. Thus, they will soon find themselves exploring certain regions thoroughly and only stopping briefly in others. At times they will slow down to observe the landscape, while at others they will press on until they find something more noteworthy. And all the while, they can be encouraged to draw maps, make notes for future journeys, and take pictures to show to friends and families back home when they describe their experiences or share impressions with other travellers.

The journey metaphor also emphasizes the unique nature of every learning experience. It focuses attention not so much on a starting or end point, as on the in-between: choices made or not made, strategies adopted, experience garnered, incidental findings. It underlines the importance of putting the learner in charge of planning, accomplishing and reporting on an activity which s/he finds worth undertaking, and highlights how activities of this kind are likely to develop strategies to make travelling easier and more enjoyable. Finally, it emphasizes the 'mind-broadening' potential of activities which stimulate the learner to observe and reflect on aspects of the language and of the culture which s/he may never have noticed or focussed on before, ultimately increasing her/his linguistic and cultural awareness.

The journey I report on in this section, which was carried out across the British National Corpus, provides a genuine example - among innumerable other options - of an LCC activity. The level of analysis is purposely kept low in order to highlight only such features as a learner could probably notice and such (partial) generalizations as s/he could probably make. There is obviously no claim as to the descriptive exhaustiveness of the analyses offered, which should be viewed exclusively in terms of their pedagogic value. Equally, there is no claim as to the generalizability of this journey to others: one of the key points of the procedure I am advocating is its fundamentally learner-centred nature, to be tuned on the cognitive skills and preferences of the individual, with varying and unpredictable outcomes. It would be inherently contradictory to prescribe a methodology when the aim of the approach is to give learners the instruments to develop their own methodologies and make their own discoveries. The reader is invited to interact with this report, imagining alternative routes which were not taken and other observations which were not made by this particular traveller. The reader will thus get a flavour - albeit an indirect one - of the potential of LCC in a pedagogy of discovery.

3.1   Exploration 1

My starting point in this journey was an analysis of the word forms *spoiled/spoilt*. Given the negative evaluation they convey, they intuitively seemed to be potentially linked with ideological positions.[3] I wanted to find out who or what is commonly described as *spoiled/spoilt*, as well as any connotations derivable from the textual environment of these words. The search was limited to adjectival occurrences, that is, ones tagged as 'adjective', 'adjective or past tense verb', or 'adjective or past participle' in the BNC.[4] I found 112 adjectival occurrences of *spoiled* and 80 of *spoilt*, which I sorted by the right, thereby grouping cases where the same word was premodified by *spoiled/spoilt*.

In very general terms, *spoiled/spoilt* either referred to something being ruined or rotten, or to someone being pampered. The 'pampered' sense of the term - as highlighted by the presence of a human (*brat(s)*, *child(ren)*, *daughter(s)*, *kid(s)* etc.) or very occasionally an animal referent (*dog*, *horse*) - appeared to be much more common than the 'ruined/rotten' sense in the output I obtained, especially as far as *spoilt* was concerned.[5] Checking the entries of *spoil* in dictionaries (Cobuild 1987, 1995), I found that they placed the 'ruined' sense first, and wondered why. Is this a case where the senses of the inflected forms have different frequencies from those of the "root" word (Renouf 1987b)? Or is the evidence yielded by the BNC partly discordant with that yielded by the Cobuild Corpus/Bank of English? We might, for instance, download random occurrences[6] of each of the forms of the lemma - *spoil, spoils, spoiling, spoilt, spoiled* (with no part-of-speech specification) - and group recurring referents and patterns of collocates in order to separate the two senses, comparing their frequencies in each case.

Such an investigation is not as irrelevant to a language learner as it might seem. Comparing information taken from a dictionary - even a corpus-based one - with first-hand evidence derived from a corpus is a 'consciousness-raising' activity, which can stimulate one to evaluate reference works critically, and consequently get to know them better and learn to use them more appropriately, as well as making one more aware of their inherent limits (Krishnamurthy 1996). At such a crossroad, the traveller must decide whether to take an unplanned turning, focussing attention on this specific point and designing queries which could satisfy curiosity about it, or whether to keep straight on, possibly making notes of the untrodden path for a future journey.

I decided to keep straight on. Among the right-hand collocates of *spoiled/spoilt* meaning *ruined* (there seemed to be no qualitative difference in use between the two forms),[7] only *votes* (4), *(ballot) papers* (4) and *ballots* (3) occurred more than once, hinting at lexicalized collocations. When I enlarged the context of these solutions, a number of terms and phrases relating to elections popped up, such as

- adjectives: *blank, spoiled or blank, spoiled or destroyed, spoilt or invalid, valid*;
- nouns: *ballots, votes, voting papers, papers*;
- verbs: *... of valid votes* cast; *... ballots were* cast; *... who* returned *spoiled ballot papers*; *who* cast *blank or deliberately* spoiled *ballot papers*; *Thatcher* received *204 votes*; *to* abstain *or* spoil *their votes*;
- noun phrases: *(no) confidence vote/motion; electoral college; round of voting; polling stations.*

The environment of the search-word in its 'pampered' sense turned out to be more interesting. Its right-hand collocates included *child/children* (33), *(little) brat* (21) and *(rich) kid(s)* (7). Despite their literal denotation of children, a number of these occurrences actually referred to adults - in particular to adult *females* - who *behave, kick and scream, fight each other* or simply are *like* spoilt children/kids/brats. The pattern is too evident to pass unnoticed: apart from *daughter(s)* (3), *girl(s)* (3), *bitch* (2), *child bride*, *heroine*, *Princess*, *wife* and *woman* (1 occurrence each), which can be spotted at first sight (and the masculine equivalents of these are not attested, with the exception of two occurrences of *spoiled [...] son*), there are a number of other clues, which require a slower reading, and sometimes a larger context than that provided by the standard one-line KWIC concordance format. These include female personal, possessive or reflexive pronouns, and names such as *Brigitte, Claudine, Diana, Julia, Maisie,* and *Melanie*. Overall, one is left with little doubt that *spoiled/spoilt* has sexist connotations. These connotations are confirmed by the numerous adjectival collocates of the search-word, which build up a colourful image of the 'spoiled woman' as *pampered* (6), *rich* or *wealthy* (3), *ungrateful, petulant, wilful, naughty, bitter, cosseted, fickle, heartless, neurotic, over-anxious* and *self-absorbed* (1 occurrence each)! Thus in the following examples, from a text from the *Liverpool Echo and Daily Post* (K97),

> *Pits protesters are branded 'spoilt children'*
> *Tory MP's fury as surgery is picketed*
> A NORTH Wales MP has accused Labour supporters of 'behaving like **spoilt** children' and of not living in the real world.

we can construct an interpretation of the reported utterance on the basis of the negative and sexist 'semantic prosody' I have just described (cfr. Bublitz 1995; Partington, this volume, chapter 3: 4). Labour supporters are not simply compared to children, they are implicitly labelled as effeminate, a shade of meaning that no doubt adds to the virulence of the accusation.

A last point concerning *spoiled/spoilt*. Reading through the solutions, one soon notices that many of them belong to the same type of text. Consider for instance the following:

BP1   his link to success was more like a chain binding him to the **spoilt** daughter of the man whose position he envied
HGK   'I did not kiss you,' he said softly. 'I was merely calming a **spoiled** child. This is a kiss, senorita.' This time his arms wrapped around her
CEC   'Forgive Czarina, Mr D'Arcy. She's terribly **spoiled** and doesn't take easily to strangers.
JYC   Melanie's beautiful, wilful, and she's been **spoiled** rotten all her life.' He smiled wryly. 'I was a challenge to her.

These all belong to what is sometimes referred to as 'women's romance fiction', and perpetuate the stereotype of the spoilt *femme fatale*. In

Stubbs's (1996) terms, they are a vehicle of cultural transmission, and a powerful one because of their reach.[8] Further analysis - for instance looking contrastively at the distribution of *spoiled/spoilt* and of any other potentially 'sexist' uses of seemingly neutral language items in texts written by female/male authors or intended for a female/male audience (both pieces of information, when available, are encoded with the BNC texts) - would be necessary to study this issue in more detail.[9] Another turning opens up at this stage, leading to unpredictable destinations.

3.2   Exploration 2

Instead of following this direction, I took a different one. Among the patterns including the words *spoilt* and *spoiled*, the most salient was certainly the phrase *spoilt/spoiled for choice* (62 occurrences). In order to see if and how the phrase varied, I downloaded all the occurrences of *spoil/ spoils/spoiled/spoilt/spoiling for*, as well as all those of *for choice*, thus striking a satisfactory balance between precision (getting *only* relevant solutions, but possibly missing some) and recall (getting *all* the relevant solutions, but possibly getting irrelevant ones as well: cfr. Aston, this volume, chapter 1: 2.1).

While a few interesting collocations cropped up in the concordance of *for choice* - *room for choice* (6 occurrences), *scope for choice* (5), *opportunity/ies for choice* (5) -, it was immediately clear that the basic form *spoilt/spoiled for choice* undergoes only limited modifications. After removing the spurious solutions from the two concordances, there was a single occurrence of *will spoil you for choice* in the middle of 50 occurrences of *spoilt for choice* and 12 of *spoiled for choice* (suggesting that the standard form is probably the former). The implication for the learner is clear: caution should be exercised in handling this phrase, which allows virtually no lexico-syntactic variation. A single occurrence of *spoilt for sports car choice* hints at the possibility of creative manipulation, but at the same time highlights its rarity: where creativity is not a priority, it might be better to stick to more standard patterns such as '(be) spoilt for choice *with* (7) or *of* (2) something'. Although other prepositions - *by, for, on* - are attested, the presence of only a single occurrence of each suggests that they may be idiosyncratic.

Another possibility suggested by the data involves placing the phrase in a separate sentence or title, with the following sentence or subtitle normally clarifying the meaning being conveyed. This appears to be chosen especially for eye-catching purposes - a strategy reproduced in the title to this chapter, as well as in the following examples:

CB4 **Spoilt for choice** Steven Seaton provides a comprehensive guide on how to choose the right shoe for you.
ACR **Spoilt for choice** Texels have established their slot as terminal sires capable of delivering lean and meaty lambs to suit an increasingly selective trade.
AYM **SPOILT FOR CHOICE** There is a mouthwatering choice of excellent value for money dishes on the Beefeater menu.

3.3 Exploration 3

From a textual viewpoint, *spoilt/spoiled for choice* was also interesting in a number of other respects. First, it occurred mostly in written texts: only three solutions out of 62 are spoken, two of them from conversational material, one from a radio phone-in.[10] Second, it was often preceded by a specification of the audience being addressed, and followed by an explanation/expansion of some kind. Figure 1 illustrates this three-part structure. While in the first three of the examples the reader is directly called upon through an explicit apostrophe (*you*), in the last three s/he is implicitly referred to as part of a group who share the same tastes.

While we cannot construct a rule out of six examples, the fact that an audience is selected and addressed hints at a specialization of this phrase for advertising purposes. Among the occurrences yielded by the BNC, it is not difficult to isolate a fair number which appear to share this function. Consider, for example, the following:

ED1 when it comes to eating out in Stuttgart you're **spoilt for choice**. | Ketterer Hotel || A friendly, family-run
AMD with all this on offer you'll be **spoilt for choice** of things to do, but there's still more! Swim
K97 On site car parking is available. | **Spoilt for choice** ... our showroom is packed with beds and
EET Guests will find themselves **spoilt for choice** with a variety of dining possibilities,
BMC DECCA CLASSICS - One is **spoiled for choice** when it comes to Decca's mid-price range

While it is hard to say whether these texts belong to exactly the same text-type or genre, they undoubtedly share the purpose, in very general terms, of selling something to someone, be it records, furniture, or a holiday. Writers about this last topic appear to be particularly fond of the phrase: at least 15 of the 62 solutions come from texts concerned with tourism. A more wide-ranging investigation might go on to select those texts in which the phrase is used to advertise holiday resorts and study how the word *choice* and its inflexions are employed to lure the reader into buying, say,

9. 'Spoilt for choice': a learner explores general language corpora 233

1	If *you* find *stately homes* and *country houses* fascinating	*you*'ll be spoilt for choice.	Sussex offers the Elizabethan Majesty of *Parham House*, [...] the Edwardian beauty of *Preston Manor* [...]
2	with over *200 types of bread*	*you*'re really spoilt for choice.	As well as the great British breads like *Bloomer, Cottage Farmhouse* and *Cotter* [...]
3	if [...] *you* prefer the *sporting life*	then *you*'re spoilt for choice here.	There's *tennis, windsurfing, volleyball* [...]
4	*Transport* enthusiasts	are spoilt for choice in the Heart of England.	The *Museum of British Road Transport* at Coventry, the *Patrick Collection* [...] are well worth a visit.
5	*Fish*-eaters	are spoiled for choice	with *cuttlefish, octopus, swordfish* [...]
6	*Motorcycling* fans here	will be spoilt for choice next Saturday	with four events being promoted on the same day. Topping the bill is the final *Ulster road race* of the season, the *Carrowdore '100'* [...]

Figure 1. *Spoilt/ed for choice*: some examples of a typical cotextual pattern

a packaged holiday in which very little choice is in fact left to the buyer ...

I searched for occurrences of *choice/choices/choose/chooses/ choosing/chose/chosen* in seven of the tourism texts in which *spoilt/spoiled for choice* appeared, and found that in six of them the number of solutions was significantly higher than would be expected given the total number of occurrences of these words in the BNC.[11] This single finding suggests that a more general investigation along these lines might be potentially rewarding, telling us something about the manipulative power of the language we are learning, as well as providing insights into the way a speech community sees itself, and prompting cross-cultural observations and reflections as to its ideals and expectations. This would also force the learner to browse longer stretches of text than provided by a simple concordance, focussing their attention on recurrent patterns and strategies within particular texts or text-types.

3.4 Exploration 4

Though less straightforward than the intertextual analysis of concordances, the intratextual investigation of single texts may lead to serendipitous learning of an equally stimulating nature. For instance, browsing an extract from one of the texts dealing with tourism mentioned above (EC9: *Short Breaks - Brighton and Hove*), I made a number of observations regarding the strategies used to describe a holiday resort in a way that a British audience would find inviting. These included, first of all, interspersing the text with lexicalized expressions and pieces of culture-specific information which are not explicitly clarified by the context, probably on the assumption that they will be immediately recognized by the reader:

Short Breaks - Brighton and Hove [EC9]	*Unrestricted search of the whole BNC*
A RIGHT ROYAL BREAK For over two hundred years in Britain, almost anybody who is anybody enjoyed a break in Brighton.	Tourists too can expect a *right Royal* welcome [AMW] would make a *right royal* half-term treat for ye kids. [CH1] start of a *right royal* relationship for Frankie [CH5] we have been given *right royal* treatment [HHS]
BREAK OUT OF THE ORDINARY If it's happening anywhere, it's sure to be	He can *break out of* the space of desperation. [KRH]

9. *'Spoilt for choice'*: *a learner explores general language corpora*   235

happening in Brighton & Hove

All that jazz. So many great places to eat. But how will you spend the rest of your time at Brighton & Hove?

Aficionados of art and antiques will *make a bee-line* for the town's museums and art galleries.

A visit to the new Sealife Centre really *makes the oceans come to life:* there are fish there you can actually touch!

And our hotels and guest-houses are *kept on their toes* by an inspection visit to ensure that standards remain high.

an attempt to *break out* of this self-imposed restriction. [ABL]
people remember the event because it was *out of the ordinary*, and special. [ADE]
It should be different, *out of the ordinary*, exciting. |[ADK]

'He had been there with Orton and *all that jazz* and I wasn't interested." [J0W]
'Well, how's it going?" said Alex, after a teaspoon of froth. It? Oh, love, life and *all that jazz* [HGF]
All that jazz and even more | | BUDDING young jazz musicians are being given the chance to shine [K2R]

take the hassle out of buying and co-ordinating your wardrobe by *making a bee-line* for this month's best buys. [ARJ]
SLUMP-bashed shoppers are *making a bee-line* for Kwik Save, [CEL]
always *makes a bee-line* for the regulars as soon as he hears the last orders bell. [A17]

All around them the world had *come to life.* [CR6]
By night, the Plaka District *comes to life* with its wealth of shops and restaurants [AMW]
By night the island really *comes to life* [AM0]

'a worthy and interesting adversary - he always *kept* us *on our toes*'. [ACS]
The general use of disapproval in order to *keep people on their toes* tends to be counterproductive after a time. [H0E]
We need our ordinary grumbling members to *keep us on our toes*. [HU1]

And the *sport of Kings* is still pursued on the nearby downland at the famous Brighton Race Course	HORSE racing may be *the sport of kings*, or more recently sheiks. [AHT] Horse riding was his route to this feeling. It was '*the sport of kings*' after all [A7H]
listening to the sound of *leather on willow* at the Sussex County Ground.	enjoy the sound of *leather meeting willow* at the Colwyn Bay Cricket club [EFC] the sound of *willow on leather* [...] as Australian batsmen yet again plaster the ball all over another English Cricket Ground. [K1S]
a sneak preview of productions bound for London's *West End*.	London is, as well, the main place for entertainment, [...] There are lots of theatres, also especially in the '*West End*'. [HDA]

A second strategy that seems typical of this text (or possibly text-type - comparisons with similar texts would be needed to check this) is the personification of places, which are represented as actively welcoming tourists, rather than passively suffering their presence:

- The jewellery and antique shops of the famous winding alleyways called the Lanes *continue to serve* discriminating tastes
- The hotels and guest houses still *treat* their visitors *like* royalty.
- There is no shortage of golf courses, tennis clubs, squash courses and riding stables *happy to welcome* visitors.
- As evening approaches, other exciting opportunities *jostle for* your attention
- There's greyhound racing at Hove's celebrated stadiums where a restaurant overlooking the track *gives* diners a ring side view

Thirdly, and unsurprisingly, there is a generalized tendency towards overstatement. This is not just the result of over-reliance on superlatives and intensifiers, but also of more subtle choices, such as:

- frequent references, figurative or not, to *royalty* - *king(s)* (6), *Prince* (4), *royal* (3), *royalty* (1), *regal* (1);
- explicit or implicit comparisons with the capital:

  - discover the delights of 'London by the sea'.

- Brighton was a centre of high society second only to London.
- A sneak preview of productions bound for London's West End.
- There are more restaurants than anywhere outside London.
- (And where in London can you enjoy seafood dishes with a tableside view of the sea?)
- Brighton & Hove is one of the best shopping centres you'll find outside of London.

- the use of positively connotated verbs (*bowl over*, *enjoy*), nouns (*splendour*, *abundance*, *pleasure*, and obviously *choice*), and adjectives (*exclusive, discriminating, riveting, fabulous,* etc.);
- figurative language:

  - A Brighton and Hove break will hi-jack your taste buds in record time
  - you can cross the intercontinental frontiers of flavour
  - A visit to the new Sealife Centre really makes the oceans come to life
  - You can also walk on water at the nearby pier

3.5   Exploration 5

Lastly, browsing single texts can provide a wealth of new directions of research, which are not necessarily linked to the original one in any apparent way, and which are not accountable for in terms of a particular research strategy. As a final example, the sentence:

> If you're enjoying Brighton & Hove on a budget there are also bistros, pizza places and good old fish and chips.

prompted me to find out what is referred to as *good old* in the BNC - 502 solutions, with collocates such as *days* (115), *British* (13), *England* (3), *English* (9), *Britain* (2), most of them carrying a clearly ironic overtone. This sentence also suggested that *fish and chips* is not only a meal in British English, but a place - a hypothesis I checked against a random selection of occurrences of the phrase in the corpus, and found to be correct. But at this point I had also noticed the word *chippy/chippie*, as in

J9A   We had fish and chips from the local chippy for lunch, dinner and supper.
D90   And we went to Frinton of all places and you could go to the chippie and get fish and chips and everything.

and gone on to make a query for *chippy/chippie/chippies*, finding 68 solutions. Most of them referred to chip shops, but a few did not:

AM5 Let's assume you'll be just a general-purpose chippie, doing jobs like building stud partition walls
GVS Its dry, 'chippy' tone goes well in association with pizzicato or col legno strings
CDY Personally I thought she was hostile and chippy.

I could now have concentrated on these occurrences and tried to guess their meanings from larger contexts; or I could have focussed on *chippy/ie* ('chip shop'), and found out which texts - and consequently what registers - it belonged to and, by the same token, was indexical of. And so on.

3.6 Other explorations

I will not pursue either of these directions here. Instead, prior to concluding this report, I will briefly list a number of other explorations which suggested themselves in the course of this journey.

First of all, a number of (semi-)fixed expressions cropped up, which prompted more or less successful attempts to check their patterns of variation. As well as various occurrences of *too many cooks spoil the broth* and *to the victor(s) the spoils*, I encountered a number of more or less daring variants, such as:

ASJ *Too many Cooks did not spoil the travellers' broth* and by the end of the nineteenth century Cooks had offices across Europe and America,
CKA There is no danger of *too many coaches spoiling the broth* as far as the Hong Kong RFU is concerned though
HTF regarded the possession of this huge state edifice as the principal *spoils of the victor* is nowhere more true than in the immediate pre- and post-colonial competition
G1X we admit that *the victor has the right not just to the spoils* but also to the truth.

More interestingly, perhaps, I noticed that such phrases were often reworded and expanded. As well as facilitating comprehension, this suggested an underlying authorial strategy of making explicit to the reader how a lexicalized expression applies to the matter in hand:

GV5 The situation in many systems was typified by the American slogan '*To the victor the spoils*'. In other words, the party in power was expected to reward its supporters with paid government positions, many of which were relatively undemanding.
HYB Contrasting proverbs with ponderous prose offers a way in: '*too many cooks spoil the broth*' is a far more expressive way of saying: "Over-maximization

of the work force is counter-productive because it inhibits the realization of a satisfactory outcome."

From the idiom *to the victor the spoils* I moved on to make queries for *spoil* and *spoils* as nouns, finding that the two forms had very different uses. The singular refers most commonly to debris of various kinds (32 solutions out of 46), with collocates such as *heap(s)* - the ten occurrences of *spoil heap(s)* suggesting a more lexicalized option than the (attested) *heaps of spoil* (1) -, *tips* (3), *colliery* (3) and *quarry* (2). The plural form, instead, shows two different patterns of use. On the one hand, it refers to a *system* (6) of *political* (3) *patronage* (2), as clarified by the following:

K8X These corps arose from the middle of the nineteenth century in response to the chronic insecurity caused by a Spanish version of the '*spoils system*': each change of government would lead to the replacement of all those appointed under the previous government by individuals loyal to the new party in power.

On the other hand, with collocates such as *victory* (6), *war* (4), *conquest* (1), *defeats* (1), *revolution* (1), *success* (2), it refers to a more or less metaphorical 'loot'. This latter kind of *spoils* can be *claimed* (1), *fought for* (or *over*) (2), *taken* (3), *won* (or *won back*) (2), *collected* (2), *acquired* (1) or *gained* (1), or alternatively *shared* (8), *(re)divided* (3) or *split* (2); only very occasionally are they *given up* (1).

Finally, having found three occurrences of *spoil sport* in the concordance of *spoil*, I made a further query to investigate the meaning and attested variations of this expression, which was new to me. This involved considering the possibility of alternative forms, such as *spoilsport* (23) and *spoil-sport* (10), as well as combinations in either order of *spoil(s/t/ed/ing)* and *sport(s)* within a span of 5 words (9 solutions).

3.7 An overall map

As a way of concluding my report on this journey, let me briefly retrace the path taken. We started off by looking at occurrences of the adjective *spoiled/spoilt*, focussing particular attention on the 'pampered' sense of the term and the ideological positions it is likely to convey. Turning aside at a certain point, we went on to analyse the phrase *spoilt/ed for choice*, its lexico-syntactic variation and textual behaviour. Two parallel routes opened up here, one heading towards other phrases in which 'spoil' appears (*to the victor the spoils, too many cooks spoil the broth, spoil sport*), and from there towards *spoil* and *spoils* as nouns; the other leading us into an intra-textual analysis of a relatively long stretch of text in which the word *choice* and its inflexions were particularly frequent. While browsing this text, many potential turnings opened up: some were taken and abandoned after finding an answer to the question at hand (*leather on willow, the sport of kings, all that jazz*). Others, however, led on to further turnings, such as *good old fish and chips*, which in its turn forked, suggesting one query for *good old* and another for *fish and chips*, the latter engendering an interest in *chippy/ie*.

Although only a tiny portion of the potential of a corpus like the BNC has been illustrated, this map may give an idea of the innumerable paths that a learner can follow. No single learning activity, especially if authentic and untampered with, can embrace more than a few aspects of corpus work, nor can it illustrate all the kinds of information one can derive. My 'journey' is no exception. I shall therefore limit the discussion in the following section to those aspects highlighted by this specific activity, repeating the warning that much will be left unsaid or only hinted at.

4. Learning as discovery: the role of large corpora

So much for the journey: but what of its theoretical implications? In this section I shall attempt to interpret the activity described in terms of the pedagogic framework outlined in section 2 above. This, it will be remembered, is mediation-oriented, viewing communication as a process of meaning negotiation, and language learning as a process of discovery (Widdowson 1990). It was argued that a 'pedagogy of discovery', being inherently process-oriented, learner-centred and meaning-focussed, has a number of methodological implications, which I grouped under the broad headings of tasks, autonomy and authenticity. In what follows I shall discuss large corpus concordancing from each of these perspectives.

4.1 Tasks

I argued in 2.1 that a pedagogy of discovery requires tasks (a) to be challenging for the learner, (b) to include reasoning gaps, and (c) to combine a focus on form (which favours accuracy and restructuring) with a focus on meaning (which favours fluency).

a) The challenging nature of independent corpus work is apparent. Since learners may follow any turning they may encounter in the course of their journey, they are likely to be faced with problems which arouse their interest but have no obvious solution. In this situation, they must either come up with a tentative strategy of analysis - involving the assessment of the problem to be solved and the use of various cognitive and technical skills - or abandon their quest. The genuineness of the stimulus guarantees the challenge (though not a successful outcome). Every query I made during the activity described above required prior thought, and even so, most had to be repeated and refined, as I realized that they did not provide satisfactory answers to the question I had in mind. Equally, the analysis of the data yielded by these queries required substantial reasoning. Answers are rarely obvious from a corpus: they must be actively, and sometimes stubbornly, sought out. By combining the beneficial effects of genuine curiosity, personal involvement and meaningfulness with the challenge of an authentic problem-solving activity, LCC seems to favour learners' active participation and to provide stimuli for communicative interaction.

b) As this analysis makes plain, LCC is built around a network of reasoning-gap activities in which the learner must engage a variety of technical and cognitive skills. Among the technical skills, we may note:

- the ability to sort and group solutions in order to highlight various kinds of patterns (for instance to group referents of the adjective *spoilt/ed*, or nouns collocating with *for choice*); to thin solutions randomly so as to make the quantity of data more manageable; and to discard irrelevant solutions;
- the ability to assess the likely precision/recall of a query (for instance, when aiming to retrieve possible variants of a phrase such as *to the victor the spoils*); and to choose a formulation that best suits one's needs, yielding evidence which is as exhaustive as possible but not overwhelming;
- the ability to assess the amount of context needed (shorter to study features such as variation in fixed expressions, longer to study less obvious issues such as connotative meanings).

Among the cognitive skills, we may note:

- the ability to guess from single as well as multiple contexts, not only so as to make sense of concordance output, but to handle low-frequency and narrow-range lexical items in general (Na and Nation 1985). As noted with regards to *spoil system* and *to the victor the spoils*, the corpus, while it does not contain 'definitions', does

provide more or less explicit clues to meaning due to the inherent intertextuality of language performance, so that obscure hints and creative turns of phrase can often be clarified by way of reference to less obscure (or less creative) material;
- the ability to check the range of an expression, distinguishing idiosyncratic or variety-specific uses from more general ones, and using the former as 'indexes' to the text or text-type they belong to. Thus *spoilt/spoiled for choice* appeared to be indexical of - if in no way exclusive to - advertising texts, particularly those dealing with travel and tourism;
- the ability to detect and interpret semantic prosodies. As Stubbs (1996) observes, this involves both the analysis of collocations in the corpus as a whole, and the analysis of patterns within single texts:

There are general expectations in the language as a whole as to how words will be used: for example, which collocations will typically occur. Texts may fit such expectations, or deviate from them. In addition, texts create their own patterns and expectations, which they can either maintain or break. The meaning of words is created in texts: the instance has a history in a text.

(Stubbs 1996: 89)

One investigation of this type which was suggested above concerned the detection and analysis of potentially sexist language. This investigation is arduous because it requires the adoption of a double perspective. First, to obtain evidence about the normal and deviant uses of an expression, it is necessary to resort to concordances drawn from many different texts. For instance, if these suggest that men describe women as *spoilt* more often than women do in their writings, and if the image of women this word helps to build can be shown to be stereotyped and negatively connotated, one can use this as evidence in the analysis of specific texts where the pattern (*spoilt* + "woman") appears. In this way, an intertextual perspective may provide evidence for the analysis of single texts. However, the process can also go the other way. If a particular text can be shown to carry clearly sexist overtones (as is the case in Stubbs's analysis of Baden Powell's letters to the Scouts and Guides: 1996), the language employed can be interpreted accordingly, thus shedding light on implications which may be generally carried by particular expressions. This combination of intertextual and intratextual perspectives is a unique feature of corpus work.

The browsing of single texts can also help the learner to observe textual patterns and strategies which are not fully appreciable in concordances. Such observations - as made, for instance, with regards to *Short breaks - Brighton & Hove* - can facilitate text comprehension and stimulate reflection on writing strategies.

The technical and cognitive skills required by LCC seem likely to develop mostly through practice, as learners repeatedly handle similar problems, devise appropriate procedures, and memorize them for future use. From a technical perspective, some initial training is clearly necessary in order to familiarize them with the corpus and the software, but the difficulties should not be overestimated: learners should quickly acquire the skills needed to limit the range and/or amount of data to be analysed to manageable proportions. From a cognitive perspective, one of the main reasons why LCC activities appear valuable pedagogically is that they provide occasions to develop skills which underlie successful communication as well as successful language learning (problem-solving, pattern-matching, planning/generating/testing/revising hypotheses: Beaugrande and Dressler 1981). These activities have the further advantage of being self-improving, becoming increasingly complex and stimulating as learners become more skilled.

c) LCC activities appear to benefit accuracy, to provide stimuli for fluency-developing communication, and to favour the restructuring of knowledge:

- accuracy seems aided by the absence of time constraints and external pressures when learners focus their attention on form. The simplest analysis requires a concordance to be gone through several times in order to group, count and interpret solutions, leading to familiarity with genuine occurrences of language from numerous text-types and genres. With the requirement to 'notice' formal features (Robinson 1995), this would seem conducive to increased accuracy, regardless of the exactness of the analysis made.
- fluency seems aided by the opportunities for communication in group investigations, and for reports and discussions following completion of LCC work. Group work does not have to be imposed as a task requirement: the objective complexity of certain investigations - which can be more easily carried out in small groups, where impressions can be compared and contrasted - represents a powerful stimulus for learners to team up. Reporting and discussing strategies and findings, on the other hand, is motivated by the information gap

resulting from different discoveries, and by the desire learners may feel to tell each other about their journeys. As Prabhu observes:

There is a sense in which meaning is perceived as one's own when one has, or sees oneself as having, arrived at it oneself; and there is a sense of pleasure in attempting to articulate such meaning.

(1987: 49)

- Restructuring of knowledge and linguistic awareness seem aided by the need to provide convincing evidence in support of claims, to spell out impressions, to count occurrences, and to assess the validity of an analysis for the purpose of a written or spoken report, a discussion, or some other communicative activity based on the LCC task. This obliges learners to reflect on their learning strategies, possibly refining them, and on their competence, comparing what they have found out with what they previously thought, and underlines the tentative nature of most generalizations about the language.

4.2 Autonomy

I argued in 2.2 above that LCC offers an opportunity to practice autonomous learning in an environment where expert advice and guidance is nonetheless available when required. As such, it seems to provide a means of bridging the gap between formal instruction and continuing education, between school and life, helping the learner to develop the skills s/he needs to learn and communicate more and more effectively.

Besides fostering autonomy, activities like the one described are also motivating. Insofar as learners are free to select areas to explore and techniques for doing so, they are more likely to see their work as meaningful and relevant to their immediate concerns. The huge amount of material LCC places at their fingertips ensures that they will never find themselves short of ideas and stimuli for research: as will be apparent from the description of this one journey, it is highly unlikely that any investigation will reach its endpoint without deviating from the originally intended path. The unplanned and unpredictable nature of such activity renders it particularly stimulating, as learners are made responsible for their own learning. As they become more experienced in corpus-work and refine their learning strategies, thereby achieving better results with less effort, they are likely to develop a sense of self-efficacy which is conducive to greater autonomy and stronger intrinsic motivation. Self-directed use of a large corpus may thus be particularly appropriate to those situations in which pedagogy aims to supply learners with the skills they require to become increasingly independent from tuition and with enough freedom to exercise them. This freedom may at first be felt as threatening, but as experience piles up, so will sets of learning procedures with which to feel secure; and nothing prevents teachers from providing guidance to help in such cases.

4.3 Authenticity

The experience of journeying through a large corpus is authentic with regards to each of the three parameters discussed in 2.3 above, those of (a) tasks, (b) discourse and (c) texts.

a) The cognitive authenticity of the task is guaranteed by the genuineness of the stimulus and by the unpredictable nature of the results. Being free to determine both objectives and strategies, the learner is more likely to see the task as relevant, and be motivated to complete it. In this respect, work with large corpora provides valuable opportunities for meaningful - not merely meaning-focussed - activity, where meaningfulness is a matter of individual perception, depending on the needs and skills of the individual.

Whilst they must see the task as meaningful in order to get the best out of it, learners need not be fully aware of its implications. Typically, they will start off by aiming at acquiring *competence* in a certain linguistic area, but in the process they will also increase their *capacity* to learn and communicate. Although the former result is psychologically important, it is the latter which is crucial in a mediation-oriented pedagogic perspective: essentially independent of the objects chosen for analysis, it is not for the learner to consciously determine.

b) There are two aspects to consider with regard to the authenticity of discourse - that is, authentic experience of meaning mediation, in Widdowson's (1984) terms. Seen from the viewpoint of discourse-to-text conversion, LCC activities offer a stimulus for structured text production in the shape of oral or written reports, as well as for less structured communicative interaction in the shape of group work and discussion. From the point of view of text-to-discourse conversion, at the same time they offer opportunities to exercise skills by analysing texts, linking lexico-syntactic and pragmatic observations. In the process, LCC is likely to increase language awareness, highlighting both standard strategies of meaning mediation (such as the 'rule' *'spoilt/ed for choice* + explanatory expansion'), and deviant 'exceptions'. Once aware of the existence of a rule, the learner can then work out for her/himself what conforming to it (as opposed to voluntarily flouting it) might imply, thereby developing a more critical attitude towards both comprehension and production.

c) Textual authenticity is guaranteed by the adoption of corpora of genuine spoken and written texts. As a result of analysing large quantities of authentic data, learners are likely to have their attention directed to the pervasiveness of lexicalization and memorization in language performance (cfr. Gavioli, this volume, chapter 5). This may make them more cautious in their handling of (semi-)fixed expressions, as they are likely to observe what function(s) such expressions have, what implications they carry, and how they characterize certain text-types, genres or registers, at various levels of specificity/generality. With a large general corpus like the BNC, learners soon learn to recognize text-types and genres on the basis of their salient linguistic features, instead of relying on aspects of the external context such as source and layout. Faced with a large amount of randomly-assembled material, they learn to group those solutions which seem to belong together; hopefully they go on to find out *what* signals their belonging together; finally, they construct an interpretation for themselves, relying on lexico-syntactic, semantic and pragmatic observations. The outcomes of these analyses may be at varying levels: in the case, for instance, of *spoilt for choice*, the same expression was observed to have a general function ('selling something to someone') and to be indexical of a more specific class of texts (those dealing with travelling and tourism). In other words, the learner may be stimulated to make tentative generalizations at various levels of specificity, becoming more aware of the risks involved in over-generalization (see Aston, this volume, chapter 1: 6; Gavioli, chapter 5: 3.2).

5. Conclusion

Following Widdowson (1990), this paper has adopted a view of language use which sees meaning as being mediated *through* the language rather than being contained *in* the language, and a view of language learning as a process of progressive discovery. I have suggested that large general language corpora offer virtually unlimited opportunities for learning by discovery, as learners embark on challenging journeys whose outcomes are unpredictable and usually rewarding. Although they may not find satisfactory answers to all their questions in the course of such journeys - answers are far from easy to find in a corpus - they are very likely to end up answering - or, typically, *asking* - other questions. Among the many features of LCC that seem relevant to language pedagogy, probably the most striking is the power large corpora have of forcing one to think for oneself, by suggesting questions and providing only hints of answers which are left to the user to elaborate. However extensive the analysis, there is always a step further one can go.

In these regards, large general language corpora differ not only quantitatively but also qualitatively from the small specialized ones discussed in other papers in this volume. The richness and range of the information available, both linguistic and cultural; the flexibility of the instrument, which lends itself to all sorts of investigations, learning styles and personal interests; the picture of the language it reveals, with patterns observable at various levels of specificity/generality and from various viewpoints (lexico-syntactic, semantic, and pragmatic); all these require us to treat large corpora as very different from small ones, calling for different kinds of training and satisfying different kinds of pedagogic priorities.

Now that large corpora are becoming more widely available, it is important that discussion of their pedagogic applications and implications should follow, and equally importantly, empirical validation. There are a number of questions which can only be answered by experimental evidence - to take just two examples, how do individual cognitive styles and learning strategies affect the fruition of corpora, and how can training and supervision improve such styles and strategies, or at least avoid interfering disruptively with them? Given their potential in both educational and training terms - which this chapter has been able to do little more than hint at - it is to be hoped that experimentation of large general language corpora will rapidly lead to more generalized exploitation of a significant resource for becoming a more competent, reflective, self-confident and effective learner and user of the foreign language.

Notes

1. Throughout this paper, I use the phrase 'large corpus/corpora' to refer to balanced, general language corpora, such as the British National Corpus and the Bank of English, which contain several thousand contemporary spoken and written texts of many different kinds and from many different sources, in carefully planned proportions. This definition excludes, for instance, newspaper collections on CD-ROM (which may amount to many millions of words, but provide samples of a single language variety only, usually from a single source), and text archives on the Internet (which include texts

selected for their topic or for their cultural status). The BNC can be consulted online at http://info.ox.ac.uk/bnc; part of the BOE at *Cobuild-Direct* (http://titania.cobuild.collins.co.uk).

2. Although it has been claimed that these corpora were assembled for ESP applications (Ma 1993: 17; Flowerdew 1996: 101), there is evidence in the literature that some have also been used for more general ELT work (Johns 1991a, 1991b).

3. Stubbs (1996) proposes a model of text analysis which aims to show how ideological positions are conveyed through language. Taking up Firth's suggestion that much could be learnt from a study of the "collocational phrases in which common words appear" (1956: 107), Stubbs claims that "if people and things are repeatedly talked about in certain ways, then it is plausible that this will affect how they are thought about" (1996: 92).

4. The part-of-speech tagging of the BNC was carried out automatically, and in cases of uncertainty the two most probable alternatives are indicated (Burnard 1995). To obtain reliable results when looking for a particular part-of-speech, it is generally advisable to include these ambiguous tags in the search, and to then thin the solutions manually to remove irrelevant instances.

5. *Spoilt*: 'pampered', 64 solutions; 'ruined/rotten', 12 solutions; doubtful cases, 2; irrelevant cases, 2; total: 80. *Spoiled*: 'pampered', 60 solutions; 'ruined/rotten', 45 solutions; doubtful cases, 2; irrelevant cases, 5; total: 112.

6. SARA allows the user to download any number of occurrences selected randomly from those present in the BNC. This is a very useful facility where there are too many occurrences to analyse properly, or when one is only wanting a quick and dirty preliminary account.

7. Unless otherwise specified, in this chapter collocates are defined as being within a span of two words on either side of the search word.

8. In the creation of the BNC, *production* criteria were favoured whenever possible, but *reception* criteria were taken into account as a secondary feature, for which reason books which had achieved high sales were normally preferred to books produced in similar circumstances which had not (Burnard 1995). As a consequence, we may assume that these books are best-sellers of their genre.

9. One possibility would be to make and test hypotheses as to the attributes used to identify and describe men and women in fiction. Concordances for

9. *Spoilt for choice': a learner explores general language corpora*

blonde, brunette, and redhead, for instance, provide a substantial number of adjectival collocates used to describe women in fiction, adding up to the most patent stereotypes.

10. This finding is confirmed by similar results obtained from the *CobuildDirect* Demo service (see note 1 above): every one of the 34 occurrences of *spoil* (as a lemma) followed by *choice* in a span of four words comes from a 26 million word sub-corpus of British books, ephemera, radio, newspapers and magazines. There are no occurrences in the American sub-corpus (9 million words; books, ephemera and radio) or in the British conversation sub-corpus (10 million words).

11.

text	length (words)	observed frequency	expected frequency	significance level (χ^2)
AMD	44,896	113 (0.25%)	14.4 (0.032%)	<0.001
EC9	9,538	15 (0.16%)	3.0 (0.032%)	<0.001
EFC	20,893	17 (0.08%)	6.7 (0.032%)	<0.001
EET	27,142	22 (0.08%)	8.7 (0.032%)	<0.001
CJK	40,279	28 (0.07%)	13.0 (0.032%)	<0.001
CMD	25,816	14 (0.05%)	8.3 (0.032%)	<0.1
BNJ	22,235	10 (0.04%)	7.1 (0.032%)	n.s.

Expected frequencies are calculated on the basis of the overall frequencies of the forms *choice/choices/choose/chooses/chose/chosen* in the BNC: a total of 31,974 occurrences in approximately 100,000,000 words.

REFERENCES

Aijmer, K. 1996. *Conversational routines in English: convention and creativity*. London: Longman.
Aitchison, J. 1994. *Words in the mind*. Oxford: Blackwell.
Aitchison, J. 1997. "Lost nails and maypoles - some current language issues". In P. Grundy (ed), *IATEFL 97: Brighton conference selections*. Whitstable: IATEFL. 88-94.
Aitchison, J. and D. Lewis 1995. "How to handle wimps: incorporating new lexical items as an adult". *Folia linguistica* 29. 7-20.
Alatis, J. (ed) 1991. *Linguistics and language pedagogy: the state of the art*. Washington DC: Georgetown University Press.
Altenberg, B. 1986. "ICAME bibliography". *ICAME news* 10. (Also in Altenberg 1991a.)
Altenberg, B. 1990. "Spoken English and the dictionary". In Svartvik 1990. 177-192.
Altenberg, B. 1991a. *ICAME bibliography 2 (up to 1989)*. ftp.nora.hd.uib.no
Altenberg, B. 1991b. "Amplifier collocations in spoken English". In S. Johansson and A.-B. Stenström (eds), *English computer corpora: selected papers and research guide*. Berlin: Mouton de Gruyter. 127-147.
Altenberg, B. 1995. *ICAME bibliography 3 (1989-1994)*. ftp.nora.hd.uib.no
Argondizzo, C. 1995. "Quale input nei dialoghi didattici?". In R. Piazza (ed), *Dietro il parlato: conversazione e interazione verbale nella classe di lingua*. Florence: La Nuova Italia. 81-102.
Arnaud, P.J. and H. Béjoint (eds) 1992. *Vocabulary and applied linguistics*. London: Macmillan.
Aston, G. 1995a. "Say 'Thank you': some pragmatic constraints in conversational closings". *Applied linguistics* 16. 57-86.
Aston, G. 1995b. "Corpora in language pedagogy: matching theory and practice". In G. Cook and B. Seidlhofer (eds), *Principles and practice in applied linguistics*. Oxford: Oxford University Press. 257-270.
Aston, G. 1996. "The British National Corpus as a language learner's resource". In Botley et al. 178-191.
Aston, G. 1997a. "Enriching the learning environment: corpora in ELT". In Wichmann et al. 51-64.
Aston, G. 1997b. "Small and large corpora in language learning". In Lewandowska-Tomaszczyk and Melia. 51-62.
Aston, G. 1997c. "How can you exploit this self-access resource? Involving learners in developing methods to use corpora". In Benson and Voller. 204-214.
Aston, G. 2000. "The British National Corpus as a language learning resource".

In M.P. Battaner and C. López (eds) *VI jornada de corpus lingüístics*. Barcelona: Institut universitari de lingüística aplicada, Universitat Pompeu Fabra. 15-40. (Available: http://www.sslmit.unibo.it/guy/barc.htm)

Aston, G. and L. Burnard 1998. *The BNC handbook: exploring the British National Corpus with SARA*. Edinburgh: Edinburgh University Press.

Atkins, S., J. Clear and N. Ostler 1992. "Corpus design criteria". *Literary and linguistic computing* 7. 1-16.

Atkinson, D. 1992. "The evolution of medical research writing from 1735 to 1985: the case of the Edinburgh medical journal". *Applied linguistics* 13. 337-374.

Atkinson, D. 1996. "The Philosophical Transactions of the Royal Society of London, 1675-1975: a sociohistorical discourse analysis". *Language in society* 25. 333-372.

Backhouse, A. 1992. "Connotation". In W. Bright (ed), *The international encyclopedia of linguistics*. New York: Oxford University Press.

Baker, M. 1992. *In other words*. London: Routledge.

Baker, M. 1993. "Corpus linguistics and translation studies - implications and applications". In Baker et al. 1993. 233-250.

Baker, M. 1995. "Corpora in translation studies: an overview and some suggestions for future research". *Target* 7. 223-243.

Baker, M. 1996. "Corpus-based translation studies - the challenges that lie ahead". Paper presented at *Unity in diversity?* International translation studies conference, Dublin City University.

Baker, M., G. Francis and E. Tognini-Bonelli (eds) 1993. *Text and technology*. Amsterdam: Benjamins.

Barlow, M. 1995. *A guide to Paraconc*. Houston TX: Athelstan.

Barlow, M. 1996a. "Corpora for theory and practice". *International journal of corpus linguistics* 1. 1-37.

Barlow, M. 1996b. *MonoConc*. Ver. 1.5. Houston TX: Athelstan.

Barlow, M. 1998. *MonoConc Pro*. Ver. 1.0. Houston TX: Athelstan.

Barlow, M. and S. Burdine 1998. "A new paradigm for teaching and language concordancing". In *Proceedings of Teaching and language corpora 98*. Oxford: Oxford University Computing Services. 11.

Barnbrook, G. 1996. *Language and computers*. Edinburgh: Edinburgh University Press.

Bassnett, S. and A. Lefevere (eds) 1990. *Translation, history and culture*. London: Pinter.

Batstone, R. 1994. "Product and process: grammar in the second language classroom". In M. Bygate, A. Tonkyn and E. Williams (eds), *Grammar and the language teacher*. Hemel Hempstead: Prentice Hall. 224-236.

Battaglia, S. 1966. *Grande dizionario della lingua italiana*. Turin: UTET.

Bazzanella, C. 1990. "Phatic connectives as interactional cues in contemporary spoken Italian". *Journal of pragmatics* 14. 377-395.

Bazzanella, C. 1994. *Le facce del parlare*. Florence: La Nuova Italia.

Bazzanella, C. 1995. "I segnali discorsivi". In L. Renzi, G. Salvi and A.

Cardinaletti (eds), *Grande grammatica di consultazione, vol. III*. Bologna: Il Mulino. 225-257.

Beaugrande, R.-A. de and W.U. Dressler 1981. *Introduction to text linguistics*. London and New York: Longman.

Bell, A. 1991. *The language of the news media*. Oxford: Blackwell.

Benson, P. and P. Voller (eds) 1997. *Autonomy and independence in language learning*. London: Longman.

Bernardini, S. 2000a. *Competence, capacity, corpora*. Bologna: Cooperativa Libraria Universitaria Editrice.

Bernardini, S. 2000b. "Systematising serendipity: proposals for large corpus concordancing with language learners". In Burnard and McEnery. 225-234.

Bernardini, S. 2000c. "I copora nella didattica della traduzione: dall'addestramento alla formazione". In S. Bernardini and F. Zanettin (eds), *I corpora nella didattica della traduzione*. Bologna: Cooperativa Libraria Universitaria Editrice. 81-103. English version 1997 "A trainee translator's perspective on corpora" available: http://www.sslmit.unibo.it/cultpaps/trainee.htm

Bernhardt, E.B. 1991. *Reading development in a second language: theoretical, empirical and classroom perspectives*. Norwood NJ: Ablex.

Bialystok, E. 1985. "The compatibility of teaching and learning strategies". *Applied linguistics* 6. 255-262.

Biber, D. 1988. *Variation across speech and writing*. Cambridge: Cambridge University Press.

Biber, D. 1993. "Representativeness in corpus design". *Literary and linguistic computing* 8. 243-257.

Biber, D., E. Finegan, D. Atkinson, A. Beck, D. Burgess and J. Burges 1994. "The design and analysis of the ARCHER corpus: a progress report". In M. Kytö, M. Rissanen and S. Wright (eds), *Corpora across the centuries*. Amsterdam: Rodopi. 3-6.

Biber, D., S. Conrad and R. Reppen 1994. "Corpus-based approaches to issues in applied linguistics". *Applied linguistics* 15. 169-189.

Biber, D., S. Conrad and R. Reppen 1998. *Corpus linguistics: investigating language structure and use*. Cambridge: Cambridge University Press.

Bolinger, D. 1975. *Aspects of language*. New York: Harcourt Brace Janovich.

Bolinger, D. 1976. "Meaning and memory". *Forum linguisticum* 1. 1-14.

Botley, S., J. Glass, T. McEnery and A. Wilson (eds), *Proceedings of Teaching and language corpora 1996. UCREL technical papers* 9. Lancaster: UCREL.

Bowker, L. 1998. "Using specialized monolingual native-language corpora as a translation resource: a pilot study". *Meta* 43. 631-651.

Bowker, L. 2000, "Towards a methodology for exploiting specialized target language corpora as translation resources". *International journal of corpus linguistics* 5. 17-52.

Breen, M.P. and C.N. Candlin 1980. "The essentials of a communicative curriculum in language teaching". *Applied linguistics* 1. 89-112.

Brighetti, C. and C. Licari 1987. "Magari: per una sensibilizzazione all'uso di alcuni connettori nella didattica della lingua italiana per stranieri". In C.G. Cecioni and G. Del Lungo Camiciotti (eds), *Lingua letteraria e lingua dei media nell'italiano contemporaneo*. Florence: Le Monnier. 62-74.
Broughton, G. 1968. *Success with English: teacher's handbook*. Harmondsworth: Penguin.
Brown, C. 1993. "Factors affecting the acquisition of vocabulary: frequency and saliency of words". In Huckin et al. 263-284.
Brumfit, C.J. 1984. "The Bangalore procedural syllabus". *ELT journal* 34. 233-241.
Bublitz, W. 1995. "Semantic prosodies and cohesive company". *L.A.U.D. Series A*, A347. Duisburg: L.A.U.D.
Burnard, L. (ed) 1995. *Users' guide to the British National Corpus*. Oxford: Oxford University Computing Services.
Burnard, L. (ed) 1999. *The BNC sampler*. Oxford: Oxford University Computing Services.
Burnard, L. and T. McEnery (eds) 2000. *Rethinking language pedagogy from a corpus-based perspective*. Bern: Peter Lang.
Burrows, J.F. 1992. "Computers and the study of literature". In Butler. 167-204.
Butler, C. (ed) 1992. *Computers and written texts*. Oxford: Blackwell.
Carpenter, E. 1993. *Confusable words*. London: HarperCollins.
Carrell, P.L. 1988. "Some causes of text-boundedness and schema interference in ESL reading". In Carrell et al. 101-113.
Carrell, P.L., J. Devine and D.E. Eskey (eds) 1988. *Interactive approaches to second language reading*. Cambridge: Cambridge University Press.
Carroll, J., P. Davies and B. Richman 1971. *The American Heritage word frequency book*. New York: American Heritage Publishing Company.
Carter, R. 1987. *Vocabulary*. London: Allen and Unwin.
Carter, R. 1993. "Language awareness and language learning". In Hoey 1993. 139-149.
Carter, R. 1998. "Orders of reality: CANCODE, communication, and culture". *ELT journal* 52. 43-56.
Carter, R. and M. McCarthy (eds) 1988. *Vocabulary in language teaching*. London: Longman.
Carter, R. and M. McCarthy 1995. "Grammar and the spoken language". *Applied linguistics* 16. 141-158.
Carter, R. and M. McCarthy 1997. *Exploring spoken English*. Cambridge: Cambridge University Press.
Cassell's colloquial Italian: a handbook of idiomatic usage. 1980. London: Cassell.
Cazden, C. 1984. "Play with language and metalinguistic awareness: one dimension of language experience". *Urban review* 1. 23-39.
Chandler, B. 1989. *Longman mini-concordancer*. London: Longman.
Chevallier, G. 1934. *Clochemerle*. Paris: Presses universitaires de France.

Chesterman, A. 1997. *Memes of translation*. Amsterdam: Benjamin.
CIDE 1995. *Cambridge international dictionary of English*. 1st edition. Cambridge: Cambridge University Press.
Clear, J. 1993. "Statistical methods and large corpora - a new tool for describing text types". In Baker et al. 1993. 293-312.
Clear, J. 2000. "Do you believe in grammar?". In Burnard and McEnery. 19-30.
Coady, J. 1993. "Research on ESL/EFL vocabulary acquisition: putting it in context". In Huckin et al. 3-23.
Coady, J., J. Magoto, P. Hubbard, J. Graney and K. Mokhtari 1993. "High frequency vocabulary and reading proficiency in ESL readers". In Huckin et al. 217-228.
Cobb, T. 1997. "Is there any measurable learning from hands-on concordancing?". *System* 25. 301-315.
Cobuild 1987. *Collins-Cobuild English language dictionary*. 1st edition. London: Collins.
Cobuild 1990. *Collins-Cobuild English grammar*. London: Collins.
Cobuild 1995. *Collins-Cobuild English language dictionary*. 2nd edition. London: Harper Collins.
Cook, G. 1998. "The uses of reality: a reply to Ronald Carter". *ELT journal* 52. 57-63.
Corder, S.P. 1986. "Talking shop: language teaching and applied linguistics". *ELT journal* 40. 185-190.
Coulthard, M. 1993. "On beginning the study of forensic texts: corpus concordance collocation". In Hoey 1993. 86-97.
Coulthard, M. 1994. "On the use of corpora in the analysis of forensic texts". *Forensic linguistics* 1. 27-43.
Cowie, A.P. 1992. "Multiword lexical units and communicative language teaching". In Arnaud and Béjoint. 1-13.
Crabbe, D. 1993. "Fostering autonomy from within the classroom: the teacher's responsibility". *System* 21. 443-452.
Craik, F.I.M. and R.S. Lockhart 1972. "Levels of processing: a framework for memory research". *Journal of verbal learning and verbal behaviour* 11. 671-684.
De Mauro, T., F. Mancini, M. Vedovelli and M. Voghera 1993. *Lessico di frequenza dell'italiano parlato*. Milan: EtasLibri.
Dickinson, L. 1987. *Self-instruction in language learning*. Cambridge: Cambridge University Press.
Dodd, A. 1997. *Sara 0.931*. Oxford: Oxford University Computing Services.
Dryberg, G. and J. Tournay 1990. "Définition des équivalents de traduction de termes économiques et juridiques sur la base de textes parallèles". *Cahiers de lexicologie* 56-57. 261-274.
Dubin, F. and E. Olshtain 1993. "Predicting word meaning from contextual clues: evidence from L1 readers". In Huckin et al. 181-202.
Duff, A. 1989. *Translation*. Oxford: Oxford University Press.

Edmondson, W. and J. House 1981. *Let's talk and talk about it*. Munich: Urban and Schwarzenberg.
Ellis, N. 1996. "Sequencing in SLA". *Studies in second language acquisition* 18. 91-126.
Ellis, R. 1994. *The study of second language acquisition*. Oxford: Oxford University Press.
Eskey, D.E. and W. Grabe 1988. "Interactive models for second language reading". In Carrell et al. 223-238.
Faerch, C. and G. Kasper (eds) 1983. *Strategies in interlanguage communication*. London: Longman.
Fillmore, L.W. 1979. "Individual differences in second language acquisition". In C.J. Fillmore, D. Kempler and W. Wang (eds), *Individual differences in language ability and language behavior*. New York: Academic Press. 203-228.
Firth, J.R. 1937. *The tongues of man & Speech*. London: Oxford University Press.
Firth, J.R. 1952/53. "Linguistic analysis as a study of meaning". In Palmer 1968. 12-26.
Firth, J.R. 1956. "Descriptive linguistics and the study of English". In Palmer 1968. 96-113.
Flowerdew, J. 1993. "Concordancing as a tool in course design". *System* 21. 231-243.
Flowerdew, J. 1996. "Concordancing in language learning". In M. Pennington (ed), *The power of CALL*. Houston TX: Athelstan. 97-113.
Fontanelle, T. 1994. "Towards the construction of a collocational database for translation students". *Meta* 39. 47-58.
Fowler, W.S., J. Pidcock, R. Rycroft and G. Del Giudice 1983. *Sprint: a complete English programme*. London: Nelson.
Francis, G. 1993. "A corpus-driven approach to grammar. Principles, methods and examples". In Baker et al. 137-156.
Francis, G. and J. Sinclair 1994. "'I bet he drinks Carling Black Label': a risposte to Owen on corpus grammar". *Applied linguistics* 15. 190-200.
Francis, W.N. 1982. "Problems of assembling and computerizing large corpora". In Johansson 1982. 7-24.
Francis, W.N. and H. Kučera 1979. *Manual of information to accompany a standard corpus of present-day edited American English, for use with digital computers*. Providence RI: Brown University.
Fraser, B. 1990. "An approach to discourse markers". *Journal of pragmatics* 14. 383-395.
Gardner, R. 1998. "Between speaking and listening: the vocalization of understanding". *Applied linguistics* 19. 204-224.
Garside, R., G. Leech and A. McEnery (eds) 1997. *Corpus annotation: linguistic information from computer text corpora*. London: Addison Wesley Longman.
Gavioli, L. 1995. "Turn-initial versus turn-final laughter: two techniques for

initiating remedy in English/Italian bookshop service encounters". *Discourse processes* 19. 369-384.
Gavioli, L. 1996. "Corpus di testi e concordanze: un nuovo strumento nella didattica delle lingue straniere". *Rassegna italiana di linguistica applicata* 2. 121-146.
Gavioli, L. 1997. "Exploring texts through the concordancer: guiding the learner". In Wichmann et al. 83-99.
Gavioli, L. 1999. "Corpora and the concordancer in learning ESP: an experiment in a course of interpreters and translators". In G. Azzaro and M. Ulrych (eds), *Anglistica e ...: metodi e percorsi comparatistici nelle lingue, culture e letterature di origine europea. Volume II: Transiti linguistici e culturali.* Trieste: EUT. 331-343.
Gavioli, L. and G. Aston 2001. "Enriching reality: language corpora in language pedagogy". *ELT journal* 55, 3.
Gavioli, L. and G. Mansfield (eds) 1990. *The PIXI corpora: bookshop encounters in English and Italian.* Bologna: Cooperativa Libraria Universitaria Editrice.
Gentzler, E. 1993. *Contemporary translation theories.* London: Routledge.
Goodfellow, R. 1994. "Design principles for computer-aided vocabulary learning". *Computers and education* 23. 53-62.
Grabe, W. 1988. "Reassessing the term 'interactive'". In Carrell et al. 56-70.
Grabowski, E. and D. Mindt 1995. "A corpus-based learning list of irregular verbs in English". *ICAME journal* 19. 5-22.
Granger, S. and C. Tribble 1998. "Learner corpus data in the foreign language classroom: form-focussed instruction and data-driven learning". In S. Granger (ed), *Learner English on computer.* London: Longman. 199-210.
Greenbaum, S. 1984. "Corpus analysis and elicitation tests". In J. Aarts and W. Meijs (eds), *Corpus linguistics.* Amsterdam: Rodopi. 193-201.
Greenbaum, S. 1991. "The development of the International Corpus of English". In K. Aijmer and B. Altenberg (eds), *English corpus linguistics.* London: Longman. 83-91.
Greenbaum, S. 1992. "A new corpus of English: ICE". In Svartvik 1992. 171-179.
Greenbaum, S. and R. Quirk 1990. *A student's grammar of the English language.* London: Longman.
Haarman, L., P. Leech and J. Murray 1988. *Reading skills for the social sciences.* Oxford: Oxford University Press.
Hadley, G. 1998. "Using corpora with Japanese beginners". *IATEFL newsletter* 141. 12.
Hadley, G. forthcoming. "Sensing the winds of change: an introduction to data-driven learning". *Insights* 2. http://web.bham.ac.uk/johnstf/winds.htm
Halliday, M.A.K. 1988. "On the language of physical science". In M. Ghadessy (ed), *Registers of written English: situational factors and linguistic features.* London: Pinter. 162-178.
Halliday, M.A.K. 1992. "Language theory and translation practice". *Rivista*

internazionale di tecnica della traduzione 0. 15-26.
Halliday, M.A.K. and R. Hasan 1976. *Cohesion in English*. London: Longman.
Halliday, M.A.K. and R. Hasan 1985. *Language context and text*. Oxford: Oxford University Press.
Harvey, K. and D. Yuill 1997. "A study of the use of a monolingual pedagogical dictionary by learners of English engaged in writing". *Applied linguistics* 18. 253-278.
Hasan, R. and G. Parrett 1994. "Learning to function with the other tongue: a systemic functional perspective on second language teaching". In Odlin. 179-226.
Hatch, E. 1992. *Discourse and language education*. Cambridge: Cambridge University Press.
Hatim, B. and I. Mason 1990. *Discourse and the translator*. London: Longman.
Higgins, J. 1991. "Looking for patterns". In Johns and King. 63-70.
Hoey, M. 1983. *On the surface of discourse*. London: Allen and Unwin.
Hoey, M. 1991. *Patterns of lexis in text*. Oxford: Oxford University Press.
Hoey, M. (ed) 1993. *Data, description, discourse*. London: Harper Collins.
Hoey, M. 1994. "Signalling in discourse: a functional analysis of a common discourse pattern in written and spoken English". In M. Coulthard (ed), *Advances in written text analysis*. London: Routledge. 26-45.
Hoey, M. 1997. "From concordance to text structure: new uses for computer corpora". In Lewandowska-Tomaszczyk and Melia. 2-23.
Hoey, M. 2000. "The hidden lexical clues of textual organization: a preliminary investigation into an unusual text from a corpus perspective". In Burnard and McEnery. 31-42.
Hofland, K. and S. Johansson 1982. *Word frequencies in British and American English*. Bergen: Norwegian Computing Centre for the Humanities.
Holmes, J. and R. Guerra Ramos 1993. "False friends and reckless guessers: observing cognate recognition strategies". In T. Huckin and J. Coady (eds), *Second language reading and vocabulary acquisition*. Norwood NJ: Ablex. 86-108.
Howatt, A. 1984. *A history of English language teaching*. Oxford: Oxford University Press.
Huckin, T. and J. Bloch 1993. "Strategies for inferring word-meanings in context: a cognitive model". In Huckin et al. 153-180.
Huckin, T., M. Haynes and J. Coady (eds) 1993. *Second language reading and vocabulary acquisition*. Norwood NJ: Ablex.
Hudson, R. 1992. *Teaching grammar*. Oxford: Blackwell.
Hulquist, M. 1985. "The adverb *just* in American English usage". Master's thesis in Applied Linguistics. Los Angeles: UCLA.
Hunston, S. and G. Francis 1998. "Verbs observed: a corpus-driven pedagogic grammar". *Applied linguistics* 19. 45-72.
Hunston, S. and G. Francis 2000. *Pattern grammar: a corpus-driven approach to the lexical grammar of English*. Amsterdam: Benjamins.

Hymes, D. 1972. "On communicative competence". In J.B. Pride and J. Holmes (eds), *Sociolinguistics*. London: Penguin. 269-293.

Joe, A.G. 1998. "What effects do text-based tasks promoting generation have on incidental vocabulary acquisition?" *Applied linguistics* 19. 357-377.

Johansson, S. (ed) 1982. *Computer corpora in English language research*. Bergen: Norwegian Computing Centre for the Humanities.

Johansson, S., G. Leech and H. Goodluck 1978. *Manual of information to accompany the Lancaster-Oslo/Bergen Corpus of British English, for use with digital computers*. Oslo: University of Oslo.

Johansson, S., J. Ebeling and K. Hofland 1996. "Coding and aligning the English-Norwegian parallel corpus". In K. Aijmer, B. Altenberg and M. Johansson (eds), *Languages in contrast*. Lund: Lund University Press. 87-112.

Johns, T. 1991a. "Should you be persuaded: two examples of data-driven learning". In Johns and King. 1-16.

Johns, T. 1991b. "From printout to handout: grammar and vocabulary teaching in the context of data-driven learning". In Johns and King. 27-46. (Reprinted as Johns 1994.)

Johns, T. 1994. "From printout to handout: grammar and vocabulary teaching in the context of data-driven learning". In Odlin. 293-313.

Johns, T. 1996. "If our descriptions of language are to be accurate ...: a footnote to Kettemann". *TELL&CALL* 1996/4. 44-46.

Johns, T. 1997. "Contexts: the background, development and trialling of a concordance-based CALL program". In Wichmann et al. 100-115.

Johns, T. and P. King (eds) 1991. *Classroom concordancing*. *ELR journal*, 4.

Jordan, G. 1993. *Concordancers: research findings and learner processes*. Unpublished MA dissertation: University of London Institute of Education.

Karlsson, F. 1994. "Robust parsing of unconstrained text". In Oostdijk and de Haan. 122-142.

Keller, E. 1979. "Gambits: conversational strategy signals". *Journal of pragmatics* 3. 219-237.

Kennedy, G. 1992. "Preferred ways of putting things with implications for language teaching". In Svartvik 1992. 335-373.

Kennedy, G. 1998. *An introduction to corpus linguistics*. London: Longman.

Kettemann, B. 1995a. "Concordancing in stylistics teaching". In W. Grosser, J. Hogg and K. Hubmayer (eds), *Style: literary and non-literary*. Lewiston NY: Edwin Mellen. 307-318.

Kettemann, B. 1995b. "On the use of concordancing in ELT". *TELL&CALL* 1995/4. 4-15.

Kettemann, B. 1997. "Concordancing as input enhancement in ELT". In Lewandowska-Tomaszczyk and Melia. 63-73.

Krashen, S. 1982. *Principles and practice in second language acquisition*. Oxford: Pergamon.

Krishnamurthy, R. 1987. "The process of compilation". In Sinclair 1987a. 62-85.

Krishnamurthy, R. 1996. "The data is the dictionary: corpus at the cutting edge of lexicography". In F. Kiefer, G. Kiss and J. Rajzs (eds), *Papers in computational lexicography*. Budapest: Linguistics Institute - Hungarian Academy of Science. 117-144.

Kučera, H. and W.N. Francis 1967. *Computational analysis of present-day English*. Providence RI: Brown University Press.

Kytö, M. 1991. *Manual to the diachronic part of the Helsinki corpus of English texts: coding conventions and lists of source texts*. Helsinki: University of Helsinki.

Kytö, M. and M. Rissanen 1990. "The Helsinki corpus of English texts: diachronic and dialectal". *Medieval English studies newsletter* 23. 11-14.

Laffling, J. 1992. "On constructing a transfer dictionary for man and machine". *Target* 4. 17-31.

Langé, J.-M. and E. Bonnet 1994. "The multiple uses of parallel corpora". Paper presented at the 1st international conference on *Teaching and language corpora* (TALC), Lancaster University.

Laufer, B. 1992. "How much lexis is necessary for reading comprehension?" In Arnaud and Béjoint. 126-132.

LDOCE 1987. *Longman dictionary of contemporary English*. 2nd edition. London: Longman.

LDOCE 1995. *Longman dictionary of contemporary English*. 3rd edition. London: Longman.

Le grand Robert sur CD-ROM. 1997. Paris: Liris interactive.

Leech, G. 1974. *Semantics*. Harmondsworth: Penguin.

Leech, G. 1991. "Corpora". In K. Malmkjaer (ed), *The linguistics encyclopedia*. London: Routledge. 73-80.

Leech, G. 1997. "Teaching and language corpora: a convergence". In Wichmann et al. 1-23.

Leech, G. and C.N. Candlin 1986. "Introduction". In G. Leech and C.N. Candlin (eds), *Computers in English language teaching and research*. London: Longman. xi-xvii.

Leech, G. and R. Fallon 1992. "Computer corpora - What do they tell us about culture?" *ICAME journal* 16. 29-50.

Leech, G. and S. Fligelstone 1992. "Computers and corpus analysis". In Butler. 115-140.

Lewandowska-Tomaszczyk, B. and P.J. Melia (eds) 1997. *PALC '97: Practical applications in language corpora*. Łódź: Łódź University Press.

Lewis, D. 1992. "Computers and translation". In Butler. 75-113.

Louw, B. 1993. "Irony in the text or insincerity in the writer? The diagnostic potential of semantic prosodies". In Baker et al. 157-176.

Louw, B. 1997. "The role of corpora in critical literary appreciation". In Wichmann et al. 240-251.

Ma, B.K.C. 1993. "Small-corpora concordancing in ESL teaching and learning". *Hong Kong papers in linguistics and language teaching* 16. 11-30.

Mackey, W.F. 1965. *Language teaching analysis*. London: Longman.

Maia, B. 1997. "Do it yourself corpora ... with a little bit of help from your friends!" In Lewandowska-Tomaszczyk and Melia. 403-410.

Mair, C. 1995. "Changing patterns of complementation, and concomitant grammaticalization, of the verb *help* in present-day British English". In B. Aarts and C. Meyer (eds), *The verb in contemporary English: theory and description*. Cambridge: Cambridge University Press. 258-272.

Manili, P. 1986. "Sintassi di connettivi di origine verbale". In K. Lichem, E. Mara and S. Knaller (eds), *Parallela 2 - aspetti della sintassi dell'italiano contemporaneo*. Tübingen: Gunter Narr. 165-176.

Marinai, E., C. Peters and E. Picchi 1991. "Bilingual reference corpora: a system for parallel text retrieval". *Using corpora: proceedings of the seventh annual conference of the UW Centre for the new OED and text research*. St. Catherine's College, Oxford. 63-70.

Marmaridou, S. 1990. "Contrastive analysis at the discourse level and the communicative teaching of languages". In J. Fisiak (ed), *Further insights into contrastive linguistic analysis*. Amsterdam: Benjamin. 561-571.

McCarthy, M. 1998. *Spoken language and applied linguistics*. Cambridge: Cambridge University Press.

McCarthy, M. and R. Carter 1994. *Language as discourse: perspectives for language teaching*. London: Longman.

McCarthy, M. and R. Carter 1995. "Spoken grammar: what is it and how do we teach it?" *ELT journal* 49. 207-218.

McCarthy, M. and R. Carter 1997. "Written and spoken vocabulary". In N. Schmitt and M. McCarthy (eds), *Second language vocabulary: description, acquisition and pedagogy*. Cambridge: Cambridge University Press. 20-39.

McEnery, A. and A. Wilson 1994. "Corpora and translation: uses and future prospects". In M.A. Lorgnet (ed), *Atti della fiera internazionale della traduzione II*. Bologna: Cooperativa Libraria Universitaria Editrice. 311-343.

McEnery, T. and A. Wilson 1996. *Corpus linguistics*. Edinburgh: Edinburgh University Press.

Meara, P. 1993. "Vocabulary acquisition and the *Activator*". In *The Longman Language Activator from the academic viewpoint*. London: Longman. 14-16.

Mindt, D. 1997. "Corpora and the teaching of English in Germany". In Wichmann et al. 40-50.

Minugh, D. 1997. "All the language that's fit to print: using British and American newspaper CD-ROMs as corpora". In Wichmann et al. 67-82.

Mitchell, T.F. 1958. "Syntagmatic relations in linguistic analysis". *Transactions of the philological society*. 101-118.

Moeschler, J. 1988. "Pragmatique conversationelle et pragmatique de la pertinence". *Cahiers de linguistique française* 9. 65-85.

Moon, R. 1998. *Fixed expressions and idioms in English: a corpus-based approach*. Oxford: Oxford University Press.

Mosteller, F. and D.L. Wallace 1964. *Inference and disputed authorship: 'The*

Federalist'. Reading MA: Addison-Wesley.
Mparutsa, C., A. Love and A. Morrison 1991. "Bringing concord to the ESP classroom". In Johns and King. 115-134.
Murison-Bowie, S. 1993a. *MicroConcord: Manual*. Oxford: Oxford University Press.
Murison-Bowie, S. (ed) 1993b. *MicroConcord: Corpus A*. Oxford: Oxford University Press.
Murison-Bowie, S. (ed) 1993c. *MicroConcord: Corpus B*. Oxford: Oxford University Press.
Murison-Bowie, S. 1996. "Linguistic corpora and language teaching". *Annual review of applied linguistics* 16. 182-199.
Na, L. and I.S.P. Nation 1985. "Factors affecting guessing vocabulary in context". *RELC journal* 16, 1. 33-42.
Nagy, W. and P. Herman 1987. "Breadth and depth of vocabulary knowledge: implications for acquisition and instruction". In M. McKeown and M. Curtis (eds), *The nature of vocabulary acquisition*. Hillsdale NJ: Erlbaum. 19-35.
Nation, P. and J. Coady 1988. "Vocabulary and reading". In Carter and McCarthy 1988. 97-110.
Nattinger, J. 1988. "Some current trends in vocabulary teaching". In Carter and McCarthy 1988. 62-82.
Nattinger, J. and J. De Carrico 1992. *Lexical phrases and language teaching*. Oxford: Oxford University Press.
Neuner, G. 1996 "The role of sociocultural competence in foreign language learning and teaching". *Language teaching* 29. 234-239.
Newmark, P. 1988. *A textbook of translation*. London: Prentice-Hall.
Newmark, P. 1991. *About translation*. Clevedon: Multilingual Matters.
Nord, C. 1997. *Translating as a purposeful activity*. Manchester: St. Jerome.
O'Malley, J.M. and A.U. Chamot 1990. *Learning strategies in second language acquisition*. Cambridge: Cambridge University Press.
OALD 1989. *Oxford advanced learner's dictionary*. 4th edition. Oxford: Oxford University Press.
OALD 1995. *Oxford advanced learner's dictionary*. 5th edition. Oxford: Oxford University Press.
Odlin, T. (ed) 1994. *Perspectives on pedagogical grammar*. Cambridge: Cambridge University Press.
OED 1989. *The Oxford English dictionary on CD-ROM*. 2nd edition. Oxford: Oxford University Press.
Oostdijk, N. and P. de Haan (eds) 1994. *Corpus-based research into language*. Amsterdam: Rodopi.
Owen, C. 1993. "Corpus-based grammar and the Heineken effect: lexico-grammatical description for language learners". *Applied linguistics* 14. 167-187.
Owen, C. 1996. "Do concordances require to be consulted?" *ELT journal* 50. 219-224.

Palmer, F.R. (ed) 1968. *Selected papers of J.R. Firth 1952-1959*. London: Longman.
Partington, A. 1991. *A corpus-based study of the collocational behaviour of amplifying intensifiers in English*. MA dissertation, University of Birmingham.
Partington, A. 1993. "Corpus evidence of language change: the case of the intensifier". In Baker et al. 177-192.
Partington, A. 1995."'True friends are hard to find': guiding translation students in machine-assisted investigation of false, true and just plain unreliable 'friends'". *Perspective studies in translatology* 95/1. 99-112.
Partington, A. 1996. "'An all-American villain': a corpus-based study of relexicalization in newspaper headlines". *Textus* 9. 43-61.
Partington, A. 1998. *Patterns and meanings: using corpora for English language research and teaching*. Amsterdam: John Benjamins.
Pawley, A. and F.H. Syder 1983. "Two puzzles for linguistic theory: nativelike selection and nativelike fluency". In J.C. Richards and R.W. Schmidt (eds), *Language and communication*. London: Longman. 191-227.
Pearson, J. 1996. "Teaching terminology using electronic resources". In Botley et al. 203-216.
Pearson, J. 2000. "Surfing the internet: teaching students to choose their texts wisely". In Burnard and McEnery. 235-239.
Peters, A. 1983. *The units of language acquisition*. Cambridge: Cambridge University Press.
Peters, C. and E. Picchi 1998. "Bilingual reference corpora for translators and translation studies". In L. Bowker, M. Cronin, D. Kenny and J. Pearson (eds), *Unity in diversity: current trends in translation studies*. Manchester: St Jerome. 91-100.
Picchi, E. 1991. "DBT: a textual database system". In L. Cignoni and C. Peters (eds), *Computational lexicology and lexicography*. *Linguistica computazionale* 7. 177-205.
Prabhu, N.S. 1987. *Second language pedagogy*. Oxford: Oxford University Press.
Quirk, R., S. Greenbaum, G. Leech and J. Svartvik 1985. *A comprehensive grammar of the English language*. London: Longman.
Renouf, A. 1987a. "Corpus development". In Sinclair 1987a. 1-40.
Renouf, A. 1987b. "Lexical resolution". In W. Meys (ed), *Corpus linguistics and beyond*. Amsterdam: Rodopi. 121-131.
Resnick, L.B. 1989. *Knowing, learning, and instruction*. Hillsdale NJ: Lawrence Erlbaum.
Robinson, P. 1995. "Attention, memory, and the 'noticing' hypothesis". *Language learning* 45. 283-331.
Robinson, P. 1996. "Learning simple and complex second language rules under implicit, incidental, rule-search, and instructed conditions". *Studies in second language acquisition* 18. 27-67.

Robinson, P., S. Chi-Chien Ting and J.J. Urwin 1995. "Investigating second language task complexity". *RELC journal* 26. 62-77.
Rudska, B., J. Channell, P. Ostyn and T. Putseys 1982. *The words you need*. London: Macmillan.
Rudska, B., J. Channell, P. Ostyn and T. Putseys 1985. *More words you need*. London: Macmillan.
Rumelhart, D. 1977. "Toward an interactive model of reading". In S. Dornic (ed), *Attention and performance, vol. 6*. New York: Academic Press. 573-603.
Sampson, G.R. 1995. *English for the computer*. Oxford: Oxford University Press.
Sanford, A.J. and S.C. Garrod 1981. *Understanding written language: explorations in comprehension beyond the sentence*. Chichester: John Wiley.
Schank, R. 1982. *Dynamic memory*. Cambridge: Cambridge University Press.
Schiffrin, D. 1987. *Discourse markers*. Cambridge: Cambridge University Press.
Schmidt, R. 1990. "The role of consciousness in second language learning". *Applied linguistics* 11. 129-158.
Schmidt, R. 1994. "Deconstructing consciousness in search of useful definitions for applied linguistics". *Revue de l'AILA/AILA review* 11. 11-26.
Scott, M. 1996. *Wordsmith tools*. Ver. 2.0. Oxford: Oxford University Press.
Scott, M. 2000. "Focusing on the text and its key words". In Burnard and McEnery. 103-122.
Scott, M. and T. Johns 1993. *MicroConcord*. Oxford: Oxford University Press. http://www.ndirect.co.uk/~lexical/downloads/_freebies/mconcord.zip
Seidlhofer, B. 2000. "Operationalising intertextuality: using learner corpora for learning". In Burnard and McEnery. 207-224.
Serianni, L. 1988. *Grammatica italiana - italiano comune e lingua letteraria*. Turin: UTET.
Sharwood Smith, M. 1994. *Second language learning: theoretical foundations*. London: Longman.
Sinclair, J.McH. (ed) 1987a. *Looking up: an account of the COBUILD project in lexical computing*. London: Collins.
Sinclair, J.McH. 1987b. "The nature of the evidence". In Sinclair 1987a. 150-159.
Sinclair, J.McH. 1991a. *Corpus, concordance, collocation*. Oxford: Oxford University Press.
Sinclair, J.McH. 1991b. "Shared knowledge". In Alatis. 489-500.
Sinclair, J.McH. 1996a. "Multilingual databases: an international project in multilingual lexicography". *International journal of lexicography* 9. 179-196.
Sinclair, J.McH. 1996b. "The search for units of meaning". *Textus* 9. 75-106.
Sinclair, J.McH. 1996c. Lectures on corpus linguistics. University of Bologna, Department of Modern Languages.
Sinclair, J.McH. and M. Coulthard 1975. *Towards an analysis of dicourse*. Oxford: Oxford University Press.
Sinclair, J.McH. and A. Renouf 1988. "A lexical syllabus for language learning". In Carter and McCarthy 1988. 140-160.

Singleton, D. 1997. "Learning and processing vocabulary". *Language teaching* 30. 213-225.
Skehan, P. 1996a. "A framework for the implementation of task-based instruction". *Applied linguistics* 17. 38-62.
Skehan, P. 1996b. "Second language acquisition and task-based instruction". In Willis and Willis. 17-30.
Skehan, P. 1998. *A cognitive approach to language learning.* Oxford: Oxford University Press.
Smith, F. 1971. *Understanding reading.* New York: Holt Rinehart.
Snell-Hornby, M. 1984. "The linguistic structure of public directives in German and English". *Multilingua* 4. 203-211.
Snell-Hornby, M. 1988. *Translation studies: an integrated approach.* Amsterdam: Benjamin.
Soglia, S. 1995. "Clochemerle/clochemerlesque/clochemerle/un clochemerle: c'est quoi?" Unpublished diploma paper. University of Bologna, Scuola superiore per interpreti e traduttori.
Somers, H.L. 1993. "Current research in machine translation". *Machine translation* 7. 231-246.
Spada, N. 1997. "Form-focussed instruction and second language acquisition: a review of classroom and laboratory research". *Language teaching* 30. 73-87.
Spevack, M. 1972. "Shakespeare's English: the core vocabulary". *RNL* 3. 106-22.
Stame, S. 1994. "Su alcuni usi di *no* come marcatore pragmatico". In F. Orletti (ed), *Fra conversazione e discorso: l'analisi dell'interazione verbale.* Rome: Nuova Italia Scientifica. 205-216.
Steffensen, M.S. and C. Joag-Dev 1984. "Cultural knowledge and reading". In J.C. Alderson and A.H. Urquhart (eds), *Reading in a foreign language.* London: Longman. 48-61.
Stenström, A.-B. 1990a. "Pauses in monologue and dialogue". In Svartvik 1990. 211-252.
Stenström, A.-B. 1990b. "Lexical items peculiar to spoken discourse". In Svartvik 1990. 137-177.
Stenström, A.-B. 1994. *An introduction to spoken interaction.* London: Longman.
Stenström, A.-B. and J. Svartvik 1994. "Imparsable speech: repeats and other nonfluencies in spoken English". In Oostdijk and de Haan. 241-254.
Stevens, V. 1991. "Concordance-based vocabulary exercises: a viable alternative to gap-fillers". In Johns and King. 47-62.
Stoller, F. and W. Grabe 1993. "Implications for L2 vocabulary acquisition and instruction from L1 vocabulary research". In Huckin et al. 24-45.
Stubbs, M. 1993. "British tradition in text analysis: from Firth to Sinclair". In Baker et al. 1-33.
Stubbs, M. 1994. "Grammar, text and ideology: computer-assisted methods in the linguistics of representation". *Applied linguistics* 15. 201-223.

Stubbs, M. 1995. "Collocations and semantic profiles: on the cause of the trouble with quantitative studies". *Functions of language* 2. 23-55.
Stubbs, M. 1996. *Text and corpus analysis*. Oxford: Blackwell.
Stubbs, M. 1998. "A note on phraseological tendencies in the core vocabulary of English". *Studia Anglica Posnaniensia* 33. 399-410.
Stubbs, M. and A. Gerbig 1993. "Human and inhuman geography: on the computer-assisted analysis of long texts". In Hoey. 64-85.
Svartvik, J. (ed) 1990. *The London-Lund Corpus of spoken English: description and research*. Lund: Lund University Press.
Svartvik, J. (ed) 1992. *Directions in corpus linguistics*. Berlin: Mouton de Gruyter.
Svartvik, J. and R. Quirk 1980. *A corpus of English conversation*. Lund: Gleerup.
Swales, J. 1990. *Genre analysis*. Cambridge: Cambridge University Press.
Taylor, M.B. 1991. "Discovering concordancing". *CAELL journal* 2. 25-26.
Thompson, P. forthcoming. "Academic writers putting modal verbs to work". In G. Aston and L. Burnard (eds), *Corpora in the description and pedagogy of English* (provisional title). Bologna: Cooperativa Libraria Universitaria Editrice.
Tognini-Bonelli, E. 1993a. "From a reliable source: uses and functions of the adjective *real*". In H. Löffler (ed), *Dialoganalyse IV*. Tübingen: Max Niemeyer. 429-436.
Tognini-Bonelli, E. 1993b. "Interpretative nodes in discourse: *actual* and *actually*". In Baker et al. 193-212.
Tomlinson, B. 1998. "Glossary of basic terms for materials development in language teaching". In B. Tomlinson (ed), *Materials development in language teaching*. Cambridge: Cambridge University Press. ix-xiv.
Treccani 1994. *Dizionario enciclopedico italiano*. Rome: Istituto della Enciclopedia italiana.
Tribble, C. 1997. "Improvising corpora for ELT: quick-and-dirty ways of developing corpora for language teaching.". In Lewandowska-Tomaszczyk and Melia. 106-118.
Tribble, C. and G. Jones 1990. *Concordances in the classroom: a resource book for teachers*. London: Longman. (2nd edition 1998. Houston TX: Athelstan.)
van Dijk, T. 1979. "Pragmatic connectives". *Journal of pragmatics* 3. 447-456.
van Lier, L. 1995. *Introducing language awareness*. London: Penguin Books.
van Lier, L. 1996. *Interaction in the language curriculum: awareness, autonomy and authenticity*. London: Longman.
Voghera, M. 1993. "La grammatica nel LIP". In De Mauro et al. 86-111.
Weber, R. 1984. "Reading: United States". *Annual review of applied linguistics* 4. 111-123.
Webster 1989. *Webster's unabridged encyclopedic dictionary of English*. New York: Portland House.
West, M. (ed) 1953. *A general service list of English words*. London: Longman.

Wichmann, A., S. Fligelstone, T. McEnery and G. Knowles (eds) 1997. *Teaching and language corpora*. London: Longman.
Widdowson, H.G. 1978. *Teaching language as communication*. Oxford: Oxford University Press.
Widdowson, H.G. 1979. *Explorations in applied linguistics*. Oxford: Oxford University Press.
Widdowson, H.G. 1984. *Explorations in applied linguistics 2*. Oxford: Oxford University Press.
Widdowson, H.G. 1990. *Aspects of language teaching*. Oxford: Oxford University Press.
Widdowson, H.G. 1991. "The description and prescription of language". In Alatis. 11-24.
Widdowson, H.G. 1992. "Communication, community and the problem of appropriate use". In J.E. Alatis (ed), *Georgetown University round table on language and linguistics 1992*. Washington D.C.: Georgetown University Press. 305-315.
Widdowson, H.G. 2000. "On the limitations of linguistics applied". *Applied linguistics* 21. 3-25.
Williams, J. 1995. "Focus on form in communicative language teaching: research findings and the classroom teacher". *TESOL journal* 4/4. 12-16.
Willis, D. 1990. *The lexical syllabus*. London: Collins.
Willis, D. 1996. "A flexible framework for task-based learning". In Willis and Willis. 52-62.
Willis, D. 1998. "Learners as researchers". Paper presented at IATEFL 32nd annual conference, UMIST, Manchester.
Willis, J. and D. Willis 1988. *Collins-Cobuild English course*. London: Collins.
Willis, J. and D. Willis (eds) 1996. *Challenge and change in language teaching*. Oxford: Heinemann.
Wills, W. 1993. "Basic concepts of MT". *Meta* 38. 403-413.
Woolls, D. 1997. *Multiconcord*. Birmingham: CFL Software development.
Word routes: inglese-italiano 1995. Cambridge: Cambridge University Press.
Wray, A. 2000. "Formulaic sequences in second language teaching: principle and practice". *Applied linguistics* 21. 463-489.
Zanettin, F. 1994. "Parallel words: designing a bilingual database for translation activities". In A. Wilson and T. McEnery (eds), *Corpora in language education and research: a selection of papers from Talc 94. UCREL technical papers* 4. Lancaster: UCREL. 99-111.
Zanettin, F. 1998. "Bilingual comparable corpora and the training of translators". *Meta* 43. 616-630.
Zipf, G. 1935. *The psychobiology of language*. Boston MA: Houghton Mifflin.
Zorzi, D. 1996. "Autonomia dello studente e uso pedagogico dei corpora". In S. Semplici (ed), *Proposte per l'apprendimento: atti del III seminario permanente dei Centri Linguistici*. Siena: Università per Stranieri di Siena. 10-29.

NAME INDEX

Aijmer K. 85, 87
Aitchison J. 16, 143-145
Altenberg B. 49, 54, 55, 87
Argondizzo C. 88
Aston G. 2, 4, 5, 16, 22, 24, 25, 34-37, 40, 41, 46, 52, 58, 82, 85, 86, 97, 101, 110, 117, 123, 144, 145, 172, 186, 191, 194, 204, 208, 210, 221, 222, 226, 231, 246
Atkins S. 113
Atkinson D. 57

Backhouse A. 68, 69
Baker M. 56, 177, 182, 195
Barlow M. 3, 5, 43, 60, 118, 194
Barnbrook G. 2
Bassnett S. 177
Batstone R. 19
Battaglia S. 94
Bazzanella C. 86, 87
Beaugrande R. 243
Bell A. 64
Benson P. 23
Bernardini S. 5, 23, 25, 35, 39, 40, 42, 117, 123, 139, 180, 215, 218
Bernhardt E. 140, 175
Bertaccini F. 5, 24, 34-37, 41, 145
Bialystok E. 225
Biber D. 2, 8, 11, 18, 32, 36, 39, 52, 57, 58, 163
Bloch J. 150
Bolinger D. 15, 110, 124, 145, 221, 226
Bonnet E. 178, 195
Bowker L. 45
Breen M. 22, 224, 225, 227
Brighetti C. 90

Brodine R. 4, 24, 28, 37, 40, 43, 52, 131, 182
Broughton G. 53
Brown C. 155
Brumfit C. 224
Bublitz W. 230
Burdine S. 43
Burnard L. 2, 6, 41, 123, 222, 248
Burrows J. 32

Candlin C. 1, 22, 224, 225, 227
Carpenter E. 18, 68
Carrell P. 139, 140
Carroll J. 49
Carter R. 2, 8, 66, 85, 87, 88, 105, 226
Cazden C. 104
Chamot A. 174, 225
Chandler B. 3, 118
Chesterman A. 177
Chevallier G. 199
Clear J. 15, 18, 21, 47
Coady J. 143, 147, 150, 151, 155
Cobb T. 45
Conrad S. 8, 11, 18, 36, 52, 58, 163
Cook G. 2
Corder S.P. 45
Coulthard M. 41, 48, 89
Cowie A. 64, 191
Crabbe D. 225
Craik F. 19, 155

De Carrico J. 15
De Mauro T. 37, 91, 93
Dickinson L. 225
Dodd A. 3
Dressler W. 243
Dryberg G. 178

Dubin F. 148
Duff A. 194, 198

Edmondson W. 88
Ellis N. 15, 19
Ellis R. 14, 174
Eskey D. 28, 140, 143, 155

Faerch C. 198
Fallon R. 55, 178
Fillmore L. 15
Finegan E. 57
Firth J. 131, 225, 248
Fligelstone S. 177
Flowerdew J. 11, 18, 36, 60, 108, 222, 248
Fontanelle T. 192
Fowler W. 192
Francis G. 53, 54, 61
Francis W.N. 46, 48, 49
Fraser B. 87

Gardner R. 85
Garrod A. 175
Garside R. 17, 51, 131
Gavioli L. 2, 4, 14, 19, 24, 29, 30, 32, 35, 37, 39-41, 43, 56, 83, 84, 86, 92, 99, 101, 105, 117, 139, 145, 156, 172, 173, 178, 180, 192, 221, 246
Gentzler E. 177
Gerbig A. 60
Goodfellow R. 144
Grabe W. 28, 139, 140, 143, 155, 175
Grabowski E. 8
Granger S. 39
Greenbaum S. 56, 176, 178, 221
Guerra Ramos R. 182

Haarman L. 138, 142, 156, 157
Hadley G. 42
Halliday M.A.K. 76, 77, 81, 159, 189, 225

Harvey K. 66
Hasan R. 76, 77, 81, 104, 225
Hatch E. 98
Hatim B. 177
Herman P. 143
Higgins J. 63
Hoey M. 14, 15, 35, 40, 102, 157, 165
Hofland K. 50
Holmes J. 182
House J. 88
Howatt A. 22
Huckin T. 150
Hudson R. 19
Hulquist M. 98
Hunston S. 54
Hymes D. 14, 223

Joag-Dev C. 175
Joe A. 19
Johansson S. 50, 178, 194
Johns T. 3, 5, 7, 17, 19, 21-25, 42, 45, 63, 82, 86, 93, 102, 107, 108, 110, 151, 173, 248
Jones G. 17, 18, 32, 108
Jordan G. 18, 82, 86

Karlsson F. 51
Kasper G. 198
Keller E. 106
Kennedy G. 1-3, 22, 42, 87
Kettemann B. 17, 18, 21, 32
King P. 108
Krashen S. 14
Krishnamurthy R. 59, 229
Kucera H. 48
Kytö M. 57

Laffling J. 195
Langé J-M. 178, 195
Laufer B. 143
Leech G. 1, 41-44, 55, 61, 68, 83, 177, 178
Lefevere A. 177

Name index

Lewis D. 16, 195
Licari A. 90
Lockhart R. 19, 155
Louw B. 15, 33-35, 69, 72, 125, 200, 217, 226

Ma B. 108, 222, 248
Mackey W. 8
Maia B. 37
Mair C. 57
Manili P. 99
Mansfield G. 56, 178
Marinai E. 177
Marmaridou S. 177
Mason I. 177
McCarthy M. 8, 85, 87, 88, 105
McEnery T. 2, 194
Meara P. 144
Mindt D. 8, 22
Minugh D. 16
Mitchell T. 14
Moeschler J. 87
Moon R. 25
Mosteller F. 41
Mparutsa C. 40, 92, 157
Murison-Bowie S. 5, 18, 21, 25, 37, 43, 63, 114, 123, 138, 151, 157, 159, 165, 175, 189, 193, 195, 212

Na L. 241
Nagy W. 143
Nation P. 150, 151, 241
Nattinger J. 15, 150, 155
Neuner G. 217
Newmark P. 177
Nord C. 177

O'Malley J. 174, 225
Olshtain E. 148
Owen C. 35, 36, 61

Palmer F. 84
Parrett G. 104

Partington A. 4, 7, 14-18, 22, 24, 37, 41, 43, 54, 57, 64, 82, 84, 102, 125, 131, 147, 148, 178, 182, 199, 200, 204, 218, 219, 230
Pawley A. 15, 226
Pearson J. 195, 204
Peters A. 15
Peters C. 195
Picchi E. 178, 195
Prabhu N. 14, 22, 23, 224, 244

Quirk R. 50, 53, 67, 89, 176

Renouf A. 8, 59, 60, 229
Reppen R. 8, 11, 18, 36, 52, 58, 163
Resnick L. 44
Rissanen M. 57
Robinson P. 14, 45, 224, 243
Rudska B. 66
Rumelhart D. 140

Sampson G. 51
Sanford A. 175
Schank R. 15, 209
Schiffrin D. 86-88, 90
Schmidt N. 19, 86
Scott M. 3, 5, 18, 19, 32, 63, 118, 211
Seidlhofer B. 173
Serianni L. 94
Sharwood Smith M. 86
Sinclair J.M. 2, 8, 9, 14, 15, 24, 52, 58, 60, 61, 69, 89, 110, 123, 124, 143, 148, 200, 218, 221
Singleton D. 19
Skehan P. 16, 22, 224
Smith F. 28
Snell-Hornby M. 177, 178
Soglia S. 217
Somers H. 195
Spada N. 2, 14

Spevack M. 48
Stame S. 90
Steffensen M. 175
Stenström A. 55, 85, 87-89, 102
Stevens V. 151
Stoller F. 175
Stubbs M. 2, 32, 47, 60, 68, 121, 132, 231, 242, 248
Svartvik J. 50, 55, 89
Swales J. 40
Syder F. 15, 226

Taylor M. 92
Tognini-Bonelli E. 55
Tomlinson B. 86
Tournay J. 178
Tribble C. 17, 18, 32, 39, 108, 222

Van Dijk T. 87
Van Lier L. 86, 104
Voghera M. 106
Voller P. 23

Wallace D. 41
Weber R. 140
West M. 7
Widdowson H.G. 2, 3, 9, 16, 45, 139, 220, 221, 223-226, 240, 245, 246
Williams J. 14
Willis D. 8, 43, 60, 108, 220, 224
Willis J. 8, 60, 108
Wills W. 194
Wilson A. 2, 194
Woolls D. 194

Yuill D. 66

Zanettin F. 4, 24, 35-37, 39-41, 56, 63, 99, 118, 124, 145, 195, 198, 215, 218
Zipf G. 61
Zorzi D. 4, 14, 18, 22, 24, 37, 43, 44, 55, 92, 110, 139, 156, 165, 172, 192

SUBJECT INDEX

accuracy 13, 19, 21, 23, 59, 140, 177, 186, 224, 240, 243
activities 2, 4-6, 21-25, 28, 35, 40, 42, 86, 88, 98, 102, 108-110, 118, 120, 121, 124, 125, 127-131, 139-143, 150, 151, 153, 155-157, 159, 161-163, 165, 166, 169-174, 180, 189, 191-194, 220, 223, 224, 226-229, 240, 241, 243-245, v. also tasks
ad hoc corpora 37, 198, 205. 209, 210, 216, 217
adjectival 28, 110, 112, 205, 228, 230, 249.
adjective 39, 51, 53-55, 67, 69, 71, 72, 75, 81, 82, 87, 112, 118, 120, 121, 123, 125, 128, 130, 132, 150, 153, 169, 180, 181, 193, 228, 229, 237, 239, 241
adverbial 51, 72, 110, 191
adverb 43, 51, 53-55, 57, 67, 72, 87
ambiguity 24, 28, 138, 141, 147, 148, 150, 159, 171, 175, 248
anaphora 29, 77, 78, 81, 150, 160
annotation 17, 18, 51, v. also tags
appropriacy 14, 36, 66, 105, 142, 177, 178, 186, 188, 189, 192, 193, 199, 204, 218, 229
Archer corpus 57
attestedness 7, 14, 15, 36, 186, 191, 192, 230, 231, 239
authenticity 42, 43, 49, 56, 58, 60, 88, 91, 101, 105, 113, 130, 172, 224-227, 240, 241, 245, 246, 999
authors 30, 41, 46, 48, 65, 129, 180, 203, 231, 238
autonomy 2-7, 23-25, 35, 40-42, 53, 108, 129, 131, 144, 172, 221, 223, 224, 226, 240, 244, 245, 999
awareness 3-5, 7, 11, 16, 23, 28, 58, 85, 86, 91, 93, 98, 101, 108, 128, 130, 138, 141, 142, 153, 159, 162, 163, 169, 171, 174, 177, 192, 226, 228, 229, 244-246

background knowledge 139, 140, 151, 170, 175
Bank of English 6, 33, 36, 50, 51, 59, 62, 68, 125, 132, 218, 220, 222, 229, 247, 248, 999
bottom-up processing 28, 29, 34, 139-141, 143, 147, 153, 170, 171, 175
British national corpus (BNC) 3, 6, 9-13, 15, 19, 26, 27, 32, 36-41, 50, 59, 61, 123, 220, 222, 223, 228, 229, 231, 232, 234, 237, 240, 246-249, 999
Brown corpus 46, 48-50, 55, 56, 61, 62, 178
browsing 47, 180, 216, 234, 237, 240, 243, v. also serendipity

Cancode corpus 50, 62, 85, 87, 105
capacity 1, 3, 5, 16, 22, 42, 45, 48, 86, 174, 223, 225, 226, 245
cataphora 29, 78, 81, 160
CD-ROM 3, 5, 6, 16, 37, 61, 62, 63, 132, 179, 180, 195, 198-200, 203-205, 208, 209, 212, 215-217, 222, 247
chunk 15, 110, 124, 125, 129, 145, 147, 148, 150, 153, 162, 171,

189, 191, *v. also* segmentation
CIDE 59, 66, 70, 72, 75, 82, 150
co-occurrence 14, 17, 51, 53, 58, 94, 109, 114, 118, 210, 219
co-reference 141
Cobuild corpus 8, 36, 50, 54, 55, 57, 59, 60, 62, 77, 78, 229, 248
Cobuild dictionary 8, 59, 66, 67, 70, 108, 220, 228
Cobuild grammar 8, 54, 108, 176, 220
Cobuild project 8, 62, 221, *v. also* Bank of English
cognates 182, 186, 188
coherence 175, 191
cohesion 18, 76, 77, 141, 156, 160, 161, 171, 191
colligation 14, 15, 33, 102, 114, 117, 118, 120, 129, 145, 148, 171, 226
collocation 14, 15, 32, 33, 44, 47, 49, 52-54, 57, 59, 60, 63, 66, 67, 69, 75, 78, 83, 84, 90, 94, 96-100, 102, 104, 105, 107, 114, 117, 118, 120, 125, 129, 132, 144, 145, 148, 153, 159, 166, 171, 204, 210, 215, 216, 218, 226, 229-231, 237, 239, 241, 242, 248, 249
communication 1, 2, 4, 5, 14, 22-25, 44, 58, 68, 90, 101, 104, 106, 131, 177, 223-225, 227, 241, 244, 245
communicative language teaching 1, 2, 22, 34, 42, 45
comparable corpora 56, 177-179, 189, 192-195
competence 1, 3-5, 11, 14, 16, 22, 40, 45, 49, 68, 104, 172, 223, 225, 226, 244, 245
concordance 6, 9, 11, 13, 14, 16-19, 21-26, 28-30, 32-37, 39, 40, 42-44, 47, 48, 59, 60, 63-67, 69, 72, 75, 76, 78, 82-84, 86, 90, 93-98, 100-102, 105, 107-110, 112-114, 117, 118, 120, 121, 123-126, 128, 129, 131, 136, 138-143, 145, 147, 150, 151, 153, 155, 156, 159-163, 165, 166, 169-176, 178, 180-182, 186, 189, 191-194, 200, 212, 219, 220, 230, 231, 234, 239-243, 249, *v. also* KWIC concordance, large corpus concordancing
connotation 16, 34, 68-71, 81, 144, 148, 151, 170, 173, 199, 201, 203, 205, 208-211, 216-219, 228, 230
convention 15, 39, 40, 105, 109, 113, 125, 128-131, 141, 223
conversation 8, 15, 37, 50, 58, 87, 88, 90, 92, 101, 103, 106, 117, 232, 249
corpora *v.* ad hoc corpora, Archer corpus, Bank of English, British national corpus, Brown corpus, Cancode corpus, Cobuild corpus, comparable corpora, Flob corpus, Frown corpus, Hansard corpus, Helsinki corpus, Hepatitis corpus, ICE corpora, large corpora, Letters corpus, LIP corpus, LOB corpus, London-Lund corpus, Lonely hearts ads corpus, MicroConcord corpus A, MicroConcord corpus B, newspaper corpora, parallel corpora, small corpora, specialized corpora, spoken corpora, written corpora
corpus linguistics 2, 4, 7, 8, 9, 14, 23, 53, 57, 58, 61, 76, 87
creativity 25, 39, 40, 125-129, 131, 226, 231, 242, *v. also* unconventional

Subject index 273

cross-cultural analogy 198, 199, 205, 208-210, 215-217, 234

data-driven learning 19, 22-25, 28, 32, 45, 108
deduction 19, 21, 22, 45, 224
definition 59, 64-67, 70, 72, 75, 91, 156, 160, 192, 199, 204, 241, 248
delexicalization 57, 94, 99
denotation 9, 44, 54, 71, 144, 148, 151, 199, 205, 210, 216, 229
dictionaries 1, 8, 11, 13, 16, 22, 39, 46, 50, 52, 57-60, 63, 64, 66, 67, 70-72, 75, 76, 82, 83, 86, 87, 91-93, 110, 143, 144, 147, 150, 162, 165, 171, 178, 192, 194, 198, 199, 211, 217, 219-221, 228, 229, *v. also* CIDE, Cobuild dictionary, LDOCE, reference materials
discourse 4, 8, 46-48, 56, 76, 77, 84, 85, 150, 157, 160, 161, 165, 166, 177, 186, 189, 191, 192, 226, 245
discourse markers 4, 18, 24, 55, 68, 82, 85-95, 97-102, 104-106, 171
discovery learning 19, 45, 220, 246
domain 18, 28, 36, 37, 40, 41, 43, 48, 60, 109, 180, 192, 195, 200, *v. also* text-type, topic

editing 24, 43, 44, 63, 76, 84, 93-98, 102, 105, 156, 160, 163, 165, 166, 172, 173, 194
English for academic purposes 4, 138, 141, 157, 171
English for specific purposes 11, 52, 60, 70, 157, 248
examples 7, 11, 13, 14, 26, 39, 49, 51, 54, 59, 60, 63, 64, 66, 67, 70-72, 76, 78, 81, 82, 85, 89, 91, 92, 97-99, 102, 104, 105, 113, 118, 125, 129, 138, 150, 151, 155, 156, 159-161, 163, 165, 188, 192, 194, 200, 203, 208, 209, 216, 217, 230, 247

face-to-face interaction 37, 85, 106
false friends 148, 162, 178, 182, 186
feasibility 14, 63, 181, 195
figurative language 186, 236, 237
first language 8, 98, 99, 142, 143, 162, 177
fixed expressions 83, 145, 226, 238, 241, 246, *v. also* idiomaticity
Flob corpus 62
fluency 28, 143, 191, 224, 240, 243
focus on form 2, 4, 7, 22, 23, 25, 28, 34, 35, 224, 225, 240
focus on meaning 2, 4, 7, 22, 23, 25, 34, 35, 142, 171, 224, 240, 245
forensic linguistics 41
French 5, 56, 64, 178, 198-201, 203, 205, 207-210, 215-218
frequency 7-9, 11, 14, 15, 18, 30, 32, 33, 47-53, 55, 59-61, 66-68, 75, 78, 84, 87, 88, 90-92, 97-101, 109, 112, 114, 118, 120, 130, 132, 143, 148, 155-157, 159, 163, 170, 171, 179, 181, 182, 192, 211, 212, 219, 229, 236, 240, 241, 249, *v. also* recurrence
Frown corpus 62

general noun 18, 76-78, 81, 82, 157
generalization 13, 19, 21, 22, 39, 41, 42, 76, 84, 89, 97, 101, 105, 108-110, 113, 114, 117, 118, 120, 121, 123, 129, 161, 169, 171, 192, 221, 228, 236,

244, 246, 247
genre 15, 18, 28, 36, 37, 40, 43, 46, 48, 50, 64, 85, 105, 109, 129-131, 140, 157, 171, 173, 180, 232, 243, 246, 248, *v. also* text-type
global meaning 28, 29, 139, 141, 147, 151, 155, 157, 170, 226
grammar 1, 8, 14, 15, 17-19, 49, 53, 105, 113, 124, 131, 140, 142, 150, 151, 156, 160, 162, 163, 166, 169, 171, 173, 191, 192, 222, *v. also* lexicogrammar, syntax
grammars 1, 8, 11, 39, 50, 54, 55, 60, 63, 82, 83, 85-87, 92, 93, 110, 123, 163, 176, 192, 220, 221, *v. also* reference materials

Hansard corpus 56, 178, 194
hapax legomena 49
Helsinki corpus 57, 62
Hepatitis corpus 37, 38, 40
hypothesis construction 5, 19, 21, 29, 30, 39, 97, 102, 147, 148, 150, 151, 155, 198, 210, 216, 217, 248
hypothesis testing 5, 19, 21, 25, 36, 39, 42, 84, 94, 100, 102, 147, 148, 150, 151, 153, 155, 173, 198, 203, 208, 210, 215, 217, 218, 248

ICE corpora 56, 62, 178
idiom principle 15, 110, 221
idiomaticity 15, 63, 72, 75, 76, 131, 221, 226, *v. also* fixed expressions
idiom 15, 72, 110, 124, 145, 221, 239.
incidental learning 25, 34, 39, 215-217
induction 19, 21, 22, 105, 110
intensifier 54, 57, 68, 72, 121, 153, 236
Internet 3, 6, 37, 62, 63, 179, 180, 198-200, 203, 205, 208, 209, 211, 212, 217, 222, 247
intertextual analysis 34-36, 41, 234, 242
intratextual analysis 34, 41, 234, 242
intuition 7, 9, 42, 61, 112, 131, 192, 208, 221
irrelevance 17, 43, 54, 93, 153, 156, 172, 210, 231, 241, 248
Italian 5, 37, 56, 76, 85, 86, 90-92, 103, 142, 162, 178, 180, 182, 186, 188, 189, 191-193, 195, 197-199, 205, 208, 209, 215, 216, 219

journalism 34, 78, 82, 84, 192, 200

knowledge restructuring 16, 22, 223, 224, 240, 243, 244
KWIC concordances 9, 18, 47, 78, 230

language change 46, 57, 62
large corpora 5, 9, 18, 25, 117, 132, 198, 219-223, 227, 240, 245, 247
large corpus concordancing 220-224, 226-228, 241, 243-245, 247
LDOCE 13, 54, 59, 65-67
learner as explorer 23, 25, 26, 40, 42, 60, 92, 215, 226-228, 231, 232, 234, 237, 238, 244
learner as researcher 4, 23, 24, 26, 82, 86, 92-94, 97, 99-101, 104, 105, 108-110, 129, 173, 179, 218
learner-centred pedagogy 2, 228, 240
learning strategies 86, 244, 247
Letters corpus 19, 32, 41, 110,

118, 121, 123-125, 131, 132, 136
lexicogrammar 7, 8, 14, 22, 25, 28, 68, 85, 94, 130, 138, 147, 170, 171, 231, 239, 245-247
lexicography 1, 7, 46, 50, 52, 58, 70, 195, 218, 222, *v. also* dictionaries
lexis 4, 8, 14, 16, 18, 19, 28, 29, 32-34, 43, 46, 51-53, 57, 60, 61, 83, 87, 89, 94, 106, 118, 138, 140, 142-145, 147-149, 155-157, 159, 161, 166, 171, 173, 182, 191, 192, 198, 200, 211, 215, 217, 241
linguistic description 2, 4, 7-9, 11, 13, 14, 16, 18, 19, 22, 23, 25, 46, 47, 52, 63, 81, 85, 89, 91, 94, 107, 130, 142, 150, 174, 181, 244
LIP corpus 91-94, 99-101, 103, 106
LOB corpus 50, 51, 55-58, 61, 62, 178
local meaning 28, 139, 141, 142, 147, 150, 151, 153, 155, 165, 166, 170, 226
London-Lund corpus 50, 55, 54, 85, 87, 89
Lonely hearts ads corpus 19, 37, 40, 41, 118-122, 124, 125, 131, 133

machine translation 56, 178, 194
mediation 108, 220, 223, 226, 240, 245
medium 83, 194, 223
metalanguage 2, 23, 141-143, 162, 163, 165, 176
metaphor 9, 11, 17, 44, 70, 72, 75, 76, 83, 128, 144, 159, 178, 180, 181, 193, *v. also* figurative language
MicroConcord 5, 63, 107

MicroConcord Corpus A 5, 63, 111, 114, 116, 123, 138, 159, 175, 189, 192, 193, 195, 211-214
MicroConcord Corpus B 5, 63, 114, 115, 138, 157, 165, 166, 168, 175
MonoConc 5
MultiConcord 194

native-like 124, 186, 221
native speaker 7, 42, 49, 50, 52, 61, 65, 98, 109, 110, 142, 145, 197, 142, 145, 217
newspaper corpora 3, 16, 25, 36, 37, 40, 63, 64, 67, 71, 72, 74, 75, 78, 80, 82, 84, 88, 103, 109, 114, 121, 123, 125, 129, 138, 159, 178-180, 186, 189, 193, 195, 205, 212, 222, 247, 249
nominal 17, 28, 29, 44, 156, 162, 163, 169, 189, 191, 192, 205
non-native speaker 61, 65, 68, 75
noun phrase 77, 78, 82, 83, 118, 229
noun 18, 28, 51, 53, 59, 66, 76-78, 81-83, 120, 140, 145, 147, 150, 151, 156, 157, 159, 160, 163, 166, 169-171, 176, 188, 191, 192, 229, 237, 239-241

open-choice principle 221

ParaConc 194
parallel corpora 56, 177, 178, 194, 195, 208, 218
paraphrase 198, 199, 205, 215-217
parsing 51, *v. also* annotation
part of speech 17, 51, 150, 229, 248, *v. also* word class
polysemy 16, 24, 28, 140, 145, 148, 150, 162, 163, 171
pragmatics 15, 18, 44, 55, 56, 60,

105, 114, 117, 129, 200, 223, 245-247
precision 17, 18, 24, 43, 153, 210-212, 231, 241
preposition 53, 55, 82, 83, 87, 94, 165, 231
printout 42, 93, 94, 98, 131, 165, 172
proper names 181, 192
prototype 8, 9

reading skills 4, 7, 24, 28, 30, 34, 39, 141-143, 151, 153, 177, 194, 198
reading strategies 148
recall 17, 18, 24, 43, 171, 210, 211, 231, 241
recurrence 14-16, 21, 22, 37, 40, 44, 90, 97, 99, 100, 102, 105, 109, 110, 114, 117, 118, 120, 121, 123-125, 128-131, 147, 148, 153, 155, 171, 200, 210, 229, 234, *v. also* frequency, repetition
reference materials 1, 3, 24, 35, 36, 86, 92, 94, 108, 148, 176, 198, 199, 217, 219, 221, 229
register 40, 46, 47, 52, 53, 58, 64, 66-68, 70, 101, 124, 131, 171-173, 175, 177, 193, 226, 238, 246
repetition 32, 52, 55, 99, 109, 120, 123, 124, 128, 129, 147, 156, 166, 182, 204, 243, 248, *v. also* recurrence
representativeness 39, 46-48, 59, 63, 84, 124, 192, 222
routine 85, 118, 123, 129, 170

salience 155, 231, 246
samples 39, 43, 48-50, 58, 62, 84, 87, 92, 93, 113, 114, 117, 118, 129, 156, 159, 160, 178, 181, 220, 222, 227, 247

SARA 3, 222, 248
schemata 16, 22, 140, 175, 209, 219, 223
second language acquisition 9, 14, 66
segmentation 141, 171, 178, *v. also* chunk
self-access 6, 41, 142
semantic prosody 69-72, 82, 84, 148, 171, 226, 230, 242
semantics 14, 15, 18, 44, 54, 56, 66, 68, 104, 105, 114, 117, 121, 124, 129, 131, 144, 145, 150, 151, 166, 169, 173, 200, 204, 211, 215, 223, 246, 247
serendipity 25, 26, 226, 234
sexism 32, 34, 230, 231, 242
small corpora 24, 37, 39, 51, 61, 84, 99, 117, 130, 198, 200, 220, 222
software *v.* MicroConcord, MonoConc, MultiConcord, ParaConc, SARA, WordSmith Tools
sorting 9, 13, 43, 44, 63, 64, 68, 72, 74, 78, 84, 93, 94, 96-98, 104, 105, 107, 114, 118, 128, 156, 159, 160, 165, 166, 171-174, 182-185, 190, 228, 241
source text 5, 56, 177, 179, 181, 182, 186, 188, 191, 194, 197, 198, 200, 201, 203-205, 208, 209, 211, 215, 216, 219
specialized corpora 18, 24, 36, 37, 39-41, 131, 156, 222, 247
speech 4, 24, 36, 37, 41, 77, 85-93, 98, 99, 101, 104-107, 131, 150, 193, 222, 229, 248, *v. also* conversation
spoken corpora 18, 48, 50, 55, 77, 85-87, 93, 98, 104
stylistics 30, 41, 46, 48, 186
syllabus 8, 11, 16, 22, 46, 52, 59-61, 90

synonymy 66-70, 150, 151, 178, 186, 188
syntax 4, 17, 29, 43, 46, 51-53, 59, 63, 66, 82, 83, 114, 123, 141, 144, 157, 159, 162, 163, 169-171, 231, 245-247, *v. also* grammar

tags 17, 51, 56, 128, 131, 175, 219, 228, 248, *v. also* annotation
target text 5, 177, 191, 193, 194, 198, 208
tasks 7, 22, 23, 39, 42-44, 58, 66, 86, 88, 98, 99, 101, 140, 155, 161, 162, 172-174, 177, 181, 195, 198, 224-226, 240, 243-245, *v. also* activities
teaching materials 1, 6, 8, 11, 16, 46, 60, 61, 90, 91, 93, 102, 108-110, 113, 144, 161, 165, 172, 220, 221
text analysis 30, 32-34, 36, 41, 226, 243
text-type 4, 5, 7, 11, 15, 19, 28, 32, 36, 39-41, 57, 58, 82, 109, 113, 118, 123, 217, 222, 232, 234, 236, 242, 243, 246, *v. also* domain, genre
textbook 3, 9, 11, 19, 21-24, 37, 55, 58-60, 82, 83, 86, 88, 92, 110, 113, 117, 138, 142, 156, 157, 159-163, 165, 172, 173, 192
top-down processing 28, 29, 34, 37, 139-141, 143, 147, 175
topic 28, 39, 64, 70, 87, 99, 106, 117, 131, 140, 150, 151, 166, 180, 232, 248, *v. also* domain
transfer 198, 205, 208
translation 4, 5, 35, 46, 56, 91, 106, 124, 141, 142, 162, 177-179, 181, 186, 188, 189, 191-195, 197-199, 201, 204, 205, 208-211, 215-219
translational equivalence 56, 57, 70, 162, 176-178, 180, 182, 186, 188, 189, 191, 192, 198, 210, 211, 215, 216, 218, 230

unconventionality 125, 128, 130, *v. also* creativity

verb phrase 176
verb 8, 13, 22, 28, 44, 48-51, 57, 58, 67, 69, 70, 72, 82, 83, 87, 94, 99, 120, 141, 145, 147, 148, 150, 162, 166, 169, 176, 188, 192, 228, 229, 237
vocabulary 19, 48, 49, 66, 69, 143, 144, 151, 156, *v. also* lexis

word class 51, 55, 76, 87, 105, 141, 144, 150, 151, 157, 162, 173, 192, *v. also* part of speech
word lists 7, 19, 30, 32, 45, 47, 48, 51, 60, 88, 89, 118, 211
WordSmith Tools 5, 18, 19, 32, 45, 211
writing skills 4, 7, 30, 33, 35, 36, 39, 78, 120, 124, 126, 128, 142, 177, 178, 191, 194, 198
written corpora 18, 19, 32, 37, 40, 41, 48, 50, 50, 56, 57, 59, 63, 88, 92, 192, 195

www.ingramcontent.com/pod-product-compliance
Lightning Source LLC
Chambersburg PA
CBHW071620170426
43195CB00038B/1524